We Keep America on Top of the World

Journalism is an essential part of the democratic process. It is simultaneously a profit-making business, a form of entertainment, and a political institution with complex ties to the state and to other powerful political actors. *We Keep America on Top of the World* brings together Daniel Hallin's most recent work on American journalism, with particular emphasis on its most influential and controversial component – television news.

We Keep America on Top of the World explores the tensions produced by the multiple roles which exist within broadcast journalism. Hallin approaches the study of broadcast news from many angles – comparative, historical, cultural and political-economic. His discussion encompasses explorations of many of the most central and most controversial issues in the study of journalism: the wars in Vietnam and Central America; US–Soviet summits; the origin of the 10-second soundbite; the differences between print and television journalism; the growth of 'reality-based programming'; the blurring line between news and entertainment; and the tension between professionalism and populism.

We Keep America on Top of the World offers a distinctive approach to understanding an institution torn between the imperatives of the market, political ideology and popular fashion, and journalistic professionalism. It will be essential reading for all students of media, communication and journalism.

Daniel C. Hallin is Associate Professor of Communication at the University of California, San Diego. He is the author of *'The Uncensored War': The Media and Vietnam*, and of many articles on journalism and politics.

Communication and Society
General Editor: James Curran

We Keep America on Top of the World

Television journalism and the public sphere

Daniel C. Hallin

London and New York

First published 1994
by Routledge
11 New Fetter Lane, London EC4P 4EE

Simultaneously published in the USA and Canada
by Routledge
29 West 35th Street, New York, NY 10001

Typeset in 10/12pt Times by Megaron, Cardiff
Printed and bound in Great Britain by TJ Press (Padstow) Ltd, Cornwall

British Library Cataloguing in Publication Data
Hallin, Daniel C.
   We Keep America on Top of the World:
   Television Journalism and the Public Sphere. –
   (Communication & Society Series)
   I. Title   II. Series
   071

Library of Congress Cataloging in Publication Data
Hallin, Daniel C.
   We keep America on top of the world: television journalism
   and the public sphere/Daniel C. Hallin.
      p.   cm. – (Communication and society)
   Includes bibliographical references and index.
   1. Television broadcasting of news – United States.   2. Press
   and politics – United States.   I. Title.   II. Series: Communication and society (Routledge (Firm))
   PN4888. T4H35   1993
   070.1′95–dc20   93-21867

ISBN 0-415-09142-X (hbk)   ISBN 0-415-09143-8 (pbk)

Contents

Acknowledgements

'The American news media: a critical theory perspective,' originally appeared in John M. Forester (ed.), *Critical Theory and Public Life*, 1985. Reprinted by permission of The MIT Press.

'The media, the war in Vietnam and political support: a critique of the thesis of an oppositional media,' originally appeared in the *Journal of Politics*, February 1984, vol. 46, no. 1, pp. 2–24. Reprinted by permission of the University of Texas Press.

Portions of 'From Vietnam to El Salvador: hegemony and ideological change,' originally appeared in David L. Paletz (ed.), *Political Communication Research: Approaches, Studies, Assessments*, 1987. Reprinted by permission of Ablex Publishing.

'We Keep America on Top of the World,' originally appeared in Todd Gitlin (ed.), *Watching Television*, 1986. Reprinted by permission of Pantheon Books, a division of Random House, Inc.

'Speaking of the president: political structure and representational form in US and Italian television news,' originally appeared in *Theory and Society*, 1984, vol. 13, pp. 829–50. Reprinted by permission of Kluwer Academic Publishers.

'Soundbite news: television coverage of elections, 1968–1988,' originally appeared in the *Journal of Communication*, 1992, vol. 42, no. 3, pp. 5–24. Reprinted by permission of Oxford University Press.

'Summits and the constitution of an international public sphere: the Reagan–Gorbachev meetings as televised media events,' originally appeared in

Communication, 1991, vol. 12, pp. 249–65. Reprinted by permission of Gordon and Breach Scientific Publishers, SA.

'The passing of the "high modernism" of American journalism,' originally appeared in the *Journal of Communication*, 1992, vol. 42, no. 3, pp. 14–25. Reprinted by permission of Oxford University Press.

Chapter 1

Introduction

American journalism and the public sphere

'We Keep America on Top of the World' was a slogan CBS used for a part of 1985 to promote its news division. In its multiple meanings it captures eloquently the ambivalent identity of American journalism. Its surface meaning, of course, refers to the role of the journalist as professional and public servant, providing the public with up-to-date information about world affairs. But underneath lie several other meanings, equally important to understanding American journalism. The journalist, first of all, is not only a provider of information but also a political ideologist. Journalism gives the world political meaning, and it stands, as the slogan suggests, in a close if not always comfortable relation to the institutions of state power. The slogan itself, moreover, is a promotional device, and points to the reality of journalism as a business. It seems unlikely to me that the journalists at CBS, if they had been asked collectively to come up with an expression of their own identity, would have picked, 'We Keep America on Top of the World.' But of course they were not asked to do any such thing. The slogan and the attitude toward news it implies were selected by people whose business is to sell television shows. Finally, if we look back at the historical context of this slogan, as we will in the essay which bears it as a title, we will see that it reflects a complicated relation of journalism to its audience. This was the height of Ronald Reagan's popularity, and a time when patriotic sentiments were very much in fashion – a time, I think it is fair to say, of collective narcissism. And it was a time when journalists felt particularly strongly the uncertainty about whether they should be standing back from popular sentiments, maintaining the detachment of the neutral professional, or, on the contrary, immersing themselves in those sentiments.

The essays of this book are about this ambivalent identity of American journalism, and about the complex set of relationships tying journalism to the rest of society which structure that ambivalence: the relation of journalism to the state and political parties, to economic institutions, and to its audience. Most focus on television news. This is a choice I have made for several reasons. Television, of course, is widely and probably rightly regarded as the most important means of mass communication today. This is true, I think, not only because of the size and breadth of its audience, but also because the way it presents the news makes it a particularly strong carrier of social meaning. Finally, television manifests particularly strongly the ambivalences reflected in the CBS slogan; it feels the pressure from its multiple roles more sharply than other media. All these points will be developed in the pages that follow. Although the focus here is primarily on television news, much of the argument of these essays applies with a little qualification to all of American journalism.

The eight essays reproduced here were written over a period of a little more than a decade, from 1981 to 1992. I have updated them some, to reflect historical change, changes in my own thinking about the media, and new scholarship; and I have revised them so that they speak more directly to one another and to some of the common themes of the book. At the same time, I have tried not to violate too much the integrity of each. Some of my reflections about the individual essays, looking back on them after a number of years, are included at the end of this introduction.

THE PUBLIC SPHERE

The essays in this book began with an attempt to apply the critical theory of Jürgen Habermas to the American news media, and most of them are concerned in one way or another with the problem of journalism and the public sphere. The concept of the public sphere has become increasingly central to the field of media studies in recent years. The reason is not hard to see: the publication in English of Habermas' *The Structural Transformation of the Public Sphere*[1] coincided with the collapse of Communism and of authoritarian regimes in other parts of the world, as well as with the beginning of a period of rapid change in mass media industries, developments which have made the problem of organizing political communication in a democratic society seem particularly insistent.

The public sphere, in the simplest terms, is the 'realm of our social life. . . in which citizens confer . . . about matters of general interest.'[2] Not surprisingly, the account Habermas put forward a generation ago, of its rise and supposed decline in bourgeois societies, has been subject to extensive criticism, a good deal of it acknowledged by Habermas as valid.[3] His account of the early rise of the public sphere has been criticized as too narrowly focused on its bourgeois origins, ignoring both pre-bourgeois origins – in the Reformation, for example – and the forums created by other classes and strata. His account of the relation of the public and private spheres has been criticized as obscuring the political significance of gender. His account of the later history of the public sphere is extremely thin. He jumps abruptly from the salons of the eighteenth century to the mass culture of the 1950s, which he understands according to the simplistic model of early critical theory. And the thesis of a unilinear decline, the 'replacement of a reading public that debated critically about matters of culture by the mass public of culture consumers'[4] is confused and ultimately unsustainable. What mass culture replaced was not the élite public sphere of the eighteenth century, but a complex popular culture that combined traditional, preliterate forms of folk culture with early efforts to enter the printed public sphere – an important change, but beyond the scope of Habermas' work, which deals only with the élite culture of the eighteenth century. And if one compares oranges with oranges – the élite eighteenth-century newspaper, for instance, with the *New York Times*, the *New York Review of Books*, or *Le Monde* – it is by no means clear that the latter are less 'rational' or less public.

But for all these – and other problems with Habermas' ideas, some of which I will raise later – I, like many others who study the media and the problem of democracy, find the core of Habermas' conception of the public sphere extremely useful, both as a standard of evaluation and as an empirical concept. Here it will be valuable to contrast Habermas' theory with traditional liberal thinking about the role of the news media in democracy. There are actually two versions of the liberal theory, identified in the classic statement of Siebert, Patterson, and Schramm as the Libertarian and Social Responsibility theories.[5] According to the traditional, libertarian theory, democracy requires only that the state be prevented from interfering with the right of individuals to communicate. Privately-owned newspapers can then spring up to represent the full range of views in society and to mobilize public opinion as a counterweight to state power.

For Habermas, on the other hand, the public sphere is a realm that stands between the state, on one hand, and the realm of private interests in the market-place on the other, and it needs to be kept autonomous of both. The public sphere cannot be collapsed into the market for two primary reasons. First, power is not confined to the sphere of the state, but exists in the economic realm as well. The implications of this become obvious as capital becomes concentrated, and the rooting of the media in private property means that access to the public sphere is clearly stratified by class. The second problem is that the logic of the 'market-place in ideas' is different from the logic of the literal market of economic exchange. In terms of Habermas' later theory, the logic of the economic system, in which human relationships are mediated by money, is different from the logic of the 'life-world,' where they are mediated by language.[6]

It is easy to make this concrete if we look at the transition within liberalism to the Social Responsibility theory. The report of the Commission of Freedom of the Press in 1947 could be taken as marking the advent of this view in the United States. By the end of the Second World War the inadequacies of the libertarian model were evident. It was clear, first of all, that the owners of the news media were not representative of the public at large, and that democracy – and, more narrowly, the credibility and morale of news organizations themselves – was at risk if the owners had the power to use the media at will as instruments of class or personal interests. Second, it was clear that what worked to sell cultural commodities didn't necessarily coincide with the interest of society in substantial and accurate reporting on public affairs. And third, it had become clear that propaganda – in Habermas' terms, the use of communication as an instrument of power and profit rather than as a medium of dialogue – had become pervasive in the private sphere as well as in political life, and also threatened to undermine the market-place in ideas.

The solution was the professionalization of journalism, which in a sense set the journalists up as a surrogate public sphere, autonomous both with regard to the state and with regard to private interests, including, in theory, those of their owners and advertisers. I will come back again and again in the essays that follow to the professionalization of journalism, in an effort to identify its internal and external limits and to illuminate its meaning for democratic politics. Professionalization is surely part of the answer to the problem of preserving the public sphere in the age of mass media. It is important to think about how it can be protected, at a time when increasing commercialization of the news media threaten to upset the balance within news organizations between the public-interest culture of journalism and the culture of commodity-production.

At the same time, the professionalization of journalism is problematic in many ways as a solution to the problem of the public sphere. Here it will be useful to contrast my own, more or less Habermasian view of the American news media with a Parsonian view put forward by Jeffrey C. Alexander. The American news media, according to Alexander, are close to the ideal-type of a differentiated media 'structurally free of directly inhibiting economic, political, solidary and cultural entanglements.'[7] Because of this 'differentiation,' according to Alexander, because, that is, they have broken their ties to particular interests and to the institutions of political debate (like parties), the American news media are able to perform the function of 'normative integration' in a particularly active and effective way. In certain ways Alexander's argument is closely parallel to the views outlined in the essays that follow. In 'Speaking of the president,' for example, Paolo Mancini and I argue that American television journalists are far more active as interpreters of the political world than their Italian counterparts. They also have a far more distinct and elaborated set of professional norms and conventions. And these differences are due in part to the fact that Italian television is closely connected to the party system, while American television is not.

In other ways, however, my own view contrasts sharply with that of Alexander and with the professional model he builds upon. First, it seems to me it is far too simple to treat the history of the American news media as a story of a more or less unilinear move toward increasing 'differentiation.' The news media have, to be sure, become separated from their old connections to political parties. The major news organizations have also become separated from ties to particular religious or ethnic, and to a degree even regional communities. At the same time, they have become far *more* entangled than in their early history with economic institutions and with the state. To return to the US/Italian contrast, there are two primary reasons for the highly active interpretive role of American journalists. One is that they are free from control by the parties. The other is that they are commercial, and commercial imperatives require strong narrative structures with clear story-lines. It is one of the central arguments of this book that the news media have to be seen as a hybrid institution, at once economic, political, and cultural-professional, and that their distinctive conventions arise out of the combination and sometimes the conflict of these forces. In the final essay, 'The passing of the "high modernism" of American journalism,' I argue that we may be passing out of a period lasting about a generation, roughly from the 1950s to the 1980s, when professional culture was relatively insulated, into a period when commercial pressures will impinge more directly on journalism, especially but not exclusively in television.

As for the relation of the media to the state, the standard view is that the First Amendment separated the two, and aside from specific clashes – for example, over the Alien and Sedition Acts and the Pentagon Papers – this is basically all there is to the story. The truth is far more complex. In the era of the party press, the relation of the media to the state was politicized: how a particular paper treated a particular government official, and how the official treated the paper, depended on their politics. Today the relationship has been rationalized in the Weberian sense: the media grant the president a right to speak, for instance, based on his office, not his politics; and the White House in turn normally grants the media rights of access based on circulation, professional standing, and similar non-partisan criteria.

But this does not mean the media and state are more separate than they were, say, in 1830. On the contrary, the connection is far closer. If I want to call the diplomatic correspondent for a major news organization, and I dial his or her Washington number, it will ring simultaneously at the news organization's own office and at the State Department. Journalists today have far more intimate and regular contact with government officials than they did in the nineteenth century; this means both that we get far more information about what government is doing, and also that the picture of the world the media give us today is far more closely tied to the perspectives of official policy-makers. This intimate connection between the media and the state is another of the major themes of the essays that follow.

It may be that here, in contrast to the relation of journalism to the economic system, we are moving toward somewhat greater professional autonomy. It seems to me the closeness of government–media relations that has prevailed in the last generation is in large part a product of the Second World War and the Cold War, and may begin to ease with the passing of the latter, and with a shift in the country's attention toward domestic affairs, strongly evident in the 1992 election. In the generation just past, 'national security' reporting was the prestige beat and in many ways the paradigm for journalism in general. (I was struck in reading the memoirs of James Reston, probably the most influential and prestigious journalist of this age, by the fact that a good three-quarters of the book deals with foreign affairs.[8] My own work over the last decade, I must acknowledge, reflects this bias as well.) Even if change may be on the horizon, however, this intimate relation between media and state remains central to understanding modern journalism.

Habermas is wrong in portraying the history of journalism as a decline from a golden age. But he is right in the contention that the logics of commodity-production and of state power now intrude into the production of news in ways they once did not.

A second disagreement with Alexander has to do with the state of the public sphere. Alexander observes, as Mancini and I do in 'Speaking of the president,' that in the United States a highly active form of journalism seems to coincide with weak institutions of political debate, with parties, for example, that do not put forward strong visions of political direction. '[M]edia differentiation,' he observes, 'appears, paradoxically, inversely related to the sharpness of public thought and the quality of intellectual insight available to the society at large.'[9] He goes on to argue, however, that this is a coincidence, and that the 'lack of sharp political focus and perspective in American political news is not a dire commentary on the impact of differentiation on the news media, but rather a reflection of the inadequate autonomy achieved by the American political system.'[10]

I would put forward a very different hypothesis: that relatively weak institutions of political debate may well be a necessary condition for the development of the kind of highly active journalism that characterizes, especially, American television. And I argue in the essays that follow that there is great deal in the differentiated, professional model of journalism that contributes to the weakening of the public sphere. The culture of profes-sionalism is largely hostile to politics, preferring technical and administrative expertise or cynical detachment to engagement in the public sphere.

These problems in turn are related to a third, which has to do with the lack of grounding of the journalists' role as 'normative organizers.' Here there is a significant difference between Alexander's view and the standard model of journalistic professionalism. That model generally treats journalists as information-providers, and minimizes any role they might play in shaping the society's normative views. Alexander believes that the latter role is important, and here again my own views overlap to a point with his. This is one of the key weaknesses of the professional model of journalism. It is wrong, as an empirical matter, to assume that the news media simply provide information.[11] It is a misunderstanding of the nature of human communication to believe that they could do so. And I am not so sure that minimizing the normative content of the news would be desirable even as an ideal: it seems to me that journalists have an important and legitimate role to play in normative dialogue. The best journalism combines a professional commitment to accuracy, balance, and the like with a sense of justice and compassion. And though it is naive to imagine that journalists are free of social location (Alexander's view of journalists might be compared with Mannheim's view of intellectuals)[12] their insulation from particular interests does have enough reality that their voice in public dialogue is at times extremely important.

The problem – both in the actual practice of professional journalism and in Alexander's theory – is that the normative role journalists rightly and inevitably play lacks grounding. Cut off from connection to the institutions of political debate and from the variety of communities in which normative points of view originate, cast in the ultimately impossible role of neutral observers, journalists often wind up moving erratically and irresponsibly among a number of positions that are highly damaging to the process of political debate. At one moment they may take the role of the neutral expert who denies that normative questions are meaningful. At another moment they may abdicate the normative role to government officials. It is not an accident that a closer relationship with the state develops along with the professionalization of journalism. Professionalization creates a problem of authority for the journalists which they did not have when the news media were simply participants in the market-place of ideas, and one of the best ways of solving it is to borrow the authority of the state. At still another moment journalists may abdicate their normative judgement instead to mass public opinion, identifying themselves with what they perceive as majority sentiment (a more accurate word, really, than opinion, for at these times the emphasis is more on feelings than on ideas). Each of these strategies – the technical angle in reporting, the journalist as a mouthpiece for authority, and pseudo-populism – is discussed in some detail in the essays that follow.

IN WHAT SENSE MUST POLITICAL DEBATE BE 'RATIONAL'?

Before discussing the essays included in this volume, I would like to turn for a little bit to a linked set of problems in the concept of the public sphere, a bit less directly tied to the role of journalism, but important to clarifying my own use of the concept. This set of problems has to do with the status of interests and identities and the concept of a 'rational' public dialogue. In his account of the early bourgeois public sphere, Habermas makes the argument that its homogeneity permitted private interests to be 'bracketed' for purposes of an 'impartial' discussion of public affairs. He is critical, of course, of the exclusions on which that homogeneity was based. Yet he goes on in his account of the decline of the public sphere to emphasize that an influx of organized private interests destroyed its public character, and he seems to leave an important ambiguity about whether those who enter the public sphere are expected to check their interests at the door.

Certainly it is essential to Habermas' conception of the public sphere that some sense of responsibility to transcend particular interests in search of the common good must exist. This is one of the things that distinguishes Habermas' idea of the public sphere from the liberal, pluralist conception of democracy as a strategic contest that produces a balance among private interests. The difference between dialogue and negotiation for Habermas is that in a dialogue interests themselves are open to criticism; and it is essential to his concept of the public sphere that it is a place where dialogue and not merely negotiation can take place.

At the same time, it seems to me that if one interprets Habermas to be saying that interests must be excluded altogether from the public sphere, the concept is reduced essentially to nonsense. This would, in the first place, violate one of the basic premises of the public sphere, that the content of what can be expressed must be unrestricted. Beyond that it would deprive the concept of any connection to the real world of politics, where the problem of public dialogue is above all a problem of conflicts of interest. A parallel set of arguments can be made about the status of particular identities, by which I mean especially conceptions of morality and of the good life (and which I do not think can ultimately be separated from questions of interest).[13]

This leads directly to the issue of whether there is or should be a single, unitary, public sphere, or many different ones. An important part of the feminist critique of Habermas is the argument that he has ignored the importance of subgroups within society having their own public spheres in which they can work out their own sense of their interest and identity.[14] And if one puts aside the image of a public sphere of abstract citizens concerned with nothing but an abstract public good, then this seems clearly correct. Subgroups within society have to have the ability to 'get their act together' before they enter into a dialogue with the rest of society; and the communication system of a society needs to be evaluated not only for its ability to contribute to dialogue at the level of the whole, but also for its contribution to the full development of a multilayered public sphere. At the same time the importance of developing a universal public sphere, not only at the national but even at the global level, cannot be ignored.[15] Modern social organization is in fact highly centralized, and if, to take as one example what seems to me one of the most significant problems in political life now, the development of an international public sphere does not eventually catch up with the globalization of economic institutions, private power will increasingly eclipse the democratic process.

Habermas has also been criticized for an overly rationalistic conception of political life. And here again I think that there is some ambiguity in his work. At times, Habermas uses 'reason' as a psychological term, for example, to mean 'consciously grappling with cognitively accessible states of affairs' as opposed to 'unconscious processes.'[16] It is important, certainly, to raise the issue of whether 'reason' in this sense can be preserved in public dialogue. In the final essay of this book, I discuss briefly the advent of the so-called 'tabloid' television news shows. They certainly represent an upsurge of irrationalism in public life, a contempt for standards of logic and evidence, and a tendency to manipulate through the emotions whose influence on mainstream journalism is potentially very dangerous.

But ultimately it is neither realistic nor necessary, maybe it is not even desirable, for public dialogue to be strictly 'rational' in this sense. Political dialogue has always involved passion and spectacle;[17] just like 'reason,' they have been used sometimes to manipulate and pacify, and sometimes to push consciousness to a higher level. It seems to me, though, that the deepest meaning of 'reason' in Habermas' work is a broader one, not incompatible with this notion of politics. This is the procedural concept of reason, in which we call a dialogue 'rational' to the extent that it is unrestricted. Reason in this sense is not opposed to passion, but to tradition and authority, to coercion, and finally – because we are dealing here with communicative and not instrumental rationality – it is opposed to the strategic pursuit of ends that are not themselves subject to dialogue.

This notion of rationality does require that agreement be secured by argument, rather than resulting, for example, from the dependence of one party on the resources of another. But it seems to me there is no reason why these arguments might not be expressed with passion or carried on the wings of imagination. Here I would agree with James Curran that entertainment should not be ignored as an integral part of the public sphere.[18] As John Dewey puts it (in a work that is otherwise too tied to the idea of neutral expertise as a solution to the problem of the public for my taste): 'Artists have always been the real purveyors of news, for it is not the outward happening in itself which is new, but the kindling by it of emotion, perception and appreciation.'[19] My own work represented here has to do with news in the narrow sense (though even here news cannot be understood without exploring its connection to entertainment). But I do not mean to imply that news makes up the whole of the public sphere.

DOES THE PUBLIC SPHERE EXIST?

Finally, Nancy Fraser has raised the question of whether a public sphere can exist while substantial inequalities of wealth and power persist in society.[20] It does follow from Habermas' theory that the idea of the public sphere cannot be fully realized in a context of substantial social inequality. It is one of the strengths of his theory to refuse to abstract the process of opinion-formation from the structure of social power. Yet there is a danger here of draining the concept of the public sphere of its empirical rooting, turning it into a pure utopia, and ignoring what it can show us about real political life.

Consider here the achievements of the two great social movements of post-Second World War American history: the civil rights and women's movements. They were organized in conditions of enormous social inequality. Yet both provoked public dialogues that shifted the social consensus very substantially. The process didn't look like an academic seminar, to be sure. Violence and other forms of power were brought to bear. None of the parties involved relied strictly on 'rational' argument in any sense of the term 'rational.' The process was enormously complex, with subsidiary public spheres forming at many levels, and reaching very different points of agreement. Both movements, of course, remain far from achieving their full aims. And changes of public opinion that were achieved are far from a pure consensus: many people continue to resist, others conform for instrumental reasons, others carry their old views to the grave and are replaced by a new generation with different opinions (it is interesting here to consider the parallel with Kuhn's account of paradigm shifts in science).[21] Yet public opinion has been changed – racism after all is today something to be used furtively and quickly denied; it has considerable power still but little legitimacy, and that is hardly a trivial change. And it seems to me that there is ultimately no way to explain this without acknowledging the reality of public dialogue: the crude versions of racism and sexism that prevailed at the beginning of these movements could not be sustained once they became subject to criticism. Certainly these movements did not accomplish what they did by achieving superior power.

I treat the public sphere in these essays not only as an ideal, but as a fact of modern society, as a particular nexus of processes and institutions, the news media being among the most important, which are involved in the construction of political meaning and formation of opinion. The concept of the public sphere involves a distinctive way of looking at political life; in contrast, for example, to the Schumpeterian view, which understands politics by analogy to the market, the dominant metaphor here is that of the conversation. We are just beginning to understand how to go about analyzing the structure of the public sphere from an empirical point of view, how to account, for example, for the distinctive structures that emerge in different political contexts.

THE ESSAYS

'The American news media: a critical theory perspective' was written in 1981, and the rest of the essays are in many ways rooted in the research agenda it proposes, concerned, for example, with the relation of professionalization to the state of the public sphere, and with the effort to integrate a political economy approach to the news media with an understanding of the media as specifically cultural institutions involved in the creation of meaning. I have revised somewhat the discussion of the history of American journalism, my view on that subject today being a good deal more complex than it was when the essay was originally written. It should also be noted that it was written before the publication in English of *The Structural Transformation of the Public Sphere*. What I did was to construct an interpretation of the news media using Habermas' later work. The result is quite different from the view put forward in *The Structural Transformation of the Public Sphere*, and that is probably just as well.

At the end of the essay, I make the comment that if the public sphere is to be brought more fully to life, the impetus will have to come from outside journalism, which is not capable in its present structure of playing the mobilizing role it once did. This view has been criticized by Jay Rosen, who has argued very eloquently that journalism can and must play a more active role in advocating and encouraging an active political life.[22] I do still believe – here I agree part way with Alexander – that the problems with political life in the United States are political and not just journalistic problems, and that their solution must lie in large part with political parties, social movements, and the like. But I also now think Rosen is right, that some initiative from journalism is essential.

'The media, the war in Vietnam, and political support' is a response to the conservative critique of the media, developed in the wake of Vietnam and Watergate, as anti-establishment institutions which were undermining the authority of governing institutions. The most important thesis of this essay is that the behavior of the media is closely tied to the degree of consensus among political élites: when consensus is strong, the media play a relatively passive role and generally reinforce official power to manage public opinion. When political élites are divided, on the other hand, the media become more active, more diverse in the points of view they represent, and more difficult to manage. A good deal of subsequent research has turned up similar findings, and the 'indexing' of news coverage to official consensus or conflict, as Lance Bennett has put it, is now one of the basic conclusions of research on political communication.[23]

Looking back on this essay, two points are worth adding. First, I separate the Vietnam War in most of the discussion into two broad periods, before and after the Tet offensive. This works well to show the changes from the early to the later part of the war, but it should not be thought that the change was abrupt. It took place gradually, the first glimmerings of a more sober view of the war appearing in about spring of 1967, and the change accelerating in mid-1969, as the policy of the new Nixon administration began to generate escalating opposition.

Second, in my later work, beginning with 'We Keep America on Top of the World' (Chapter 5), I began to turn from considering the relation of the media to government to looking at their relation to their audience and to the 'common person.' I also began about this time to focus more on the narrative dimensions of television news, and not only on the explicit political arguments it represents. And I think that today, without minimizing the importance of the élite politics whose influence is stressed in this essay, I would look more at the role of the individual soldier, who was after all the main character in the 'living-room war.' It was not particularly common for soldiers to be shown discussing the war as a political issue. Nevertheless, I now think that the collapse of morale among American troops as the process of withdrawal dragged on from 1969 to 1972 had considerable impact on the tone of the news.

'From Vietnam to El Salvador: hegemony and ideological change' is a new work, combining two earlier papers and adding unpublished data from a content analysis of television coverage of Central America from 1979 to mid-1985. It serves as a sequel to the chapter on Vietnam, exploring whether the political processes shaping foreign affairs reporting in the 1960s and early 1970s had changed significantly by the 1980s. It traces the process by which news frames were shaped over the course of the Central America crisis, and proposes a way to use quantitative content analysis to measure news frames. And it applies the Gramscian concept of hegemony to foreign affairs reporting.

I don't find myself using the term hegemony much in my more recent work. I have grown tired of the enterprise of demonstrating that the media are neither neutral nor are they most of the time 'watchdogs' acting to check the power of the state or other dominant interests. It seems to me this case has been adequately made, and though it may need reiterating in the public arena, research can go on to other questions. Nevertheless I do consider the basic Gramscian insight to be valid and essential: I mean here the idea that cultural institutions like the media are part of a process by which a world-view compatible with the existing structure of power in society is reproduced, a process which is decentralized, open to contradiction and conflict, but generally very effective. Gramsci's view, of course, is in many ways similar to those of Weber, who calls this process 'legitimation,' or Parsons (following in some ways the Durkheimian tradition) who calls it 'integration.' The main difference is that Gramsci treats 'hegemony' as something to be contested, while Weber regards it as inevitable and Parsons as natural and un-problematic. The strongest critique of the concept of hegemony, it seems to me, would be to say not that it is false – is it really plausible, after all, that major cultural institutions would not be closely tied to the structure of power? – but that it is too obvious to be interesting. But I am not persuaded by this view, in part because I do consider the relation of power to discourse to be contestable and subject to historical change.

The argument of the essay runs in two directions. On the one hand, it makes the case that the hegemonic process was in fact at work in Central America reporting, limiting a potential challenge to the dominant powers in the foreign policy area. On the other hand, it contrasts the hegemony perspective with the related but more extreme view that sees the media more or less as a simple mouthpiece for a unified power élite. The most significant statement of this position in recent years is Herman and Chomsky's 'propaganda model' of the media, and it is worth elaborating a little here on my disagreements with their view.[24]

The 'model' Herman and Chomsky outline consists of a list of factors which filter oppositional views out of the news – capitalist ownership, use of official sources, and the like. There is plenty of evidence that these factors do indeed limit the openness of the media, though perhaps not as simply or auto-matically as Herman and Chomsky suggest. The problem is that the model is perfectly unidimensional; no forces working in other directions are taken into account in any serious way. The professional ideology of journalism, to give just one example, is dismissed as merely a false consciousness which conceals from the public and the journalists themselves their true role. My own view is that this ideology, while it is obviously not to be taken simply at face value, is central to understanding the way the media operate. Another way of coming at the problem is to say that Herman and Chomsky focus on one 'function' of the media, that of reproducing dominant conceptions of the political world, and forget that they have other 'functions:' including, for example, providing information which élites use to make decisions, and serving as a forum for debate among élites. And at times these functions may get in each other's way. The result is that Herman and Chomsky give us a view of the media that is flat and static, which gives us no way of understanding change or variation.

Looking back on the Central America debate of the 1980s, I have the same contradictory impressions I had at the time. On the one hand, this was a great political dialogue that failed. Around 1982 or 1983, the nation really did seem on the verge of confronting its understanding of revolution, the legacy of Vietnam, and related issues with a seriousness that is unusual in political life. But in the end, rather than deepening, the dialogue was diverted into a strategic game between the administration and congressional critics seeking to avoid political harm from the issue, and faded with few traces on the national consciousness. At the same time, I think it is very clear that important changes took place from Vietnam to Central America. Kennedy, after all, was able to send 16,000 American 'advisors' to Vietnam with little publicity and hardly a ripple of protest. The people running Reagan's policy had to worry about what would happen if an advisor was seen in the field with an M-16, and to resort to elaborate clandestine plots to supply the Contras. It seems to me there is little doubt that it was far harder for the administration to control public opinion in the 1980s than the 1960s.

We can now see, at least provisionally, how the conflicts in Central America have come out. And the outcomes seem as mixed as everything else about the conflict. Reagan did succeed in driving the Sandinistas from power, though no doubt historians will disagree about the balance between internal and external factors in the failure of the Sandinista revolution. On the other hand, the Nicaraguan opposition took over by political means rather than by the military means the Reagan administration favored, and the Sandinistas were left with considerable countervailing power. In El Salvador the government and the guerrillas fought to a standstill and once again a political settlement is being attempted. If some semblance of a real public sphere hadn't opened up in the United States (and around the world) in relation to Central America, I'm not so sure that these conflicts would have been decided, for the moment, by political means.

'We Keep America on Top of the World' is a little different from the other essays; it is a topical commentary on television news at a particular historical moment, which happened to be near the height of Ronald Reagan's popularity, rather than a systematic scholarly study. But it played an important role in the development of my thinking about television news, and I believe the essential lines of the analysis hold up well. It has two major themes. One is the blurring of lines between news and entertainment in modern television, and the tensions between these two. As I point out in an epilogue added to the essay, this is far more marked today than it was in 1985 when the essay was originally written.

The second theme is the populism of television news, and its political consequences. By populism here, I mean the tendency of American television to appeal to and identify with the ordinary person, the John Doe, which is one important facet of television's complex cultural stance. The essay explores the consequences of this stance for political authority, and finds them complex. It can undermine political authority, when those in power are portrayed as insensitive to the problems of the 'little guy.' But it can also serve the interests of those in power. The Gulf War, discussed briefly in the epilogue, is a prime example. To a large extent the power of the state to manipulate public opinion was mediated through populism: once the lives of soldiers were put on the line, television and the public at large identified with them and their families, critical distance collapsed, and media and public opinion were integrated into the war effort.

The populism of American journalism in some ways strengthens the public sphere. It prevents it, for example, from becoming strictly a conversation among formally organized political forces, which, as Mancini and I argue in 'Speaking of the president,' is what tends to happen in Italy. But it also has the potential to degenerate into manipulative flattery of 'the people' that renders dialogue impossible. Dialogue is drowned out by a sort of feedback – not in the cybernetic sense, but as an audio engineer understands it – as journalists, often paying close attention to the polls, tell the audience what it wants to hear, and the same signal goes round and round in the system getting louder and louder until no one can hear anything.

'Speaking of the president' and 'Soundbite news,' Chapters 6 and 7, can be understood as a pair. The first, co-authored with Paolo Mancini, attempts to explain the differing conventions of television news in the US and Italy in terms of the political structures of the two societies and the differing economic and political foundations of television. 'Soundbite news' attempts to explain historically the origins of the highly mediated form of American TV news which 'Speaking of the president' approaches from a comparative and synchronic point of view.

The owl of Minerva, as Hegel wrote, takes wing only with the falling of dusk. And in important ways the era in political communication described in 'Soundbite news' came to an end with the 1992 election. The evening news was displaced as the main point of contact between candidates and the voters. Voters could for the first time watch the candidates many times a week, usually live, with little or no intervention by journalists, on a variety of talk-show platforms, from CNN's *Larry King Live*, to the daytime talk shows normally interested in transvestites and diets, to MTV's 'Choose or Lose' forums.[25] Perhaps the candidates' increasing marginality in evening news coverage, as journalists took center stage as communicators, encouraged them to venture into these new channels. The result, in any case, is that the 10-second soundbite no longer has the importance to electoral politics that it did in 1988. I do not think, however, that the analysis of 'Soundbite news' is now of merely historical significance. Between elections, for one thing, the evening news will continue to play an extremely important role in political communication. And I suspect that even if television journalists no longer mediate between voters and candidates as they have in the past, their interpretive role in election campaigns is likely to retain considerable importance.

'Summits and the constitution of an international public sphere,' also co-authored with Paolo Mancini, examines the Reagan–Gorbachev summits as media events in light of two contrasting notions of community: the Durkheimian notion of community based on shared values, and the Habermasian notion of community as participation in a common conversation. It is of course dated in certain ways by the end of the Cold War; even before it was published, the tenses had to be changed from present to past. I suspect that the 'summit' will never again have the meaning it did in the age of two superpowers. But the problem of developing an international public sphere is sure to become increasingly important as economic and cultural integration advance, weapons of mass destruction proliferate, and world environmental problems become more pressing.

Chapter 9, 'The passing of the "high modernism" of American journalism,' is a brief essay prepared for a symposium in the *Journal of Communication* on the future of journalism around the world,[26] which I think serves well as a conclusion to this volume. It makes the argument that the era has ended when professionalism seemed to have solved the problem of the public sphere. The economic problems now facing news organizations, which have threatened the journalists' insulation from market pressures, coupled with political problems faced by the society as a whole, have reopened in a practical and pressing way the problem of the journalists' identity and their role in the public sphere, which is the subject of this book. I would add that the events of the 1992 election underscore one of the key points raised in this essay. I mean here the question of whether the journalists stand apart from or belong to civil society, and whether they themselves *are* in effect the public sphere, or it exists somewhere outside of journalism. There has been increasing resentment of the journalists' role in the election process – of their focus, for example, on the personal charges and countercharges of strategic political communication – and a number of efforts to diminish the journalist's role. This is perhaps most clearly symbolized by the second of the three presidential debates, in which voters, not journalists, questioned the candidates.

My thanks to James Curran, the series editor, whose idea it was initially to put this collection together. Other acknowledgements appear in notes to each chapter.

NOTES

1 J. Habermas, *The Structural Transformation of the Public Sphere: An Inquiry into a Category of Bourgeois Society*, Cambridge, Mass., MIT Press, 1989.

2 J. Habermas, 'The public sphere: an encyclopedia article (1964),' *New German Critique*, 1974, vol. 3, p. 49.

3 Habermas' response can be found in J. Habermas, 'Further reflections on the public sphere,' in C. Calhoun (ed.), *Habermas and the Public Sphere*, Cambridge, Mass., MIT Press, 1992. Critical discussions include Calhoun, op. cit.; J. Curran, 'Mass media and democracy: a reappraisal,' in J. Curran and M. Gurevitch (eds), *Mass Media and Society*, New York, Routledge, 1991; J. Curran, 'Rethinking the media as a public sphere,' in P. Dahlgren and C. Sparks (eds), *Journalism and the Public Sphere in the New Media Age*, London, Routledge, 1991 (as well as Dahlgren's introduction to the volume); N. Fraser, 'What's critical about critical theory? The case of Habermas and gender,' in *idem, Unruly Practices: Power, Discourse and Gender in Contemporary Social Theory*, Minneapolis, Minn., University of Minnesota Press, 1989; Eli Skogerbo, 'The concept of the public sphere in a historical perspective: an anachronism or a relevant political concept,' *Nordicom Review*, 1990, vol. 2.

4 *Structural Transformation*, op. cit., p. 168.

5 F. S. Siebert, T. Peterson, and W. Schramm, *Four Theories of the Press*, Urbana, Ill., University of Illinois Press, 1956.

6 J. Habermas, *The Theory of Communicative Action: Volume 2: Lifeworld and System: A Critique of Functionalist Reason*, Boston, Mass., Beacon Press, 1987.

7 J. C. Alexander, 'The mass news media in systemic, historical and comparative perspective,' in E. Katz and T. Szecskö (eds), *Mass Media and Social Change*, Beverly Hills, Calif., Sage, 1981.

8 J. Reston, *Deadline: A Memoir*, New York, Random House, 1991.

9 Alexander, op. cit., p. 35.

10 Ibid., pp. 35–6.

11 See, for example, J. S. Ettema and T. L. Glasser, 'Communicating innocence and guilt: narrative strategies in investigative reporting,' *Critical Studies in Mass Communication*, March 1989, vol. 6, no. 1 pp. 1–20.

12 K. Mannheim, *Ideology and Utopia*, New York, Harcourt, Brace & World, 1936.

13 Cf. J. Whitebook, 'Reason and happiness: some psychoanalytic themes in critical theory,' in R. J. Bernstein (ed.), *Habermas and Modernity*, Cambridge, Mass., MIT Press, 1985.

14 N. Fraser, 'Rethinking the public sphere: a contribution to the critique of actually existing democracy,' in Calhoun, op. cit.

15 N. Garnham, 'The media and the public sphere,' in Calhoun, op. cit.

16 *Structural Transformation*, op. cit., p. 221.

17 See, for instance, C. Geertz, 'Ideology as a cultural system,' in D. E. Apter (ed.),

Ideology and Discontent, New York, Free Press, 1964; D. I. Kertzer, *Ritual, Politics and Power*, New Haven, Conn., Yale University Press, 1988.

18   'Mass media and democracy,' op. cit.

19   J. Dewey, *The Public and Its Problems*, Athens, Oh., Swallow Press, 1954, p. 184.

20   Calhoun, op. cit., pp. 468–9.

21   T. Kuhn, *The Structure of Scientific Revolutions*, Chicago, Ill., University of Chicago Press, 1970.

22   J. Rosen, 'Making journalism more public,' *Communication*, 1991, vol. 12, pp. 267–84.

23   W. L. Bennett, 'Toward a theory of press–state relations in the United States,' *Journal of Communication*, spring 1990, vol. 40, no. 2, pp. 103–25; M. Kern, P. W. Levering, and R. B. Levering, *The Kennedy Crises: The Press, the Presidency and Foreign Policy*, Chapel Hill, NC, University of North Carolina Press, 1983; B. L. Nacos, *The Press, Presidents and Crises*, New York, Columbia University Press, 1990. I also expand upon this idea in my larger work on Vietnam, *The 'Uncensored War': The Media and Vietnam*, New York, Oxford University Press, 1986.

24   E. S. Herman and N. Chomsky, *Manufacturing Consent: The Political Economy of the Mass Media*, New York, Pantheon, 1988.

25   P. Taylor, 'Political coverage in the 1990s: teaching the old news new tricks,' in J. Rosen and P. Taylor, *The New News v. the Old News: Press and Politics in the 1990s*, New York, Twentieth Century Fund, 1992; J. Katz, 'Rock, rap and movies bring you the news,' *Rolling Stone*, 5 March 1992.

26   *Journal of Communication*, 1992, vol. 42, no. 3.

Chapter 2

The American news media
A critical theory perspective

Critical theory is concerned with the ability of human beings to reflect on their social life for the purpose of discovering, as Tolstoy once put it, 'what we should do and how we should live.' For this reason it has devoted a good deal of attention to the institutions of what Habermas calls the public sphere: the arena, formed as the liberal political order was replacing the feudal, in which private individuals come together to discuss the public affairs of the community.[1] At the heart of the critique of contemporary capitalism advanced by Horkheimer, Adorno, Marcuse, Habermas, and others is the thesis that the capitalist form of social organization that brought the public sphere into being nevertheless distorts and limits its development to the point that the society is unable to establish the process of dialogue and collective self-reflection that the advent of liberal institutions seemed to promise.

From the beginning the newspaper was among the key institutions of the emerging public sphere. 'We should underrate their importance,' wrote Tocqueville, 'if we thought [newspapers] just guaranteed liberty; they maintain civilization.'[2] And the young Marx, in the wonderfully overblown style of German romanticism, called the fledgling press 'the omnipresent open eye of the spirit of the people . . . the ruthless confession of a people to itself . . . the mind of the state that can be peddled in every cottage, cheaper than natural gas.'[3] Both expected the newspaper to assist in the birth of a fundamentally new political order, to enable the society as a whole, for the first time in human history, to open a dialogue about itself and decide in a public way the direction of public life. But this, according to critical theory, is not how it has turned out. The public sphere has given way to the 'consciousness industry,' the press as a potential medium of public dialogue to the 'mass media,' deeply embedded in a structure of domination.

Critical theorists have offered two types of explanation for the distortion of political dialogue in liberal capitalist societies. The first and more familiar concerns the structure of power in a class society. Unequal distribution of political and economic power gives to some members of society greater access and control over the institutions of political communication and organization than others. All interests and perspectives are not equally represented. Power intrudes upon discourse, and the outcome of debate can neither be considered a genuine consensus or compromise, nor can it be expected to reflect an assessment of all the information or insight potentially available.

The second argument is less familiar but more original to critical theory, and I will take it as my primary focus here. This argument, summed up by Habermas' phrase the 'scientization of politics,' concerns the type of social action and discourse characteristic of capitalist society. There are, according to Habermas, two types of action fundamental to human life. First, human beings must interact with nature to produce their material means of subsistence. This type of action, involving the manipulation of nature and of human beings as 'forces of production' to achieve established purposes, Habermas calls purposive–rational action. Second, human beings must interact with one another to produce the frameworks of reciprocal expectation that make it possible for them to live as members of collective social institutions. This Habermas calls communicative action. Habermas draws these concepts in part from Aristotle's distinction between *techne* – 'the skillful production of artifacts and the expert mastery of objectified tasks'[4] – and praxis – action directed toward human education and the realization of human potential. He accordingly distinguishes between two types of knowledge, technical and practical, which correspond to the two types of human action. Capitalism, Habermas argues, develops the capacity for purposive–rational action to a degree never approached by any previous social order. But it also tends to universalize that form of action and the standards of discourse and knowledge that correspond to it. All questions come to be framed as essentially technical or strategic questions, questions of the most effective means by which a given end can be attained. As a result society is unable to develop a capacity for communicative action through which it could resolve practical questions, those that have to do not with means but ends, not with techniques but standards of human conduct.

This, then, is the perspective from which I will examine the American news media. I will begin by making the argument that modern American journalism does in fact take technical knowledge as a model for the reporting of news. This conception of news reporting, I will argue, is a relatively recent historical development, connected with the rise of commercial mass media – and thus with capitalist forms of social organization – and with the professionalization of journalism. I will conclude by discussing the political implications of this transformation of journalism. As we shall see, critical theorists have taken two very different positions on the political role of mass media. Marcuse, Horkheimer, and Adorno, writing in the 1940s, 1950s, and early 1960s, argued that the media were capable of producing an ideological consensus tight enough that the possibility of opposition to the existing structure of society became extremely problematic. Habermas, on the other hand, has cast doubt in his recent writings on the possibility of any such centralized production of social values and in fact has argued that liberal capitalist societies are susceptible to conflict and crisis precisely in the sphere of ideology and culture.

In discussing this debate over the media's ability to legitimize the existing social order, I shall introduce Habermas' recent work on the pragmatics of human communication, which points toward important new ways of approaching the study of the mass media. For Habermas all forms of human communication, however asymmetrical the social relations may have become, are essentially derived from the basic form of dialogue and must be seen as relationships between active human subjects. This suggests that we must direct our attention not only to the content of media messages but also to the character of the relations established between communicator and audience and the message that relation implies about the nature of social relationships generally. The news tells us not only what happened in the world today but who we are in relation to that world. I shall argue that the crucial consequence of the scientization of journalism, the shift to a technical angle in the reporting of news, may well lie in the message this form of journalism conveys about the nature of politics and the citizen's relation to it. The grounding of mass communication in dialogue also suggests that there may be limits beyond which the process of communication may not be stretched without destroying the legitimacy of the communicator. This point is important to understanding the relation of the mass media to the structure of social power: the ability of the media to support that structure ideologically is limited by their need to maintain the integrity of the process of communication on which their own legitimacy depends.

This argument is very preliminary. One might think, given the centrality to critical theory of the problem of public dialogue, that critical theorists would by now have produced a substantial body of research on the institutions of political communication. In fact, critical theory, which has been preoccupied for most of its history with the philosophical critique of positivism and the effort to develop a nonpositivist conception of social enquiry, has so far produced relatively little in the way of extended analysis of concrete social institutions, and the news media are no exception.[5] What follows, therefore, should be taken not primarily as a report on research already undertaken but as a proposal for future work in an area where most of the interesting questions remain to be addressed.

TECHNICAL ANGLE IN NEWS REPORTING

A few examples will illustrate how the modern journalist reports political events. In December 1968 *CBS Evening News* featured a two-part special report on 'pacification' in Vietnam. The series, which totaled an unusually long 13 minutes in length, reflected the growing maturity of the American news media. A couple of years earlier Vietnam coverage had been primarily a chronicle of daily battlefield events. By late 1968 the media were beginning to make a conscious effort, at least occasionally, to offer background, analysis, and perspective. CBS had chosen well the topic for this particular background report. Pacification involved the struggle for political support or hegemony in the villages of South Vietnam, which was what the war was ultimately about. By this time, too, the media were beginning to venture beyond official sources of information. The CBS pacification report included a lengthy interview with a critic of administration policy (John Tunney, a senator from California); a few years earlier use of information from critics, even élite ones, had been extremely rare in foreign policy coverage.

How did CBS provide background on the complex and controversial struggle for South Vietnam's countryside? Here are Walter Cronkite's introduction to the report and correspondent Murray Fromson's wrap-ups to the two segments:

> Cronkite: American officials in Saigon came out with their most optimistic pacification report of the war today. They said that almost three-fourths of South Vietnam's seventeen million people now live in relatively secure areas controlled by the Saigon government. According to those officials Vietcong control has dropped to just over thirteen percent of the population with the remaining South Vietnamese living in contested areas. Tonight we get a look at one of those contested areas . . . .
>
> Fromson [concluding part I]:   So pacification does not stand still. It moves forward, it moves back. But what is the balance? What is the trend . . . ? An effort is being made to measure this, and we'll look at the measurements in our next report.
>
> Fromson [concluding part II]:   Another offensive by the Communists would undermine the program . . . . But the momentum seems to be in the other direction. Since the November 1 bombing halt government and U.S. troops have taken over nearly 800 hamlets previously regarded as contested. The goal is to occupy another three hundred of these hamlets by the anniversary of the Tet offensive.[6]

The story, in short, was structured from beginning to end around the question of effectiveness; each element was explained within this framework. A US tank, for instance, had fired into the village in response to small arms fire, killing two civilians. 'What may be regarded as a military necessity,' Fromson reported, 'also creates problems for the pacification team.' The whole of part II was devoted to the computerized Hamlet Evaluation System (HES), which produced the official figures on the progress of pacification. That was where Senator Tunney came in; he was not there to discuss the wisdom or justice of US policy in Vietnam but to offer an opposing view on the accuracy of the figures produced by the HES.

The tendency to frame and analyze events in terms of strategy and tactics, success and failure, is characteristic of modern US journalism. In Vietnam coverage, even stories about the political debate at home were shaped to this pattern. Reports about the anti-war movement, when they were not preoccupied with the possibility of a violent disruption of social order (another common focus in coverage of political controversy), focused heavily on the issue of whether the movement was gaining or losing ground: would as many people participate in this year's demonstration as in last year's? Would the demonstration have any impact on the president's decision, or would the president be watching a football game?[7] As we shall see in the following chapter, relatively few reports on the anti-war movement gave its spokespeople the opportunity to comment on the political issue of the war itself.

Studies of election coverage have shown a heavy preponderance of attention to the horse-race angle and the strategic battle of wits.[8] 'The Presidential debate produced no knockout blow, no disastrous gaffe and no immediate, undisputed victor,' wrote the *New York Times*'s Hedrick Smith, analyzing one of the 1980 Reagan–Carter debates. 'It was a contest of content against style, of a President repeatedly on the attack to put his challenger on the defensive while Ronald Reagan used his calm demeanor to offset Jimmy Carter's contention that he was "dangerous." '[9] In November 1981, when President Reagan's budget director in a published interview termed the administration's budget policy 'trickle-down economics' and conceded the numbers on which it was based were dubious, the media's handling of the affair was not surprising. 'The question all day at the White House,' reported Lesley Stahl of CBS, 'was: Can Stockman survive? Will he be fired?' And from congressional reporter Phil Jones: 'The question is: Can Stockman regain credibility in Congress? If today's Senate Budget Committee hearing is any indication, it will be difficult for Stockman to be effective again.'[10]

What I have called here the technical angle in news reporting is by no means the only way contemporary journalists frame political events. Journalism, like any other long-standing cultural institution, is intricate in its complexity. But the technical angle does tend to dominate political coverage, particularly when background and analysis are offered.[11] It also serves well to illustrate what is distinctive about contemporary journalism as a form of political communication. In order to understand why this form of journalism has become dominant and to assess its implications, it is necessary to trace the transformation of the news media from the small-scale political press of the eighteenth and early nineteenth centuries to the large-scale commercial mass media of today.

DISPLACEMENT OF THE POLITICAL PRESS BY COMMERCIAL MASS MEDIA

When, in 1749, Benjamin Franklin outlined the curriculum for a proposed Pennsylvania Academy, he stressed the importance of political oratory, noting that this required a knowledge not only of the rhetoric of the ancients but of the craft of newspaper publishing, 'Modern Political Oratory being chiefly performed by the Pen and the Press.'[12] Alexis de Tocqueville, writing in the 1830s, saw the American newspaper as catalyst of collective political action, essential for maintaining an active political life under conditions of mass democracy. Tocqueville wrote:

> The leading citizens living in an aristocratic country can see each other from afar, and if they want to unite their forces they go to meet one another, bringing a crowd in their train. But in democratic countries it often happens that a great many men who both want and need to get together cannot do so, for all being very small and lost in the crowd, they do not see one another at all and do not know where to find one another. Then a newspaper gives publicity to the feeling or idea that had occurred to them all simultaneously but separately . . . . The newspaper brought them together and continues to be necessary to hold them together.[13]

The US newspaper of the eighteenth and early nineteenth centuries was a vehicle of political debate and action. Neither objectivity nor political neutrality, the key values of contemporary journalism, was considered a virtue.[14] The main purpose of a newspaper, to the extent that it concerned itself with public affairs (newspapers also provided entertainment, commercial information, and religious and moral edification), was to express a particular point of view as forcefully and eloquently as possible. In the early nineteenth century as political parties were established, the press became primarily partisan. Most newspapers were backed financially by parties or politicians whose politics they represented and whose followers they served to mobilize. The press of this period was also relatively decentralized. Newspapers were small, numerous, and, given the small amount of capital required, relatively easy to establish; Franklin began as a printer's apprentice. The early American newspaper was both public and political: public in the sense that it was neither an official agency of the state nor primarily a private business venture but an organ established by citizens to communicate with one another; political in that it took a stand on the issues of the day. It was a quintessential institution of the public sphere, a means by which the ordinary citizen could be involved in the discussion of political issues.

The public sphere in the eighteenth and early nineteenth centuries, however, was restricted to a relatively small segment of the population. It was not until the 1820s and 1830s that property qualifications were dropped and the franchise extended to the entire white male population, nor until then that the newspaper became fully accessible to the masses. The papers of the pre-1830 period cost 6 cents an issue, nearly 10 per cent of a wage-worker's average daily income. They were read primarily by commercial and political élites. It was the penny press of the 1830s, the forerunner of today's commercial mass media, that first put newspapers in the hands of the mass public on a regular basis. This transformation of the American press was to prove paradoxical: on the one hand, it democratized the market for newspapers, but, on the other, it centralized the means of political communication in the hands of large corporations and caused the atrophy of the mobilizing and advocacy roles previously fulfilled by the newspaper.

The penny papers and their successors were commercial rather than primarily political enterprises. Introducing newly-developed steam-powered cylinder presses, they lowered prices and expanded circulations by an order of magnitude. This gave them a new but very valuable product to sell: the attention of a mass audience. Advertising became the solid economic foundation of the new mass-circulation papers, and the newspaper became a major commercial undertaking, requiring substantial capital investment and promising handsome profits. These profits had important political implications; they meant that the mass-circulation newspaper, unlike its less lucrative predecessor, had no need of political subsidies to stay afloat. The penny papers thus began to turn away from the political tradition of the early American press, proclaiming their independence and often their distaste for 'political discussions of a merely partisan character,' and turning from 'oratory' to news in the modern sense of the term.[15] Eventually, as newspaper markets became increasingly concentrated, the economics of advertising would create strong incentives for the final abandonment of politically-committed journalism as a paper intent on maximizing its circulation could not afford the restriction of its audience that would result from identification with a particular political position.[16]

In the era following the rise of the penny papers, newspapers were both lucrative commercial enterprises and instruments of personal political power. Their owners continued to be deeply involved in partisan politics, but as independent actors with their own power bases; the rhetoric of commitment to 'the public good' often served as a weapon in the battle with opposing party leaders and factions.[17] The final phase in the break with political journalism was professionalization and the development of the idea of 'objectivity,' a transition which took place roughly between the 1920s and 1950s.

It is the ideal of objectivity that explains the emphasis on technique and efficacy in the news stories cited. The rise of commercial mass media transformed not only the institutional structure of political communication but also the structure of discourse itself. Commercial or professional journalism employed standards of truth and of the writer's proper relation to the audience which were very different from those of political journalism. It had entirely changed standards for what needed to be said in a newspaper and how it should be said.

At the heart of this conception was the respect for 'facts,' which the penny papers proclaimed along with their political independence and which grew in importance as the commercial media developed. Just as the changing organization of the press paralleled the central change taking place in the wider economy, the growth of large-scale capitalist organization, the changing conventions of journalism paralleled the rise of science as a cultural paradigm against which all forms of discourse came to be measured. 'We shall endeavor to record facts on every public and proper subject, stripped of verbiage and coloring,' wrote James Gordon Bennett in his 1835 prospectus for the *New York Herald*.[18] The *Herald* was by no means free of verbiage or coloring, but it did emphasize news and the gathering of information rather than the political 'oratory' that had been the stock-in-trade of the '6-penny' papers. By the 1920s Walter Lippmann and others would be speaking explicitly of scientific method and 'the habit of disinterested realism' as a model for journalism. The journalist of the late nineteenth century, despite a commitment to factual reporting, did not yet radically separate fact and value; one could be a realist and yet a moralist, a recorder of facts and yet a political crusader. But by the early twentieth century realism had become objectivity: 'a faith in "facts," a distrust of "values," and a commitment to their segregation.'[19] And journalists came to think of themselves not as participants in a process of political discussion, even of a nonpartisan character, but as professionals, standing above the political fray.

The precise meaning of objective journalism has changed considerably over the course of the twentieth century. From about the Second World War through the early 1960s, objectivity was assumed most of the time to require strict separation not only between fact and value but between fact and interpretation. This was the heyday of 'straight' journalism; news analysis for the most part was restricted to the signed column, and the ordinary reporter was supposed to tell 'who, what, when, where' and leave it at that. The naive realism of 'straight' objective journalism was shattered by the political conflict of the 1960s and 1970s, which produced both a credibility gap (a questioning of traditional sources of political information) and a clash of interpretations unknown in the years of wartime and Cold War consensus. The stories examined above represent a concern for analysis and investigation born of the disillusionment and confusion of the 1960s. They offer the audience not just facts, not just a record of the latest press releases, but perspective and summation, an interpretation of how the facts fit together and what they mean. But the 1960s and 1970s did not produce a questioning of objectivity itself; the 'new journalism,' which harkened back to the committed journalism of earlier periods, never gained more than a slippery toehold in the commercial media. In some ways, in fact, the 1960s and 1970s, precisely because the interpretation of reality had become subject to political debate, increased the journalist's and the news organization's need to appear strictly objective. The journalist had to provide analysis without appearing to depart from disinterested professionalism. And the easiest way to accomplish this was to focus on questions of strategy, effectiveness, and technique, questions that did not touch directly on conflicts of interest or clashes over the ends and values of political life. The political future of David Stockman is easier to assess with an attitude of detached realism than the actual policy of trickle-down economics, which inevitably raises the issue of how the interests and values affected by economic policy are to be weighed.

ONE-DIMENSIONALITY OR LEGITIMATION CRISIS?

What are the consequences of the commercialization of the press and the scientization of journalism? Critical theorists have given two very different answers. The prevailing view in the 1940s, 1950s, and early 1960s held that the mass media had become fully integrated into a form of welfare state capitalism, which was rapidly expanding technical rationalization from the sphere of production into all aspects of social life.[20] The media had been stripped of the independent position the early press had held regarding the dominant social interests and had become not merely policemen of the ideological realm but something more sinister than that (policemen, after all, are only necessary to the extent that people resist social control). The media had become producers of consciousness. The consciousness they produced, moreover, was what Marcuse called a 'one-dimensional' consciousness; it accepted the existing social order as defining the limits of rationality and sought merely to reflect that order, rejecting any attempt to speak of values or possibilities beyond it as inherently meaningless.

Centralization of control over the production of news

The one-dimensionality perspective was never developed within critical theory beyond a few provocative essays or applied very systematically to an analysis of news reporting. But more recent research certainly confirms that there is a good deal of truth to it. The rise of the commercial media reversed the decentralization that had prevailed in the early days of the press, placing political communication once more under the control of established institutions, albeit institutions very different from those that had regulated political discourse before the advent of the newspaper and the pamphlet.

It is interesting to look at the rise of commercial media in Great Britain, where the political implications of that development were more directly evident than in the United States.[21] The British newspaper was burdened by onerous political restrictions until well into the nineteenth century, including heavy taxes designed to keep newspapers too expensive to be either published or purchased by the lower classes. But repression proved not only ineffective but possibly counter-productive. Working-class papers were published illegally, and the taxes, which they therefore did not have to pay, gave them a competitive edge over the respectable papers. Repression, in other words, ensured that the working class would continue to control its own press. By 1836 the growing illegal press exceeded the legal press in circulation. The liberal campaign for repeal of the 'taxes on knowledge,' which triumphed in the 1850s, made use of all the familiar arguments for freedom of the press, but the reformers did not leave their case simply to noble sentiments. To these they added the argument that a free market in information would place the education of the masses in the hands of men of 'wealth and character.' Said one reformer in Parliament, quoted by James Curran:

> We have made a long and fruitless experiment with the gibbet and hulks. Is it not time to consider whether the printer and his types may not provide better for the peace and honour of a free state, than the gaoler and the hangman. Whether in one word, cheap knowledge may not be a better political agent than costly punishment.[22]

Freedom of the press meant not merely the lifting of censorship but the transformation of knowledge into a commodity, and the small-scale political press, like the independent petty producer of the precapitalist era, soon had to face the devastating economic power of highly capitalized mass production.

The radical press never attained a political importance in the United States comparable to its importance in Britain in the 1830s.[23] Perhaps this was in part because the United States had for a long time given market forces free reign in the sphere of information; no doubt it was largely due to the differing political and economic structure of the two societies. But when the penny papers appeared in the 1830s, there was nevertheless a growing labor press in the United States, and the penny papers played precisely the role described by the English reformers: they spoke to the cultural and political needs of the constituents of the labor press, artisans who in the 1830s were facing loss of economic independence. But they spoke to those needs from a consensual, reformist, and often a relatively apolitical perspective, emphasizing what the artisans had in common with the other and probably the primary constituency of the new commercial press, the rising middle class. 'An emerging American working class,' writes Dan Schiller:

> confronted newspapers that accepted and amplified belief in individual property, the market and the state, and that simultaneously drew heavily on its own experience . . . . The American working class had barely begun to employ the press as an agency of class identity when the commercial penny papers began to enlist the interest and identification of the laboring men.[24]

The liberal conception of a free market in ideas rested on the principle that the exchange of ideas should be insulated from the structures of wealth and power. In fact the rise of a market in ideas tied the production and dissemination of political information closely to the centers of economic and political power. There is a deep historical irony here. The coming of mass production, which so democratized the market for news, making the newspaper, as Marx put it, 'cheaper than natural gas,' at the same time centralized the production of news, placing the press under the control – today, in fact, generally monopoly control – of the corporation.[25] The American news media, moreover, have also come to have an intimate institutional connection with the state, despite the absence of formal state control. Modern American news organizations are so strongly geared toward reporting the activities and perspectives of government officials that one journalist gave his influential book the ironic title, *The Fourth Branch of Government*.[26] The news generally reflects the views of political élites faithfully enough that in a period like the 1950s and early 1960s, when conflicts within that élite are relatively insignificant, the political discourse that filters through the media to the public does come very close to the one-dimensionality described by Marcuse.

The role of ideology

There is also another, more impersonal but perhaps ultimately more significant face of power: the power of ideology. This is where the technical angle on politics and the principle of objectivity enter the picture. The scientistic model of political discourse is a deeply-rooted element of modern capitalist culture, which imposes itself on political discourse without any direct or conscious political intervention for the most part. I introduce the qualification 'for the most part' because there have been times when this model of journalism has been emphasized for directly political reasons, and these are revealing. Objectivity was stressed by editors and publishers during the 1930s for instance, when the Newspaper Guild was strong and relatively political, and there was concern reporters would slant the news toward the interests of labor.[27]

What are the implications of this use of the technical angle? Again, they are not simple, and I shall discuss some of the complexities below. But certainly that model of journalism does have the effect that Marcuse decried; it tends to exclude from political discourse discussion of the ends of public policy. It conveys, moreover, along with the news of particular events, a general conception of politics more or less compatible with the prevailing low level of popular mobilization. It portrays politics either as a matter of administration or as a more or less sordid personal struggle for power (as in the story on the Reagan – Carter debate), and not, to use Habermas' phrase, as a process of 'collective will-formation' and not therefore as a process in which the average citizen need be involved. It conveys to citizens a message about their own role in politics, and that message is essentially one of exclusion.

The news report as a speech act

This last point touches on a dimension of communication much neglected in the study of the media. It is a basic principle of pragmatics, stressed by Habermas, who borrows it from J. L. Austin and John Searle,[28] that any 'speech act' has a twofold structure: it contains both a propositional and a 'performative' content. It makes a statement about the world and simultaneously invokes or solicits a relationship between speaker and hearer.[29]

Consider the contrast between a modern news broadcast and an eighteenth-century newspaper. Let me take as examples the CBS broadcast containing the special report on pacification and an edition of the *New-England Courant*, an early American newspaper published by James Franklin and later Benjamin Franklin. The CBS broadcast analyzes for the audience in a factual and authoritative tone the progress of the pacification program. It contains virtually no statements that address the audience members directly; they are treated as strictly anonymous. It ends with Walter Cronkite's famous sign-off, 'And that's the way it is, Tuesday, December 16, 1968.'

The *New-England Courant* dealt with political material of an entirely different kind. One fairly typical edition contained a tract on the philosophical basis of law:

> Law is right Reason, commanding Things that are good, and forbidding Things that are bad . . . . The Violation therefore of the Law does not constitute a Crime when the Law is bad; but the violation of what ought to be a Law, is a Crime even where there is no Law.[30]

Along with this different kind of content went a different way of addressing the audience. The political tract, which was reprinted from a London journal, was introduced to the readers by a letter to the editor, signed in the fashion of the time, 'Your Humble Servant, &c.' It may in fact have been a contribution sent in by a reader, or it may have been written by the publisher. Most major articles were presented in the form of open personal letters.

In the two cases, very different relationships are established between speaker and hearer. The *New-England Courant* speaks to its readers in a personal tone, at an equal level. It invites them to participate in political discussion. CBS speaks to its audience as a provider of authoritative information. It solicits nothing beyond their attention, solicits of them no active role regarding the political material reported; indeed the authoritative and detached style of the report and the finality of the sign-off leave the impression that the matters discussed are essentially closed, at least until the next broadcast.

The technical angle is only one element of the ideology that shapes modern US journalism. The role of ideology in political communication is a subject that cries out for more systematic investigation. A number of recent studies of the media have addressed the question perceptively, but there is as yet little systematic theory in the area. Most discussions of the role of ideology tend, for lack of theory, to slip by default into functionalism. They tend, that is, to identify certain ideological assumptions, supportive of the capitalist social order, which seem generally to dominate the news, and sometimes to show how these assumptions are effective – how, for example, they are built into the routines of journalism. But they then generally default the question of why these particular ideological principles become dominant, why a congruence develops between the ideological structures of capitalism and its political and economic structures, assuming that the fact of congruence is explanation enough (this problem is taken up in the discussion of the concept of hegemony in Chapter 4).

IMPOSSIBILITY OF AN 'ADMINISTRATIVE PRODUCTION OF MEANING'

One reason functional assumptions can be dangerous in the study of the media and of ideology generally is that cultural institutions do not always develop in ways that are functional for the established social order. This brings us to Habermas' theory of legitimation crisis, which departs sharply from the picture of ideological integration painted by the critical theory of the 1940s, 1950s, and early 1960s. The critique of late capitalist society advanced by Horkheimer, Adorno, and Marcuse is based largely on the 'closing of the universe of discourse,' which they believed that society had produced. Habermas' critique of late capitalism rests on the impossibility of this very ideological closure, the impossibility of an 'administrative production of meaning.'

This argument, which Habermas presents in an admittedly sketchy and preliminary form in his *Legitimation Crisis*, runs essentially as follows.[31] Liberal capitalist societies have been able to maintain political stability largely because they have permitted the state to intervene increasingly in the workings of the market, softening the social disruptions it produces and ensuring a level of private satisfaction high enough that the mass public will remain generally uninterested in politics. But state action to maintain an orientation of civil privatism has an ironic consequence; it results in an increasing 'politicization of the relations of production:' more and more areas of social and economic life, previously regulated by the market or by traditional institutions like the family and the church (whose functions, threatened by the tradition-shattering rationality of capitalist production, the state often takes over), are drawn into the political arena. Politicization creates an increased need for legitimation, for justification of social decisions that had previously seemed inevitable products of the market mechanism or expressions of cultural tradition. But legitimation is becoming increasingly hard to come by, precisely because the institutions that have borne the burden of cultural 'production' – the family, the church, and to some extent the market itself – are on the decline. And the resulting deficit of legitimation cannot, at least ultimately, be made up by any sort of managed production of ideology, for the latter is incompatible with the communicative action essential to the creation of shared normative structures.

It might seem that the media would be the logical institution to fill the legitimation gap, especially in the United States where they have almost complete formal independence from the state, and enjoy a much higher level of public trust than most other institutions. Habermas himself does not address the role of the media in *Legitimation Crisis*. But I would like to outline here, in a preliminary way, several reasons why it seems unlikely that the media could be counted on to play this role adequately and consistently.[32]

The anarchy of ideological production

Corporate control of the mass media does not guarantee that the media's cultural products will consistently serve the interests of the capitalist system as a whole, any more than corporate control of energy guarantees against an energy crisis. Certainly no major news organization is ever likely to become an open critic of capitalism, but the purpose of a news organization is to make profit, not politics, and there is no reason to assume that the narrow economic interest of the corporation will always coincide with the political interest of the system. If the anarchy of production leaves the capitalist system vulnerable to economic crisis, why should the anarchy of ideological 'production' not leave it similarly vulnerable to cultural crisis?

Tensions within the dominant ideology

Neither does the hold of ideology over the journalist seem likely to guarantee that the media will consistently serve to legitimate the dominant institutions of capitalist society. Ideologies are as fraught with contradiction as are any other historical phenomena. Certainly that is true of the ideology that dominates US journalism. The ambivalence of US journalism is especially acute with respect to the state. Modern journalism is characterized by a great reverence for political authority, expressed in explicit terms at times of ceremony or crisis (the transition of power from Nixon to Ford, for example), and, perhaps more important, manifested implicitly in the whole focus and organization of the news-gathering process, which revolves like a satellite around the center of political power. But the US journalist is also traditionally cynical about the holders and seekers of power, and that tradition has been reawakened and perhaps deepened by the political conflicts of the 1960s and the drift and ineffectiveness of the 1970s. This cynicism may itself be functional for the system in that it demobilizes the public, lowering what political scientists call the sense of political efficacy.[33] But that does not mean it could not simultaneously be hollowing out the myths that have sustained the welfare–national security state of the postwar period. When it comes to the economic structure of modern capitalism, the journalist is much less likely to express doubts. But even here there are ideological tensions. The American journalist believes in 'free enterprise' and the rationality of modern capitalist technology and social organization; at the same time she or he clings to an ideology of traditional individualism that predates the corporate era and coexists with it somewhat awkwardly.[34]

Universal pragmatics and the limits of ideological manipulation

The media, finally, have a need for legitimation of their own, which may conflict with the legitimation of the system. Here it will be useful to return to Habermas' pragmatics. Critical theory is concerned with developing a form of social enquiry that will be able to bridge the gap between is and ought, enabling us to offer rational answers, grounded in the analysis of human experience, to practical questions, questions of how we should live and act. Habermas believes the solution to this puzzle is to be found in the analysis of communication. The effective use of language presupposes certain relations of reciprocity between human individuals; these conditions for the possibility of effective communication, which can be established by a reconstructive science of speech acts, provide a basis for both normative discourse and for empirical analysis of the dynamics of human history. It is this 'universal pragmatics' that provides the justification for the central premise of *Legitimation Crisis*, the premise that there can be no 'administrative production of meaning.' The use of communication as an instrument of domination, Habermas argues, violates the conditions of trust and reciprocity essential to the achievement of shared meaning. This is not to say communication cannot be used successfully for manipulative purposes. On the contrary, what Habermas calls instrumental or strategic communication is a routine fact of social life and certainly a central characteristic of contemporary political history; one need only to recall the effectiveness of government management of the news in the early years of the Vietnam War.[35] But it follows from Habermas' theory that there are limits beyond which the basic structure of human communication cannot be stretched.[36]

The idea of a universal pragmatics is fraught with theoretical difficulties, far too numerous and fundamental to be discussed here. But Habermas does seem to have stated a simple but neglected truth crucial to the analysis of ideological institutions. Every process of communication involves a social relationship, in fact, a network of relationships, among active human subjects.[37] The maintenance of these relationships imposes demands on institutions like the media that may conflict with the need of the system for legitimation. The media have to attend to their own legitimacy. They must maintain the integrity of their relationship with their audience and also the integrity of their own self-image and of the social relationships that make up the profession of journalism.[38] Maintaining these relationships requires a certain minimum of honesty, which, especially in periods of political crisis, can lead to conflicts of considerable ferocity between the media and other major social institutions and may seriously conflict with the legitimation requirements of the system. To a limited extent, this did in fact occur in the United States during the 1960s and 1970s. We do not yet know how substantial the ideological consequences have been. It has often been observed that the fact of conflict between the media and other institutions does not necessarily mean the media are playing a delegitimating role in relation to the political and socio-economic system, and this is clearly true. Indeed the media often see themselves in such cases as upholders of that system and present the correction of abuse as the ultimate proof of its soundness.[39] One study of the impact of Watergate coverage found that those who followed Watergate on television were more likely than others to lay the blame on individuals rather than the political system.[40] There is, however, no theoretical reason to assume this will always be the case, and the potential for disjunctions between the needs of the media and the needs of other institutions deserves more attention than it has gotten from critical analysts of the media.

To the extent that the media do not maintain the integrity of their relationship with their audience, moreover, legitimation may break down in another way: the media may become ineffective ideological institutions. This may in fact be one important consequence of the scientization of journalism. The shift to an attitude of detached realism places the ends and values of political life outside the normal bounds of political communication, and this is functional for the system. But at the same time it may render the media incapable of contributing to the establishment of new legitimating values if the old ones are beginning to break down. The modern mass media and the professional journalist clearly have great power (subject to the many political, economic, and social constraints within which they operate) to set the agenda of political discussion and to determine the context within which day-to-day events will be perceived. As purveyors of authoritative information, their strength is great indeed. But their ability to establish positive social values and political commitments may be another matter altogether.

CONCLUDING COMMENTS

The rise of commercial mass media, which began in the United States in the 1830s, had paradoxical political consequences. It democratized the market for newspapers; at the same time it centralized the production of political information and ruptured the connection between the press and an active public. It led to the decline of politically-committed journalism and its replacement by a professional journalism that claimed to stand above politics. Professionalization transforms the nature of political discourse. It narrows discussion to questions of technique and effectiveness that can be approached with detached realism. It also changes the performative content of journalism; it transforms the newspaper from a political message addressed from citizen to citizen, inviting the reader to participate in political debate or action, into an authoritative account of the state of the world, addressed to an audience whose own role in that world normally is not at issue. For these reasons, the modern news media do not produce the kind of active, critical public debate that the newspaper seemed to promise when it first emerged as an institution of the public sphere. The American news media may, in fact, communicate to the public a conception of politics and of their own political role that strongly discourages active political involvement. Beyond this the precise consequences of the commercialization and scientization of journalism are not easy to judge. There is no simple answer, in particular, to the much-debated question of whether a commercial–professional news media can be expected to serve as an effective ideological support for the power structure of advanced capitalism.

This argument I put forward simply as a research proposal; all the links in the chain of development I have outlined here need to be investigated more thoroughly. I have suggested, for example, that the technical angle in news reporting results from professionalization, which in turn results from commercialization. In fact little is known about the interconnections among these three aspects of American journalism, and these most likely are considerably more complex than I have presented them here. Professionalization, for instance, no doubt has cultural and political as well as economic roots; it is particularly advanced in the United States and much less so in other advanced capitalist states.[41] And the technical angle is no doubt to some extent a reflection of the general political culture of the twentieth-century United States, not a result purely of the structure and ideology of the news media. Little is known, similarly, about how the public actually responds to the underlying messages about politics, embedded in the form of news presentation, which I have stressed. And the problem of legitimation is still shrouded in ambiguity. We do not know, for example, to what extent a system of political and economic power actually needs a coherent legitimating ideology that penetrates the consciousness of the mass public. Perhaps passivity and pragmatic acceptance of power are sufficient; in that case Habermas' strictures about administrative production of meaning would be more or less irrelevant to assessing the role of mass media in the maintenance of structures of power.

The mass media are an institution with a dual social identity. They are both an economic (or in Western Europe, often political) and a cultural institution; they are a profit-making business and at the same time a producer of meaning, a creator of social consciousness. Much research has been done in recent years on the political economy of the news media, the structure of the media as economic institutions, and the impact of that structure on their cultural product. This, however, is only part of the story: the 'production' of culture – to use a common but misleading metaphor – also surely has imperatives of its own, which must be understood if we are to capture in its full complexity the functioning of an institution like the news media. It is for this reason that I have placed such heavy emphasis on Habermas. Habermas seems to offer at least the beginnings of a systematic approach to the dynamics of ideological production, conceptualized in such a way that those dynamics can be linked with the economic and other processes that also shape the news media.

Underlying Habermas' contribution to the understanding of political culture and communication is the concept of dialogue, which is crucial in two respects. First, it is the concern with dialogue that leads Habermas, like others in the critical theory tradition, to focus on the character of political debate, the fate of the public sphere in liberal capitalist societies. But Habermas also uses the concept of dialogue in a new and powerful way: as the heart of a method of analysis of communication and culture. For Habermas, all forms of human communication, even under conditions of mass dissemination, are essentially relationships between human subjects, derived ultimately from the elementary structure of dialogue. The structure of dialogue therefore provides a basis for a theory of communicative action and hence of the 'production' of culture. Whether one accepts the idea that a universal structure of dialogue underlies all communication, communication is clearly a relationship, not merely a product. It is essential to grasp not only the effects of mass communication (the focus of the positivist tradition) and the economic and political constraints under which it operates but also the specifically communicative or interactive constraints involved in the creation of shared meanings.

Discussions of the media and public policy are traditionally dosed with exhortations to the media to provide the public with more and better information, 'an informed and active public being essential to a vigorous democracy' (as the phrase goes). This is sensible enough advice, subject of course to the problem of saying what is to count as better information about public affairs. But it is also insufficient. The problem with the American news media, if one does in fact value active public participation, lies not so much with the quality of the product being offered the consumer as with the fact that the major relation of political communication has indeed become a relation of seller and consumer.

The modern mass media are relatively good at collecting and disseminating information. When one compares them with the news-gathering efforts of the pre-commercial, 'pre-mass' press, the organizational, technological, and even cultural advances are staggering. The mass public today receives an unprecedented quantity of information. Even the scientism of contemporary journalism represents a significant – and in certain ways democratizing – cultural advance. The shift from the oratory of early political journalism to the commercial media's focus on news and 'facts' meant a shift of attention from abstract principles (the 'right Reason' of the *New-England Courant*'s discussion of law) to the real historical events and social conditions that touched the mass public in their daily lives.

What the modern mass media cannot do is to play the role of sparking active public participation in deciding the direction of public policy. I use the word *cannot* deliberately. Individual journalists working in established news organizations can certainly from time to time break out of the focus on technique and strategy to raise the direction of public policy as an issue; they can be sensitive to the underlying message their reporting conveys about politics and the citizen's relation to it; they can give a hearing to those who do seek to play a mobilizing role. But all of this must remain within relatively narrow limits; the anti-political tendencies explored here are deeply rooted in the structure and the professional ideology of the American news media. Few of us, in fact, would want the established news media to presume to play the mobilizing role of the decentralized press of Tocqueville's day. It is not a role appropriate to institutions with such massive social power.

To the extent, then, that life is to be breathed into the public sphere of liberal capitalist societies, the initiative must come from outside the institutions now dominating that sphere. The 'Habermasian' analysis I have stressed suggests reason for at least cautious optimism that citizens' organizations can make themselves heard despite the centralization of control over the channels of political communication. However powerful they may have become, the mass media must maintain some semblance of a dialogue with the public. There is always, therefore, some degree of openness, of two-dimensionality in the communication process: when an active public challenge to the limits of political discourse arises, the media can ignore it only at the peril of their own legitimacy.[42]

NOTES

1 J. Habermas, 'The public sphere: an encyclopedia article (1964),' *New German Critique*, 1974, vol. 3, pp. 49–53; J. Habermas, *The Structural Transformation of the Public Sphere: An Inquiry into a Category of Bourgeois Society*, Cambridge, Mass., MIT Press, 1989.

2 A. de Tocqueville, *Democracy in America*, Garden City, NY, Doubleday, 1969, p. 517.

3 Karl Marx, 'Debates on freedom of the press and publication [1842]', in S. K. Padover (ed.), *Karl Marx on Freedom of the Press and Censorship*, New York, McGraw-Hill, 1974, p. 31.

4 J. Habermas, *Theory and Praxis*, Boston, Mass., Beacon Press, 1973, p. 42. See also his *Knowledge and Human Interests*, Boston, Mass., Beacon Press, 1971. See also Hugh Baxter, 'System and life-world in Habermas's *Theory of Communicative Action*,' *Theory and Society*, 1987, vol. 16, pp. 39–86.

5 One work that does attempt an empirical analysis of political communication from a critical theory perspective is C. Mueller, *The Politics of Communication*, New York, Oxford University Press, 1973. Mueller's work, though, contains relatively little discussion of the media.

6 CBS, 11 and 16 December 1968.

7 See D. C. Hallin, *The 'Uncensored War': The Media and Vietnam*, New York, Oxford University Press, 1986; and T. Gitlin, *The Whole World Is Watching: Mass Media in the Making and Unmaking of the New Left*, Berkeley, Calif., University of California Press, 1980.

8 T. E. Patterson and R. D. McClure, *The Unseeing Eye: The Myth of Television Power in National Politics*, New York, Putnam, 1976.

9 *New York Times*, 29 October, 1980, p. 1.

10 CBS, 12 November 1981.

11 One might object: 'What about the editorial, the "op-ed" page and the specialized press of political opinion? Doesn't modern American journalism merely differentiate news and political commentary?' Political commentary certainly survives in the modern media, but it survives in a subordinate and restricted status. It is no

longer considered the primary task of journalism. It is banished from the front page. It also tends to be restricted to the prestige press. The *New York Times*, the *Washington Post*, and a few other papers with relatively élite readerships have fairly substantial 'op-ed' pages, most US newspapers do not; and television, which is the major source of information for the mass public, places a particularly low value on political commentary. The 'op-ed' page itself, moreover, is not unaffected by the growing importance of the technical angle in news analysis.

12 B. Franklin, *The Autobiography and Other Writings*, New York, Signet, 1961, p. 213.

13 Op. cit., p. 518.

14 In discussing the early American news media, I draw heavily on two fine studies: M. Schudson, *Discovering the News*, New York, Basic Books, 1978; and D. Schiller, *Objectivity and the News*, Philadelphia, Pa., University of Pennsylvania Press, 1981.

15 *Baltimore Sun*, quoted in Schudson, op. cit., p. 22.

16 In the late nineteenth century, as Elliot King points out, when competition among newspapers was intense and markets fragmented, political crusades were a good way to sell papers (E. King, 'The political values of the public press: 1835–1920', Ph.D. dissertation, University of California, San Diego, 1992). Once a newspaper aspires to cover an entire market, however – as advertisers prefer and as most papers (and television) do today – identification with a particular political position becomes much more problematic. It is interesting here to consider the competition in the 1940s and 1950s between the *New York Times* and *New York Herald-Tribune*, as described in R. Kluger, *The Paper: The Life and Death of the New York Herald-Tribune*, New York, Knopf, 1986. Kluger's account suggests that the *Herald-Tribune* lost out by trying to stick to a strategy of political 'product differentiation' while the *Times* tried to build circulation and demographics without regard to political lines. The professionalization of the advertising business itself seems to have been a factor: once the buying of advertising space was turned over by owners to professionals, the *Herald-Tribune*'s appeals for support of a Republican paper were met with demands to produce the numbers.

17 King, op. cit.

18 Quoted in Schiller, op. cit., p. 74.

19 Schudson, op. cit., p. 6.

20 The most important statements of this perspective are M. Horkheimer and T. W. Adorno, 'The culture industry: enlightenment as mass deception,' in *idem, The Dialectic of Enlightenment*, New York, Seabury Press, 1972; and H. Marcuse, *One-Dimensional Man*, Boston, Mass., Beacon Press, 1964.

21 See J. Curran, 'Capitalism and control of the press, 1800–1975,' in J. Curran, M. Gurevitch, and J. Woollacott (eds), *Mass Communication and Society*, Beverly Hills, Calif., Sage, 1979; G. Boyce, 'The fourth estate: reappraisal of a concept,' and J. Curran, 'The press as an agency of social control: an historical perspective,' both in G. Boyce, J. Curran, and P. Wingate (eds), *Newspaper History: From the 17th Century to the Present Day*, Beverly Hills, Calif., Sage, 1978.

22 Curran, 'Press as an agency of social control,' op. cit., p. 55.

23 There has been relatively little research on the radical press in the United States. See J. R. Conlin (ed.), *The American Radical Press, 1880–1960*, Westport, Conn., Greenwood Press, 1974; and R. Armstrong, *A Trumpet to Arms: Alternative Media in America*, Boston, Mass., Houghton Mifflin, 1981.

24 Op. cit., p. 74.

25 By 1986 only twelve American cities still had competing daily newspapers, and about twice that many had editorially separate papers with joint operating

agreements. There are many fewer today. B. H. Bagdikian, *The Media Monopoly*, Boston, Mass., Beacon Press, 1987, p. 124.

26 D. Cater, *The Fourth Branch of Government*, New York, Vintage, 1959. An enormous literature bears on this point. Two of the most important works are B. Cohen, *The Press and Foreign Policy*, Princeton, NJ, Princeton University Press, 1963; and L. Sigal, *Reporters and Officials*, Lexington, Mass., D. C. Heath, 1973.

27 Schudson, op. cit., pp. 156–7.

28 J. L. Austin, *How to Do Things With Words*, New York, Oxford University Press, 1962; J. L. Austin, 'Performative utterances,' in *idem, Philosophical Papers*, Oxford, Clarendon Press, 1961; J. R. Searle, *Speech Acts*, Cambridge, Cambridge University Press, 1969.

29 J. Habermas, 'What is universal pragmatics?,' in *idem, Communication and the Evolution of Society*, Boston, Mass., Beacon Press, 1979. A similar point is made by Bakhtin: V. N. Volosinov, *Marxism and the Philosophy of Language*, New York, Seminar Press, 1973.

30 7–14 May 1722.

31 J. Habermas, *Legitimation Crisis*, Boston, Mass., Beacon Press, 1975. See also 'Legitimation problems in the modern state,' in *Communication and the Evolution of Society*, op. cit.

32 Cf. D. Kellner, 'Network television and American society: introduction to a critical theory of television,' *Theory and Society*, 1981, vol. 10, no. 1.

33 Political scientists have tried, without success, to demonstrate a connection between the media and the level of political efficacy. But no one has devised a way to assess long-term media effects through the use of quantitative methods. See M. J. Robinson, 'Public affairs television and the growth of political malaise: the case of "The Selling of the Pentagon," ' *American Political Science Review*, 1976, vol. 70, pp. 409–32; A. H. Miller, L. Erbring, and E. N. Goldenberg, 'Type-set politics: impact of newspapers on public confidence,' *American Political Science Review*, 1979, vol. 73, pp. 67–84. My critique of both appears in Chapter 3.

34 Much of the ideology of the modern American journalist can be traced to the Progressive era, when the journalistic profession was just beginning to take shape. It is, it seems to me, the ideology of an independent middle class absorbed into corporate capitalism but not entirely comfortable with the new order. This is a connection that deserves more attention than it has gotten. There is some discussion of the importance of progressivism in H. J. Gans, *Deciding What's News*, New York, Pantheon, 1979.

35 See Hallin, op. cit.

36 There is considerable ambiguity in Habermas' writing on this point, as there is in general on the relation between the normative and the empirical sides of his argument about legitimation. When Habermas writes in 'Legitimation problems in the modern state:' 'Only the rules and communicative presuppositions that make it possible to distinguish an accord or agreement among free and equals from a forced or contingent consensus have legitimating force today,' he is falling into a purely normative concept of legitimation (or perhaps confusing intellectual history with the history of actual legitimation processes), for the actual process of legitimation is much more complex, involving, for one thing, a continuing importance of tradition.

37 Again Bakhtin is also relevant.

38 On the possibility of disjunction between the media professional and the structure of power, see A. W. Gouldner, *The Dialectic of Ideology and Technology: The Origins, Grammar, and Future of Ideology*, New York, Seabury, 1976.

39 D. Paletz and R. Entman, *Media Power Politics*, New York, Free Press, 1981.

40 J. McLeod, J. D. Brown, L. P. Becker, and D. A. Zieke, 'Decline and fall: a

longitudinal analysis of communication effects,' *Communication Research*, 1977, vol. 4, pp. 3–22.

41 A number of European countries are trying to find ways to preserve a political press, despite strong economic tendencies toward the elimination of such a press. See A. Smith (ed.), *Newspapers and Democracy: International Essays on a Changing Medium*, Cambridge, Mass., MIT Press, 1980.

42 Gitlin discusses the interaction of the media and citizen activists in *The Whole World is Watching*, op. cit., and 'News as ideology and contested area: towards a theory of hegemony, crisis and opposition,' *Socialist Review*, 1979, vol. 9. See also Paletz and Entman, op. cit., ch. 8.

Chapter 3

The media, the war in Vietnam, and political support

A critique of the thesis of an oppositional media

Since the late 1960s the thesis has been put forward repeatedly in academic and public discourse that the American news media have been transformed from a relatively passive and conservative institution into an institution of opposition to political authority. This transformation, the argument continues, is in large part responsible for the well-documented decline of public confidence in political institutions[1] and, more generally, for a weakening of political authority. 'The most notable new source of national power in 1970, as compared to 1950, was the national media,' wrote Samuel Huntington, in a mid-1970s report to the Trilateral Commission. 'In the 1960's the network organizations, as one analyst put it, became "a highly creditable, never-tiring political opposition, a maverick third party which never need face the sobering experience of governing." '[2]

THE STATE OF THE EVIDENCE

The most important empirically-backed statement of this thesis is Michael Robinson's 'Public affairs television and the growth of political malaise.'[3] Robinson presented data to show that people who relied primarily on television for information about public affairs (like most proponents of the oppositional media thesis, Robinson considers television a particularly important source of delegitimizing news coverage) tended to be more cynical about political institutions and more doubting of their own political capacity than those who utilized other media. These differences, according to Robinson, could not be explained by the low educational level of those who depended on television; it was reduced but not eliminated by a control for education (which may be a surrogate, of course, for social class). The explanation, therefore, had to lie in the content of television news: 'events are frequently conveyed by television news through an inferential structure that often injects a negativistic, contentious or anti-institutional bias. These biases . . . evoke images of American politics and social life which are inordinately sinister and despairing.'[4]

Robinson's study, however, has a critical flaw. It is based on the association between political attitudes (efficacy and trust in government) and self-reports of media habits (reliance on television as opposed to other media), and it contains no measure of what according to Robinson's theory is the real independent variable: the content of television news.[5]

A stronger test of the link between critical news coverage and declining support for political authority is Miller, Erbring, and Goldenberg's 'Type-set politics: impact of newspapers on public confidence.'[6] In 1974 the National Election Study conducted by the Center for Political Studies at the University of Michigan included a content analysis of the front-page articles appearing in newspapers collected from the areas surveyed. This made it possible for the authors to assess directly the association between news content and the political attitudes of those exposed to it. The association proved substantial. News content varied considerably from paper to paper, and those whose newspapers contained more criticism of political authorities and institutions tended to score lower in indices measuring trust in government and, to a lesser degree, political efficacy. This finding persevered in the face of numerous controls. The authors concluded that there was a 'significant relationship between negatively critical media content and evaluations of government.'[7]

Here, however, we run up against the basic limitations of the media effects paradigm, with its focus on the link between news content and individual attitudes. Establishing that critical news content does indeed affect popular attitudes toward government only takes us one step toward resolving the larger issue of the role of the media in the legitimation or delegitimation of political authority, and therefore whether they can be seen, in Huntington's terms, as institutions of political opposition. Two crucial questions remain unanswered.

The first is the question of aggregate news content, which becomes essential as soon as we attempt to move from statements about the link between content and individual attitudes to statements about the impact of the media on public opinion at the aggregate level. Given that critical news coverage leads to critical attitudes – and favorable content to favorable attitudes; that is, that Miller, Erbring, and Goldenberg could have stated their conclusion in the opposite way: 'There exists a significant relationship between positive media content and evaluations of government' – we need to know how much of news content, overall, is favorable and how much unfavorable to political authority.

Miller, Erbring, and Goldenberg do, in fact, provide interesting evidence on aggregate news content. The papers in their sample contained more criticism of political authority than praise, but more neutral content than either of these: 31 per cent of the stories contained criticism, 6 per cent praise, and 63 per cent were neutral. Their data also showed that most criticism was directed at individuals rather than at institutions and that most came from other political authorities rather than from journalists – both very significant findings, as we shall see below (p. 54). But theirs was not primarily a study of news content, and Miller, Erbring, and Goldenberg are limited in the conclusions they can draw about the political messages to which the American public is generally exposed. Most important, that analysis was confined to a relatively brief and unusual period of time, the denouement of the Watergate affair in the middle of 1974. It thus contains no information about changes in news content over time, which is clearly important for assessing claims about the role of the media in a secular decline of public confidence.

The second question concerns the process by which news content is produced – the functioning of the media as institutions, the constraints under which they operate, their relations with other political institutions, and so on. Does a high level of negative news content, for example, reflect an ideology of adversary journalism? Or does it simply reflect policy failures and conflicts between élites, faithfully recorded by an essentially apolitical news media? Certainly in the two cases our assessment of the media's role in the overall process of opinion formation would be very different.

METHODOLOGY

This study addresses the relatively neglected questions of shifts in news content over time and the functioning of the media as political institutions. On the basis of a content analysis of television coverage of the war in Vietnam, it offers a critique of the thesis that the American news media shifted toward an oppositional stance during the Vietnam period, and a reinterpretation of their changing relation to political authority.

Vietnam and television are both obvious choices for a case study of this sort. Vietnam was the most extensively covered and the most controversial news story of the period from 1960 through 1976, during which the bulk of the decline of public confidence in American political institutions took place. The argument that the media were in large part the cause of that decline is essentially an historical one, and in that sense this study is less subject to the problems of generalizability that often limit the value of case studies. The argument made by Robinson, Huntington, and other proponents of the oppositional media thesis is not that the media have always played a delegitimizing role (though Robinson, perhaps, can be taken to imply that television is by its nature destructive of political support); it is that they began to play this role sometime during the middle or late 1960s. And for such a hypothesis Vietnam is clearly a critical case. It is, moreover, television which these researchers have generally singled out as the most important source of delegitimizing news coverage.

The data which follow are based on a stratified random sample of 779 television broadcasts from the period beginning 20 August 1965 and ending with the cease-fire on 27 January 1973. The analysis begins in August 1965 because archives of television news are not available before that date (the

Vanderbilt Television News Archive was established in August 1968). All material after that date is taken from Vanderbilt. Interestingly, it is possible to extend this analysis back to 1965 only because the Defense Department, alarmed by the now-famous report by CBS correspondent Morley Safer which showed the Marines burning peasant huts with cigarette lighters, began recording news coverage relevant to military activities in August of that year. This material is now in the National Archives. It is unfortunately not as complete as the Vanderbilt collection is, at least for weekday news. It omits an unknown amount of coverage less directly related to the military, including some coverage of domestic debate, the actions of civilian policy-makers, and the diplomatic and political sides of the war. When there is reason to believe these omissions might bias figures presented here, this will be noted.[8]

The argument will proceed as follows. On the surface, the pattern of change in television content seems consistent with the thesis of an increasingly oppositional news media. The data suggest a substantial shift from one-sidedly favorable coverage of US policy in the early years – before the 1968 Tet offensive – to more critical coverage after Tet. This change, moreover, cannot be dismissed as a mere reflection of the actual course of events. In some cases the increase in negative content clearly has no relation to changes actually taking place in Vietnam. So one must conclude that the media were indeed applying different journalistic standards in the latter part of the war.

When we probe more deeply, however, the thesis of an oppositional media begins to fall apart. The evidence does not suggest any dramatic shift in the basic ideology and news-gathering routines of American journalism. The routines of objective journalism – routines which are incompatible with an actively oppositional conception of the journalists' role – seem to have persisted more or less unchanged throughout the Vietnam period. The media continued, in particular, to rely heavily on official information and to avoid passing explicit judgement on official policy and statements. Data will also be presented which suggest that the media were not inclined to favor opponents of administration policy, and it will be argued that critical coverage in the latter part of the war did not extend to the political system or to basic consensus beliefs.

The concluding section presents a model for explaining changes in the level of critical coverage, emphasizing the response of an objective media to the degree of consensus or dissensus that prevails particularly among political élites.

NEWS CONTENT: THE GROWTH OF CRITICAL COVERAGE

The following four tables illustrate the shift in Vietnam coverage from a balance quite favorable to administration policy prior to the Tet offensive to a considerably less favorable balance after Tet.[9] Table 3.1 gives a summary of journalists' editorial and interpretive comments on the news. It includes all

Table 3.1   Direction of television journalists editorial comments on major actors of Vietnam war (percentages down)

Favorability to action or policy of:	Administration, supporters	South VN gov't	Dove critics of war	North VN, NLF
Pre-Tet period				
Favorable	11	2	0	0
	78.6%	50.0	0.0	0.0
Unfavorable	3	2	2	20
	21.4	50.0	100.0	100.0
Tet period				
Favorable	0	0	0	2
	0.0	0.0	0.0	40.0
Unfavorable	6	3	3	3
	100.0	100.0	100.0	60.0
Post-Tet period				
Favorable	23	17	7	10
	28.8	29.8	31.8	25.6
Unfavorable	57	40	15	29
	71.3	70.2	68.2	74.4

Note: Pre-Tet period is 20 August 1965–30 January 1968 (about thirty-six months); Tet, 31 January–31 March 1968 (two months); post-Tet, 1 April 1968–26 January 1973 (about fifty-one months).

statements by journalists which offered explicit opinions on the war (commentaries included), drew explicit conclusions about controversial issues (for example, a conclusion that one side or the other was winning), or used strong evaluative language (words like 'butchery' or 'massacre') without attribution. I shall return to this table on a number of occasions. For now, it is enough to observe that the figures show a shift from a heavily favorable balance (by a ratio of four to one, though the number of cases for this period is small) before Tet, to an unfavorable balance of more than two to one.

Tables 3.2 and 3.3 chart the development of two important themes in news coverage which were lightly covered early in the war but reflected unfavorably on administration policy after 1968. These tables, in contrast to Table 3.1, take into account not only comments made directly by journalists, but also comments attributed to others and the subject of the stories themselves. Table 3.2, for instance, gives a count of positive and negative references concerning the status of democracy in South Vietnam. A reporter's observation that the South Vietnamese regime was unpopular would appear in this table as a negative reference, as would a report on anti-government demonstrations. A report on administration statements lauding South Vietnamese democracy would appear as a positive reference. When a relevant statement or event is the major subject of a story, it is scored as one reference; when it is mentioned but

Table 3.2   Positive and negative references to democracy in South Vietnam

	Positive references	Negative references
Pre-Tet period	4.5	6.0
Tet period	0.0	0.5
Post-Tet period	3.5	37.0

Note: Figures are raw frequencies. For dates and relative lengths of periods see note to Table 3.1.

Table 3.3   Positive and negative references to morale of US troops

	Positive references	Negative references
Pre-Tet period	4.0	0.0
Tet period	0.0	1.0
Post-Tet period	2.5	14.5

Note: Figures are raw frequencies. For dates and relative lengths of periods see note to Table 3.1.

is not the major subject, it is scored as half a reference. The table shows that negative references to South Vietnamese democracy increased by an order of magnitude after 1968. Table 3.3 shows a more modest but still substantial increase in negative references to the morale of US troops. These figures reflect primarily an increase in stories about drug use, attacks on officers, protests by soldiers, and refusals to follow orders.

Table 3.4, finally, shows how often representatives of different points of view on the war appeared on television. Briefly summarized, the table suggests that spokespeople for administration policy were heavily predominant during the early period, while after Tet there was relative parity between the administration and its critics.

Similar patterns emerge for many dimensions of news content. Before Tet, for example, of those military operations reported on television in which some conclusion was offered as to who had won or lost, 62 per cent were reported as victories for the US and its allies, 28 per cent as defeats, 2 per cent as stalemates. After Tet the figures were 44 per cent victories, 32 per cent defeats, and 24 per cent stalemates. Before Tet positive assessments of the overall military situation in Vietnam outnumbered negative assessments by ten to one in television coverage; it must have been difficult for the average viewer even to conceive of the possibility of a US defeat. After Tet positive and negative assessments were roughly balanced.

It could of course be argued that the increase in negative news had nothing to do with any change in the media, but simply reflected the evident failure of

Table 3.4 People speaking or quoted in television coverage of Vietnam

	Pre-Tet period	Tet period	Post-Tet period
Administration and supporters[a]	59 26.3	4 13.8	250 28.4
South Vietnamese, allied governments	8 3.6	0 0.0	33 3.8
Critics of administration[b]	10 4.5	7 27.6	230 26.1
North Vietnamese, NLF officials	4 1.8	1 3.4	35 4.0
American officers, GIs in field[c]	110 49.1	11 41.4	152 17.3
Others	34 15.2	4 13.8	179 20.3
Total	224 100.0	26 100.0	880 100.0

Notes: Figures may not add to totals because of rounding. Frequencies are rounded because of weighting (see note 4 in the text). For the pre-Tet period, figures for both administration spokespeople and for domestic critics are biased downward because the 'Defense Department Kinescopes' excluded much domestic reporting.
[a] Includes domestic but not foreign supporters of administration policy.
[b] Includes both 'doves' and 'hawks,' though most are 'doves.' Includes only domestic critics of administration policy.
[c] Also includes lower-level civilian officials, for example, pacification advisors.

US policy and the growth of domestic opposition. This is the mirror theory of news – a theory cherished by news people themselves. And there is a good deal of truth to it. The data in Table 3.3, for instance, which show an increase in the coverage of morale problems among US troops, more or less parallel the actual figures for fragging incidents (attacks on officers) and insubordination convictions.[10] Table 3.4 similarly reflects the spread of public and congressional opposition to the war.

But this explanation cannot be carried too far. Consider Table 3.2, which shows a massive increase in negative coverage of the South Vietnamese political system. Did the South Vietnamese regime suffer a dramatic loss of public support between, say, 1966 and 1970? Not at all; indeed, 1966 was a year of intense political strife in South Vietnam, more intense than anything that occurred after 1968. In this case it was clearly the selection of news – rather than South Vietnamese politics – which was changing. It is similarly hard to explain the change in the portrayals of the military situation as a reflection of objective reality.

OBJECTIVE JOURNALISM

On the surface then, Vietnam seems to confirm the thesis of a shift in American journalism toward an oppositional stance: news content became substantially more critical as the war went on, and the pattern of change cannot be explained away as a simple reflection of the course of events. But as soon as one begins to probe beneath the surface of news content, to explore the production of news as well as the ideology and organization of American journalism, the thesis of an oppositional media begins to unravel.

It is true that during the Vietnam period journalists became more inclined to report information critical of official policy. Any history of journalism in this period and any journalist's memoir will confirm this. In 1961 the *New York Times*, showing the typical caution with which the media approached any story related to national security in the early 1960s, suppressed on its own initiative information on the impending Bay of Pigs invasion which was public knowledge in Miami and Guatemala; in 1971 the *Times* was willing to defy threats of criminal prosecution to publish the *Pentagon Papers*.[11] But there were certain basic elements of the structure and ideology of American journalism which persisted more or less unchanged through the Vietnam period, and which make it very hard to sustain the thesis of an actively oppositional news media.

Most important here is the continuing importance of the professional ideology of objective journalism. What is most striking about the modern American news media, if one compares them with the media of other historical periods or other countries, is their commitment to a model of journalism which requires disengagement from active political involvement and assigns to the journalist the relatively passive role of transmitting information to the public. Studies of the socialization and professional ideology of the modern American journalist have consistently confirmed the centrality of the ideal of a politically neutral press,[12] as have analyses of news content. Miller, Erbring, and Goldenberg found that even at the height of the Watergate affair most news stories were neutral toward political authority. Studies of campaign coverage have generally found rough but consistent balance in coverage of major candidates.[13]

Did the rise of critical news coverage during the later years of Vietnam represent a break with the tradition of objective journalism, a return perhaps to something resembling the partisanship of the nineteenth-century press? This is not what the data on television coverage suggest.

It will be useful here to reconsider Table 3.1, which gives a count of the kinds of people who appeared or whose statements were cited in television coverage, and which shows a substantial increase in the number of opponents of administration policy represented. This would seem to indicate a divers-ification of sources. But when these data are broken down it becomes clear that they mask an important element of continuity.

Table 3.5   People speaking or quoted in television coverage of Vietnam, domestic
stories excluded

	Pre-Tet period	Tet period	Post-Tet period
Administration and supporters[a]	48 26.2	3 18.8	145 32.4
South Vietnamese, allied governments	8 4.4	0 0.0	33 7.4
Critics of administration[b]	1 0.5	0 0.0	16 3.6
North Vietnamese, NLF officials	4 2.2	1 6.2	34 7.6
American officers, GIs in field[c]	101 55.2	11 68.8	143 32.0
Others	22 12.0	1 6.2	75 16.8
Total	183 100.0	16 100.0	447 100.0

Notes: Figures may not add to totals because of rounding.
[a] Includes domestic but not foreign supporters of administration policy.
[b] Includes both 'doves' and 'hawks,' though most are 'doves.' Includes only domestic critics of administration policy.
[c] Also includes lower-level civilian officials, for example, pacification advisors.

The evidence does not suggest that the reporters in Saigon and Washington who covered the basic news of the Vietnam War did their work much differently in 1973 than in 1963. What happened instead is that a new issue arose alongside the basic Vietnam story: the story of domestic dissent. As domestic conflict increased, television reported the rising tide of dissent, and opponents of the war became increasingly visible in the news. The news from the field and from executive branch beats in Washington – from which the hard news of the war was primarily covered – continued to reflect a heavy predominance of official sources. This can be seen in Table 3.5, which presents the same data as Table 3.4, but excludes from the analysis all purely domestic stories, primarily stories about the conflict on the home front. These findings are supported by other studies of news coverage during the latter period of the Vietnam War. Leon Sigal, for instance, found in a study of *Washington Post* and *New York Times* coverage in 1969 that 72 per cent of the sources used in stories with Washington datelines were US government officials, as were 54 per cent of the sources used in Saigon stories.[14]

One way to summarize the contrast between Tables 3.4 and 3.5 is to say that administration representatives and their opponents appeared in different kinds of television stories: dissenters appeared in stories primarily about dissent itself, while official spokespeople appeared in stories which reported the actual news of the war. This may seem at first glance an obvious and trivial finding. But it is more significant than it appears. Stories on domestic dissent, first, often did not give opponents of administration policy any real opportunity to present alternative interpretations of the news. A large proportion of these stories focused on the issue of domestic dissent itself: the prospects for legislative opposition, the tactics of the demonstrations and how many people were attending them, whether violence would occur, and how order would be restored.[15] Opponents of administration policy would appear in these stories to explain and justify themselves, not to discuss the war in Vietnam. Only about 40 per cent of all stories on domestic debate contained any substantive discussion of the war, and often this was extremely brief. Even to the extent that domestic critics did appear in stories that contained discussion of policy issues (this happened most often in reports on congressional hearings), critics and officials appeared in essentially different roles. Critics were shown giving their opinions about a political issue. Officials were shown defending their policies against criticism, but they also appeared in the authoritative and nonpolitical role of providing the basic information about events in Vietnam and explaining those events to the public.

This reliance on officials for authoritative information has several implications. First, it suggests that administration spokespeople were likely to have been taken more seriously by the news audience than their critics. One of the basic findings of the long tradition of media effects research is that a communicator presented in a nonpolitical, information-providing role has higher credibility than one presented as an exponent of partisan opinions.[16] Second, it means that when the administration decided to exploit fully its ability to initiate news, it was often very successful, even in the skeptical context of the post-Tet period. For example, the key element in the Nixon administration's efforts to sell its Vietnam policy to the American public was Vietnamization – the replacing of American with Vietnamese troops. The data in Table 3.6 suggest that the initiation of Vietnamization not only put the South Vietnamese armed forces on the news agenda, but also resulted in a continued preponderance of favorable references to their performance, despite the generally more critical tone of coverage in the latter part of the war. These favorable references were largely the result of what Boorstin[17] has called 'pseudo-events:' statements by US officials, ceremonies turning over US bases to the South Vietnamese, etc., which, because they represented official policy, were considered mandatory news stories.

Finally, the practice of turning to officials as the primary source of authoritative information is an important symbolic recognition of their legitimacy: it is an affirmation both of their claim to superior knowledge ('trust us – we have access to information you don't have') and of their right to be considered representative of the community as a whole and thus above politics. The right to be considered the primary source of authoritative

Table 3.6   Positive and negative references to performance of South Vietnamese armed forces, before and after 'Vietnamization'

	Positive references	Negative references
Prior to Vietnamization	11.5	3.0
After Vietnamization	40.5	14.5

Note: For purposes of this table the beginning of Vietnamization is dated 7 June 1969, the day before the Midway conference at which Nixon announced his first withdrawal of US troops. Figures are raw frequencies. The two periods are about equal in length, forty-six and forty-four months, respectively.

Table 3.7   Frequency of editorial comments in television coverage of major actors of the Vietnam War

	Number of editorial comments	Comments per hour of coverage
Coverage of US policy, activity	99	4.0
Coverage of opposition to US policy	27	5.0
Coverage of South Vietnamese gov't	63	10.2
Coverage of North Vietnam, NLF	65	19.7

Note: Amount of time devoted to activities of various actors must be estimated, since many television stories deal with several actors at a time.

information about world events should probably be considered a central component of the legitimacy of modern political institutions, comparable in a secular age to the right of the church in medieval Europe to interpret the scriptures.[18]

Two further sets of figures illustrate the persistence of journalistic respect for official sources. It was not simply the use of official sources which gave officials so much influence over news content. It was the fact that the norms of objective journalism required the journalist to pass on official information without comment on its accuracy or relevance. Did these restraints also persist through the Vietnam period? The fact that only 8 per cent of the stories sampled contained explicit commentary by journalists suggests that they did. And when that figure is disaggregated, it becomes clear that it very much overstates the willingness of journalists to comment on official policy and statements. The data in Table 3.7 indicate that commentary was substantially less common in coverage of the US executive than in coverage of other political actors relative to the amount of time devoted to each.

Data on the frequency of news reports questioning the accuracy of official statements tell a similar tale. Fourteen and one-half such references turned up in the sample for the post-Tet period (with the half references, again, scored when the theme was not the primary subject of the story, and all references to inaccuracy or dishonesty of official statements counted, whether made by journalists or attributed to others). To put this figure in perspective, it can be estimated that a faithful viewer who watched the evening news every night would have seen an average of about one such reference a month – considerably more, no doubt, than a viewer would have seen before Tet (only three references occurred in the pre-Tet sample), but not a figure that suggests journalists were going out of their way to question official information, or even to air such questions raised by others. Of those 14.5 references only 3.5 involved charges of deliberate efforts to mislead the public.

COVERAGE OF THE OPPOSITION

If the media had become an oppositional institution during the latter years of the Vietnam War, it is reasonable to assume that they would have given relatively favorable coverage to other opponents of administration policy. But here again the data do not square with the thesis of an oppositional media.

The media did give increasing coverage to the opposition as the war went on. But this coverage was not particularly favorable. As shown in Table 3.1, journalists' interpretive comments were unfavorable to domestic opponents of the war by roughly two to one in the latter part of the war, approximately the same ratio that prevailed in coverage of administration policy. A count of all statements about the anti-war movement presented on television, including both journalists' and attributed comments, yields a similar two to one negative ratio for the post-Tet period – forty-eight unfavorable comments, twenty-five favorable.[19] Whatever tendency there may have been for journalists to become more skeptical of administration policy, it does not seem to have been translated into sympathetic coverage of the opposition.

COVERAGE OF THE SYSTEM

It is important to note, finally, that the increase in critical coverage during the latter part of the Vietnam War did not involve coverage critical of the political system in any meaningful sense of that term. Just as critical coverage during the immediate post-Watergate period, as measured by Miller, Erbring, and Goldenberg, was directed at particular incumbents rather than at the system or its major institutions,[20] critical coverage in Vietnam reporting was directed at the administration and its policies. For the most part, the political system was simply not an issue in Vietnam coverage, which, like most news coverage, focused on what journalists call hard news – news of specific events, policies, and personalities. When the political system – or important consensus beliefs, like the belief that American foreign policy is motivated by a concern with democracy – did become an issue in the news, coverage was generally of a legitimating character. Journalists reporting on the anti-war movement, for example, often distinguished between those who, in the phrase of the day, 'worked within the system' and those who did not, and made clear their preference for the former. Journalists also made a special point on certain particularly delegitimizing occasions (the Tet offensive and the evacuation of Saigon in 1975) to stress that the motives of US policy had been good.[21] This finding parallels the evidence from public opinion surveys: despite their loss of confidence in the conduct of government during the 1960s and 1970s, the American public continued to express a high level of faith in the system.[22]

CONCLUSION: OBJECTIVE JOURNALISM AND POLITICAL SUPPORT

The case of Vietnam, in short, does not support the thesis that the American news media shifted to an oppositional role during the 1960s and 1970s. There was, to be sure, a very substantial turn toward more critical coverage of US policy in Vietnam. But it is hard to argue that journalists began to take on an actively oppositional role; the professional ideology of objective journalism and the intimate institutional connection between the media and government which characterized American journalism before the turbulence of the 1960s and 1970s both persisted more or less unchanged.

That conclusion made, however, we are left with an important problem of how to account for the substantial change in news content over the course of the Vietnam War. The puzzle is the more acute as we have already rejected the most obvious alternative explanation: the mirror theory that changing news content reflected a changing course of events.

As paradoxical as it may seem, the explanation for the media's changing level of support for political authority during the Vietnam War lies in their constant commitment to the ideology and the routines of objective journalism. Tom Wicker of the *New York Times*, referring to the early 1960s, once observed that 'objective journalism almost always favors Establishment positions and exists not least to avoid offense to them.'[23] He was, as we shall see, essentially correct. But from the point of view of a particular administration and its policies, objective journalism can cut both ways politically. A form of journalism which aims to provide the public with a neutral record of events and which, at the same time, relies primarily on government officials to describe and explain those events obviously has the potential to wind up as a mirror not of reality, but of the version of reality government officials would like to present to the public. At the same time, objective journalism involves a commitment to the political independence of the journalist and to the representation of conflicting points of view. The journalist's relation to political authority is thus not settled in any definite way by the professional norms and practices of objective journalism. It is on the contrary something of a paradox for the journalist, and it is resolved in different ways depending on political circumstances.

Consider the early period of the Vietnam War, when coverage was by most measures heavily favorable to administration policy. How could coverage so imbalanced be reconciled with a conception of journalism which requires neutrality and balance on controversial issues? The one-sided character of news coverage in this period is not hard to understand if one simply keeps in mind that Vietnam was not yet a particularly controversial issue within the mainstream of American politics. There were debates in Congress over certain tactical questions – whether the military should have greater freedom in selecting bombing targets, whether enough was being done on the political and diplomatic fronts, and so on. But on the broad outlines of US policy there was still relatively little disagreement among the major actors of American politics. To reflect the official viewpoint did not seem in this context to violate the norms of objective journalism: it did not seem to involve taking sides on a controversial issue.

This consensus, of course, did not last forever. Its erosion became serious politically, by most accounts, about the middle of 1967, and was accelerated by the Tet offensive.[24] Given this change in the parameters of political debate it is perfectly reasonable to expect that the media, without abandoning objective journalism for some more activist and anti-establishment conception of their role, would produce a far higher quantity of critical news coverage. Here, then, is an explanation for the change in Vietnam coverage that seems to fit nicely both with the data on news content and with our knowledge of the institutional relations between the media and political authority: *the change seems best explained as a reflection of and a response to a collapse of consensus – especially of élite consensus – on foreign policy.* One journalist expressed it this way:

> As protest moved from the left groups, the anti-war groups, into the pulpits, into the Senate – with Fulbright, Gruening and others – as it became a majority opinion, it naturally picked up coverage. And then naturally the tone of the coverage changed. Because we're an Establishment institution, and whenever your natural constituency changes, then naturally you will too.[25]

It is useful to imagine the journalist's world as divided into three regions, each of which involves the application of different journalistic standards. The first can be called the sphere of consensus. This is the region of motherhood and apple pie; in its bounds lie those social objects not regarded by journalists and by most of the society as controversial. Within this region journalists do not feel compelled to present opposing views, and indeed often feel it their responsibility to act as advocates or ceremonial protectors of consensus values. The discussion of patriotism that marked coverage of the homecoming of the hostages after the Iranian crisis is a good example. So is the journalists' defense of the motives of US policy in Vietnam. Within this region the media play an essentially conservative, legitimizing role; here the case for a

Gramscian model of the media as maintainers of the hegemony of a dominant political ideology is strong.

Beyond the sphere of consensus lies what can be called the sphere of legitimate controversy. This is the region where objective journalism reigns supreme: here neutrality and balance are the prime journalistic virtues. Election coverage best exemplifies the journalistic standards of this region.

Beyond the sphere of legitimate controversy lie those political actors and views which journalists and the political mainstream of the society reject as unworthy of being heard. It is, for example, written into the Federal Communications Commission's (FCC) Fairness Doctrine that '[it is not] the Commission's intention to make time available to Communists or to the Communist viewpoints.'[26] Here neutrality once again falls away and the media become, to borrow a phrase from Parsons,[27] a 'boundary-maintaining mechanism:' they play the role of exposing, condemning, or excluding from the public agenda those who violate or challenge consensus values,[28] and uphold the consensus distinction between legitimate and illegitimate political activity. The anti-war movement was treated in this way during the early years of the Vietnam period; so were the North Vietnamese and the Viet Cong, except during a brief period when peace talks were near completion.

All of these spheres, of course, have internal gradations, and the boundaries between them are fuzzy. Within the sphere of legitimate controversy, for instance, the practice of objective journalism varies considerably. Near the border of the sphere of consensus journalists practice the kind of objective journalism that involves a straight recitation of official statements; farther out in the sphere of controversy they become more willing to balance official statements with reactions from the opposition or with independent investigations of controversial issues.

Using this framework the major changes in Vietnam coverage can easily be summarized. First, the opposition to the war expanded, moving from the political fringes of the society into its mainstream – into the electoral and legislative arenas, which lie within the sphere of legitimate controversy. As this occurred the normal procedures of objective journalism produced increasing coverage of oppositional viewpoints; when a presidential candidate comes out against the war, as occurred for the first time at the New Hampshire primary in 1968, the opposition becomes not only a respectable but an obligatory subject for news coverage. The reader may recall that Miller, Erbring, and Goldenberg found most criticism of political authorities reported in post-Watergate newspaper coverage to be criticism of one political authority by another – of Congress by the president and vice versa. (For all the drama of investigative journalism it is unlikely that the Watergate story would have gone very far if Congress had been controlled by the Republicans.) Similarly, the data on television coverage of Vietnam show 49 per cent of all domestic criticism of administration policy attributed to other public officials, compared with 16 per cent which came from reporters in commentaries and interpretive comments, and 35 per cent from all other sources, including anti-war activists, citizens in the street, and soldiers in the field.

Second, the sphere of consensus contracted while the sphere of legitimate controversy expanded. Not only did the media report the growing debate over the war, they were also affected by it. As the parameters of political debate changed, so did the behavior of the media: stories that previously had been reported within a consensus framework came to be reported as controversies; subjects and points of view that had been beyond the pale in the early years came to be treated as legitimate news stories. Neither the institutional structure nor the professional ideology of the media had changed substantially, but in a changed political environment these could have very different implications for the reporting of the news. The media did not shift to an oppositional role in relation to American foreign policy during the Vietnam War, but they did start to treat foreign policy as a political issue to a greater extent than they had in the early 1960s. This meant that the journalistic standards they applied were less favorable to administration policy-makers. ⌈In short, then, the case of Vietnam suggests that whether the media tend to be supporting or critical of government policies depends on the degree of consensus those policies enjoy, particularly within the political establishment. In a limited sense, the mirror analogy is correct.[29] News content may not mirror the facts, but the media, as institutions, do reflect the prevailing pattern of political debate: when consensus is strong, they tend to stay within the limits of the political discussion it defines; when it begins to break down, coverage becomes increasingly critical and diverse in the viewpoints it represents, and increasingly difficult for officials to control.[30] This does not necessarily imply that the media's role is purely passive or unimportant. It seems likely, on the contrary – though the question of media impact is beyond the scope of this study – that the media not only reflect but strengthen prevailing political trends, serving in a time of consensus as consensus-maintaining institutions and contributing, when consensus breaks down to a certain point, to an accelerating expansion of the bounds of political debate.[31] If this interpretation is correct, however, the media are clearly intervening and not – as the oppositional media thesis implies – independent variables in the process by which political support is generated or broken down. One must therefore look to other factors besides the structure and ideology of the media for the more basic causes of the current crisis of confidence in American politics.⌉

NOTES

1 A. H. Miller, 'Political issues and trust in government, 1964–1970,' *American Political Science Review*, 1974, vol. 68, pp. 951–72; S. M. Lipset and W. Schneider, *The Confidence Gap*, New York, Free Press, 1983.
2 S. J. Huntington, 'The United States,' in M. J. Crozier, S. P. Huntington, and J. Watanuki (eds), *The Crisis of Democracy*, New York, New York University Press, 1975. Huntington is quoting from M. J. Robinson, 'American political legitimacy

in an age of electronic journalism,' in D. Cater and R. Adler (eds), *Television as a Social Force*, New York, Praeger, 1975. Other statements of this position include P. B. Clarke, 'The opinion machine: intellectuals, the mass media and American government,' in H. M. Clor (ed.), *Mass Media and American Democracy*, Chicago, Ill., Rand McNally, 1974; E. C. Ladd Jr with C. D. Hadley, *Transformations of the American Party System*, New York, Norton, 1975; S. Rothman, 'The mass media in post-industrial society,' in S. M. Lipset (ed.), *The Third Century*, Chicago, Ill., University of Chicago Press, 1979; and A. Ranney, *Channels of Power: The Impact of Television on American Politics*, New York, Basic Books, 1983; and S. R. Lichter, S. Rothman, and L. S. Lichter, *The Media Elite*, Bethesda, MD, Adler and Adler, 1986.

3 *American Political Science Review*, 1976, vol. 70, pp. 409–32.

4 Ibid., p. 430.

5 There are other problems with Robinson's study as well, some discussed by A. H. Miller, L. Erbring, and E. N. Goldenberg, 'Type–set politics: impact of newspapers on issue salience and public confidence,' paper presented at the Annual Meeting of the American Political Science Association, Chicago, Ill., 1976. Robinson used reliance on television as opposed to other media as a surrogate measure of exposure to television content. But in 1974, when a direct measure of television exposure was available in the CPS National Election Study, it was not associated with lower levels of political trust or efficacy. Robinson's article also contains an experimental study of the impact of the CBS documentary, *The Selling of the Pentagon*, on subjects' political attitudes. *The Selling of the Pentagon*, however, cannot be taken as representative of television content in general; and in any case Robinson's data show only slight effects.

6 *American Political Science Review*, 1979, vol. 73, pp. 67–84.

7 Miller, Erbring, and Goldenberg, op. cit., p. 78.

8 Eight, ten, or twelve dates were selected randomly from each month during this period and for each date one network broadcast was then selected randomly. The National Archives material was sampled more heavily (ten dates per month) because, in part due to the limitations of the Pentagon's archiving, certain types of stories occur in it relatively rarely. The 1968 campaign period was also sampled heavily to permit separate analysis. All data presented below are weighted to correct for these sampling differences. The three networks did not differ greatly in their coverage of the Vietnam War, and they are combined in the analysis which follows. More detailed information on the content analysis is given in D. C. Hallin, *The 'Uncensored War': The Media and Vietnam*, New York, Oxford University Press, 1986.

9 A word about statistical significance. Many cells in the tables which follow have small Ns, and for that reason the data should be interpreted cautiously, particularly given the limitations of the National Archive sample. Nevertheless, most of the comparisons cited in the text are statistically significant. Take as an example the first column of Table 3.1. The four to one favorable ratio in journalists' editorial comments on the administration during the pre-Tet period is significant at a level of better than 0.03 (if the null hypothesis is a balanced 50–50 ratio), for the two to one unfavorable ratio in the post-Tet period, $p < 0.001$, and for the difference over time (eliminating the Tet period), $p < 0.001$ ($\chi^2_{1df} = 12.83$). Ns for the Tet period are clearly too small for statistical inference; data for this period are presented separately for illustrative purposes, and because that period is too distinctive to be lumped with either of the others. Ns for the pre-Tet period, incidently, are so much smaller than those for the post-Tet for three reasons: (1) the pre-Tet perod is shorter; (2) there were fewer news stories, in part because the war was not as important a domestic issue; and (3) the National Archives collection

does not include every story, excluding, especially, many domestic stories.

10 Reported fragging incidents rose from 126 in 1969, the first year data were kept, to 333 in 1971; insubordination convictions from 82 in 1968 to 152 in 1970, according to G. Lewey, *America in Vietnam*, New York, Oxford University Press, 1978, pp. 156–67.

11 See for instance H. Salisbury, *Without Fear or Favor: An Uncompromising Look at The New York Times*, New York, Ballantine, 1980.

12 For example, B. Cohen, *The Press and Foreign Policy*, Princeton, NJ, Princeton University Press, 1963; G. Tuchman, 'Objectivity as a strategic ritual,' *American Journal of Sociology*, 1972, vol. 77, pp. 660–79; H. J. Gans, *Deciding What's News*, New York, Pantheon, 1979.

13 For example, D. A. Graber, *Mass Media in American Politics*, Washington DC, Congressional Quarterly Press, 1980; R. C. Hofstetter, *Bias in the News: Television Network Coverage of the 1972 Election Campaign*, Columbus, OH, Ohio State University Press, 1976.

14 *Reporters and Officials*, Lexington, Mass., D. C. Heath, 1973.

15 Cf. T. Gitlin, *The Whole World Is Watching: Mass Media in the Making and Unmaking of the New Left*, Berkeley, Calif., University of California Press, 1980; D. N. Paletz and R. Dunn, 'Press coverage of civil disorders: a case study of Winston-Salem, 1967,' *Public Opinion Quarterly*, 1969–70, vol. 33, pp. 328–45.

16 C. I. Hovland, I. L. Janis, and H. H. Kelly, *Communication and Persuasion*, New Haven, Conn., Yale University Press, 1953.

17 D. Boorstin, *The Image*, New York, Athenaeum, 1962.

18 Cf. D. L. Paletz, P. Reichert, and B. McIntyre, 'How the media support local government authority,' *Public Opinion Quarterly*, 1971, vol. 35, pp. 80–92.

19 The figures in Table 3.1 are for all domestic opponents of the war; this set of figures is specifically for coverage of the anti-war *movement*.

20 One study found that those who followed Watergate in newspapers were more likely than those who did not to blame Nixon rather than the system: J. McLeod, J. D. Brown, L. B. Becker, and D. A. Zieke, 'Decline and fall at the White House; a longitudinal analysis of communication effects,' *Communication Research*, 1977, vol. 4, pp. 3–22. See also D. L. Paletz and R. M. Entman, *Media Power Politics*, New York, Free Press, 1981.

21 Thus Cronkite's famous commentary following the Tet offensive (27 February 1968) included both a call for de-escalation of the war and an affirmation that its intent – to 'defend democracy' – had been honorable, whatever the outcome.

22 J. Citrin, 'Comment: the political relevance of trust in government,' *American Political Science Review*, 1974, vol. 68, pp. 973–88; P. M. Sniderman, W. R. Neumann, J. Citrin, H. McClosky, and J. M. Shanks, 'Stability of support for the political system: the initial impact of Watergate,' *American Politics Quarterly*, 1975, vol. 3, pp. 437–57.

23 *On Press*, New York, Viking, 1978, pp. 36–7.

24 H. Y. Schandler, *The Unmaking of A President: Lyndon Johnson and Vietnam*, Princeton, NJ, Princeton University Press, 1977.

25 Max Frankel of the *New York Times*, quoted in Gitlin, op. cit., p. 205.

26 Quoted in E. J. Epstein, *News From Nowhere*, New York, Vintage, 1974.

27 T. Parsons, *The Social System*, New York, Free Press, 1951.

28 Cf. Gans, op. cit.

29 Cf. G. Tuchman, *Making News*, New York, Free Press, 1978.

30 Gitlin makes a similar argument, op. cit., ch. 10.

31 See here the recent work of J. Zaller, *The Nature and Origins of Mass Opinion*, New York, Cambridge Univesity Press, 1992.

Chapter 4

From Vietnam to El Salvador
Hegemony and ideological change*

In February 1981, the Reagan administration, as its first major foreign policy action, released the State Department 'White Paper' entitled 'Communist interference in El Salvador.' I was struck by the similarity between the reporting of the 1981 White Paper and the reporting of the White Paper released by the Johnson administration in February of 1965 in preparation for escalation in Vietnam, and decided to write an essay on the remarkable persistence of the old practice of reporting official statements on foreign policy at face value, without consulting alternative sources or historical parallels, and without commenting on their accuracy, significance, or motivation. I was quickly 'scooped' by numerous critiques of White Paper coverage.[1] But in the meantime a much more complicated and theoretically more significant story was developing.

The purpose of the El Salvador White Paper, like that of its 1965 predecessor, was to 'frame' the situation in El Salvador as a Cold War confrontation between the United States and the Soviet Union, on the assumption that a 'Cold War' interpretation would maximize public support for American intervention (the concept of 'frame' is explained in an appendix to this essay). But, within a few days, alternative frames – most notably the parallel with the 'quagmire' of Vietnam – were becoming common enough in news coverage that the Reagan administration, which had made a major effort to put Central America in the spotlight, was beginning to complain of 'excessive publicity.' The publicity following the White Paper was in fact very extensive, much more so than at a comparable stage of American involvement in Vietnam. And, as the focus of coverage began to shift somewhat from Washington to El Salvador itself, much of it was strikingly *different* from the foreign policy coverage of the early and mid-1960s. The crisis in Central America has thus become an excellent case for an exploration of the dynamics and the limits of change in the ideological orientation of the American news media and in their relation to the structure of political authority.

I will center my discussion around Antonio Gramsci's concept of 'hegemony,' which crossed the Atlantic to establish a beachhead in American media research about the time the Reagan administration raised the alarm about a 'Soviet beachhead' in Central America.[2] Gramsci was concerned with the nature of power in a liberal-democratic political system. Briefly, he argued that political power in liberal capitalist societies depends relatively little, except in times of extreme crisis, on the coercive apparatus of the state. It rests instead on the strength of a world-view, a system of assumptions and social values accepted as 'common sense' which legitimates the existing distribution of power and, indeed, renders opposition to it *inconceivable* for most of the population. The state plays a role in the propagation of that world-view, but the legitimating cultural system so crucial to political power is maintained largely by private, autonomous, and in many cases 'nonpolitical' institutions: the family, the church, the political party, and, of course, the mass media.

The concept of hegemony plays a double role in the study of the media. It is used, first, to conceptualize the political 'function' of the media. (I will have a few things to say later about the problem of functionalism.) The media, according to this neo-Marxist perspective, play the role of maintaining the dominant political ideology: they propagate it, celebrate it, interpret the world in its terms, and, at times, alter it to adapt to the demands of legitimation in a changing world. At the same time, the concept of hegemony is employed to explain the 'behavior' of the media, the process of cultural production itself. The media themselves are subject to the hegemonic process. The dominant ideology shapes the production of news and entertainment; this explains why the media can be expected to function as agents of legitimation, despite the fact that they are independent of direct political control.

Central America coverage is a significant case on which to test this perspective. After Vietnam, a major ideological rift developed over what is likely to prove a sensitive political question in the decades following the end of the Cold War: the United States' relation to revolution in the Third World. On Central America the Reagan administration and the media at times stood on opposite sides of that rift. As a result, the Reagan administration had a great deal of trouble 'managing' public opinion on Central America. More significant still for the long-term development of American political ideology, questions about the American stance toward revolution not publicly aired in the United States since the onset of the Cold War broke into the arena of mass political communication during this period.

Nevertheless, I shall argue that the hegemonic process can be seen very strongly at work in the Central American case. The Vietnam era shook the ground from beneath a number of the key assumptions of the view that has been taken as 'common sense' on foreign affairs since the late 1940s. The shaking of those assumptions initiated a period of both ideological and institutional change that has profoundly affected the way the American news media report world politics. But at the same time, there are powerful 'centrifugal forces' at work which limit the scope of those changes and the threat they could potentially pose either to the power of foreign policy élites within the United States or to the basic shape of the US role in world politics.

I will begin by examining the extent of the changes in foreign policy coverage since Vietnam, and the implications of those changes for the analysis of the hegemonic process, and then move to a discussion of the limits of change.

This essay is based on a content analysis of network television coverage of Central America from the October 1979 coup in El Salvador through June 1985,[3] a somewhat less systematic monitoring of coverage in major American newspapers, and on a series of interviews with reporters, producers, and editors involved in Central America coverage, both in Central America and in Washington, New York, and Miami bureaus.

THE FRAGMENTATION OF THE COLD WAR CONSENSUS

The Vietnam War, like the Central America crisis of the 1980s, was marked from beginning to end by considerable tension between the media and the government. As intense as these conflicts seemed to those involved in them, however, they took place within the narrow bounds of a powerful consensus on foreign policy. News coverage was held within those bounds by two factors. First, the dominant professional ideology of objective journalism held that it was the reporter's job simply to provide a record of what was said and done by those in positions of authority.[4] The news therefore tended most of the time – especially from Washington, where this principle was strongest, and especially on the front page – to reflect official views, whatever the reporter's personal beliefs. Second, reporters themselves almost all accepted the basic outlines of the 'bipartisan' consensus on foreign policy that had been established with the onset of the Cold War. That consensus held that the central fact of world politics was the conflict between the 'Free World,' led by the United States, and an expansionist Communist bloc, led by the Soviet Union. Given the centrality and the irreconcilability of this conflict, any local conflict, whether in Europe or what would later come to be called the Third World, had to be interpreted in terms of its 'global' – that is, its Cold War – significance.

A word is necessary here about the power of ideology. All human communication requires a structure of rules for the production of meaningful statements or utterances. Language is such a structure; its rules at the same time make it *possible* for us to apprehend and represent the world in a social way, and also *limit* the range of representations open to us. An ideology is also such a structure, on a higher level. It provides the basic framework within which political thought and communication take place. A language, of course, is very broad: it develops over a period of centuries, shaped by the speech acts of millions of very different individuals. Its limits are therefore wide enough that it generally does not make sense to see them as constraints, although, as recent controversies over the assumptions about gender embedded in ordinary language attest, this is not always the case. But an ideology is a much more specific historical structure, often developed, to some extent at least, by a limited number of individuals for conscious political purposes. Its limits are much narrower; and in a period when a single ideology dominates a particular area of discourse, the constraints it imposes can be powerful and of great political significance.

The early 1960s were precisely such a period – a period of consensus on foreign policy, when the Cold War ideology was accepted as defining the limits of 'responsible' political discussion. The assumptions of that ideology pervaded the news, and the critical coverage which so galled the administration remained firmly within its bounds. The news in this period often cast doubt on the effectiveness of American policy, particularly the wisdom of supporting Ngo Dinh Diem. It did not cast doubt on the goals of that policy or the world-view on which it was based: these were taken for granted. Here, for example, is the lead from a *New York Times* background story on Asia from 1962: 'Domestic instability in key non-Communist countries fringing Communist China continues to hamper United States efforts to build up these lands against further Communist penetration into free Asia.'[5] The headline was 'Three Areas of Asia [Laos, South Korea, South Vietnam] Disturb the Free World; U.S. Attempts to Stem Communist Aggression Hampered by Weak Regimes on China's Fringes.' The media's focus on the weakness of the Saigon regime was a real political liability to the Kennedy administration. But at the same time, the 'framing' of the Vietnam story is as good an example as one could wish of the hegemonic process at work. Ideological assumptions shape the news, and the news in turn reinforces those assumptions, 'confirming' them by interpreting a new historical case in their terms.

The contrast between Vietnam and El Salvador coverage is dramatic. To illustrate the extent of the change, I will take as an example a CBS documentary aired in March 1982, *Central America in Revolt* (parts of it were also shown on several evening news broadcasts). This documentary is not typical of television coverage of this period; it is not surprising that one of its principal reporters, Bill Moyers, did not last at CBS, but shifted back to public television. Yet *Central America in Revolt* is especially useful for this analysis, precisely because it did press against the furthest political limits of foreign affairs coverage in the American media. We shall see, moreover, that many significant characteristics of its approach did carry over into day-to-day news coverage.

Here is the introduction to the section dealing with El Salvador:

> This is the war the Reagan administration calls the 'decisive battle for Central America.' It's a civil war. But we are told the Soviet Union is working through Nicaragua and Cuba to help the insurgents win a victory for Communism. We're told our own security is at stake here.
>
> By now the sights and sounds of the war itself are as familiar as the evening news. But most of us have not seen how the war came about. It did

not just happen yesterday. It happened over many yesterdays, all of them filled with violence and terror.

That's the frustrating thing about reporting this story. There is much of it we cannot show you. We cannot show you the Spanish invaders, making slaves of the Indians to begin an era of brutal rule. We cannot show you the big coffee growers of a hundred years ago taking the land on which the peasants grew food. And we cannot show you that crucial bloody year of 1932, when the peasants rose up and were slaughtered, thousands and thousands of them, by the dictator who served the ruling class.

Politicization of the Cold War perspective

The most basic ideological change, reflected in the contrast between this background report and the *New York Times* report quoted above, is that the Cold War interpretation is now no longer assumed, but posed as a particular political position. This was a very new development for American journalism. Even in the later part of the Vietnam War, when journalists were generally disillusioned with American policy in Vietnam, discussion about the origins of revolution or the basic outlines of the US relationship with the Third World were simply not a part of the news agenda. Debate – as represented in the news – concerned the pace and the terms of American withdrawal, not the ideological underpinnings of US policy. It was, in contrast, common for background reports on Central America to pose the Cold War interpretation as the major political issue to be explored. ABC State Department correspondent Barrie Dunsmore introduced a week-long series of special reports, aired on the evening news on 9 March 1981, two weeks after the White Paper was released, with the statement that it would 'try to determine if an East–West confrontation over El Salvador is desirable or likely.' Note the assumption that confrontation with the Soviets is a *policy*, not an inevitable fact of world politics.

Reporting internal causes of revolution

The 'politicization' of the Cold War ideology has been accompanied by a number of other major changes in the presentation of foreign news. The *New York Times* report quoted above said virtually nothing about the specific history or the social or economic structure of South Vietnam, except that there was 'domestic discontent' which might render the Diem government ineffective against the 'Communist threat.' This was true of most Vietnam coverage, except during certain periods when policy debate in Washington centered around what to do about the 'instability' in Saigon. If the cause of the war was outside aggression, local history was not a significant part of the story. Thus, in the entire corpus of *New York Times* coverage from 1960 through 1963, there were only two references to the problem of land tenure, each about a paragraph long. *Central America in Revolt*, on the other hand, began its discussion of each country with an overview of its history. Those histories, moreover, gave considerable attention to certain themes which until recently had been rigidly excluded from foreign policy coverage, including social stratification (not simply 'poverty' or 'underdevelopment') as a cause of revolution, and the history of US intervention and economic involvement in the Third World. The segment on Guatemala centered around the contrast between the sanguine views of an American businessman and the realities of political and economic repression in that country.

Coverage of the 'enemy'

The Cold War consensus, later combined with the involvement of American troops in combat, made coverage of the North Vietnamese and the NLF extremely sensitive politically. Reports from North Vietnam (again, especially on television) were usually heavily laced with warnings about 'Communist propaganda;' reports on the NLF were extremely rare. Coverage of the official Nicaraguan position, on the other hand, was routine in Central American coverage (Table 4.1, p. 65, shows how frequently Nicaraguan officials appeared). In *Central America in Revolt*, Nicaraguan and US officials were 'balanced' in the same way Republicans and Democrats are balanced in domestic reporting. Coverage of the guerrillas in El Salvador was also fairly frequent, at least by historical standards.[6] Most of it was not very substantial; it tended to focus on the reporter's adventure 'behind the lines.' And, as Table 4.2, p. 76, shows, it was on balance much more negative than positive. But the mere fact that the guerrillas appeared with a human face, rather than existing purely as they were characterized by Washington, was a significant difference from the Vietnam period. *Central America in Revolt* went further, including clips of interviews with two Guatemalan revolutionaries whose views were presented with some substance, and 'balanced' against those of the Guatemalan military.

The 'credibility gap'

Finally, there has been substantial change in the journalists' attitudes toward political authority. Dan Rather introduced *Central America in Revolt* with three questions: 'Are we witnessing another Communist takeover in our hemisphere? Is the United States again becoming hopelessly entangled in another civil war? Is the information that we are getting from our government the truth?' An entire segment of the documentary was devoted to the question of government credibility. About thirty evening news stories in the sample focused on inaccuracies in official statements, and 154 of the 917 stories in the sample made at least some reference to inaccuracy of official statements or to official secrecy or image management. An interesting illustration of the change is the use of the term 'propaganda.' That term, throughout the Vietnam period, was a good example of how 'the concept [can] be absorbed by the word, [and lose all] other content than that designated by the word in its . . . standardized usage,' as Marcuse once put it.[7] Throughout the 1960s, the term applied almost exclusively to statements from Communist sources. By the 1980s it was not uncommon for journalists to speak of a two-sided 'propaganda war' over, for instance, Central America or arms control.

LIMITS OF CHANGE

Would it, then, be reasonable to say that the concept of hegemony is dated – that the hegemonic process so evident in Vietnam coverage was a transitory result of the specific political character of that period? Certainly, if the concept of hegemony is formulated in such a way that it assumes ideological change to be marginal and insignificant, it is of limited use. The post-Vietnam fragmentation of the Cold War consensus is not an event that can be dismissed as historically insignificant. Yet, even in a period of significant ideological crisis, which this period certainly was for the United States, the media are subject to powerful constraints which limit the impact of change.

The persistence of journalistic routines and power over news frames

Hegemony is power sustained by ideology. But this does not mean that it can be understood entirely at the level of ideas, of symbolic structures. It is a process, embedded in practices, routines, and ways of living and working. As we saw in the preceding essay, the routines most central to understanding political coverage by the American media have to do with their reliance on official sources and channels of information. Just as this relationship persisted without fundamental change through the Vietnam period, so did it persist through the crisis in Central America. Table 4.1 shows how often different kinds of people appeared in television coverage of Central America. US government officials strongly dominated as in earlier eras, with the main alternative voices being members of Congress. And if we turn from those appearing on camera to sources cited by journalists in their narration, US officials, including advisors in the field, made up 44.4 percent of citations. The next most important sources were Salvadoran, Guatemalan, and Honduran government officials, who together made up 10.1 percent, and Nicaraguan government officials at 8.3 percent.

When we look at the broad trends in the development of the story, moreover, it is clear (1) that these were shaped primarily by the terms of political debate in Washington, and (2) that the administration was able more often than not to prevail in the battle to determine the dominant frame of television coverage.

Table 4.1   People appearing in television coverage of Central America (N = 1,114)

US officials	26.1%
Members of Congress and other US political élites	20.3
Central American civilians	8.1
Central American gov't officials (excluding Nicaraguan)	6.6
Church and human rights workers	6.1
Nicaragua opposition	4.9
Nicaraguan gov't officials	4.8
Central American political opposition(including guerrillas)	3.1
US opposition groups	1.9
Others	18.1

Here we can turn to a set of figures, 4.1a, 4.1b, 4.2a, and 4.2b, which show the amount of attention given in television coverage to three key frames: Cold War, human rights, and potential Vietnam. The methodology involved in producing these figures is outlined in the appendix to this essay.

As the 'mountain range' character of these figures suggests, the story is enormously complex. But let's look at some of the peaks, to see what forces created them. The first occurred at the beginning of 1981, with the release of the White Paper. The Carter administration had through much of its tenure interpreted political conflicts, which in earlier eras would have been seen in Cold War terms, as issues instead of human rights.[8] From October 1979, when a coup overthrew El Salvador's right-wing government, through the end of 1980, the administration went back and forth in its policy and rhetoric toward Central America, sometimes expressing concern about Cuban ties to the Salvadoran guerrillas, but more often emphasizing human rights and the need for social reform. (There was one other important frame in this period, the contrast between the 'moderate' government supported by the US and 'extremists' of the right and left. I will discuss this frame a bit later (p. 78).)

Then in November–December 1980 two events, the election of Ronald Reagan and the murder by government security forces in El Salvador of four American religious workers, focused attention strongly on human rights. The murder of the nuns provoked a temporary cut-off of US military aid, and the election of Ronald Reagan touched off a major conflict over the direction of US foreign policy. Carter officials committed to the human rights perspective began to stress to reporters their philosophical differences with the incoming Reagan regime. Here, of course, it is important to note that the prominence of the human rights frame in news coverage was from the beginning due to a shift in official policy: it was the Carter administration that took the lead in de-emphasizing the Cold War perspective. By the end of January, when the Reagan administration came to office, the question of human rights had become the dominant frame.

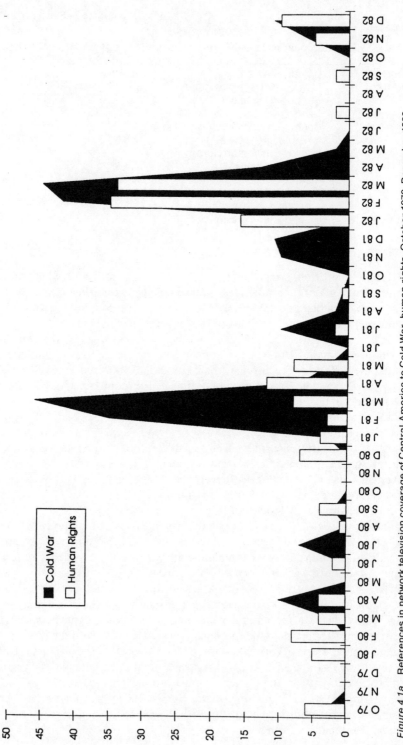

Figure 4.1a   References in network television coverage of Central America to Cold War, human rights, October 1979–December 1982

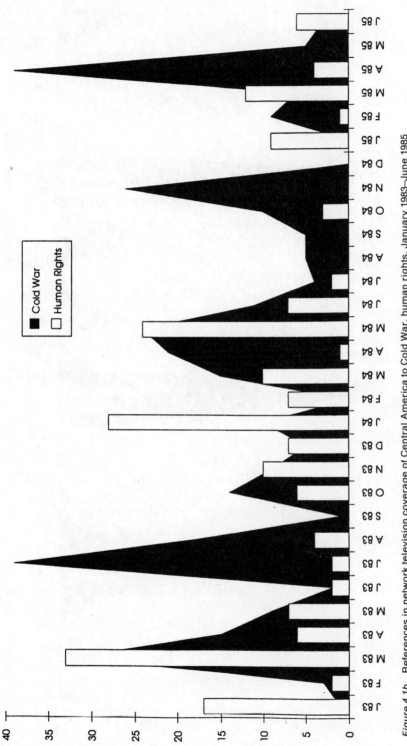

Figure 4.1b References in network television coverage of Central America to Cold War, human rights, January 1983–June 1985

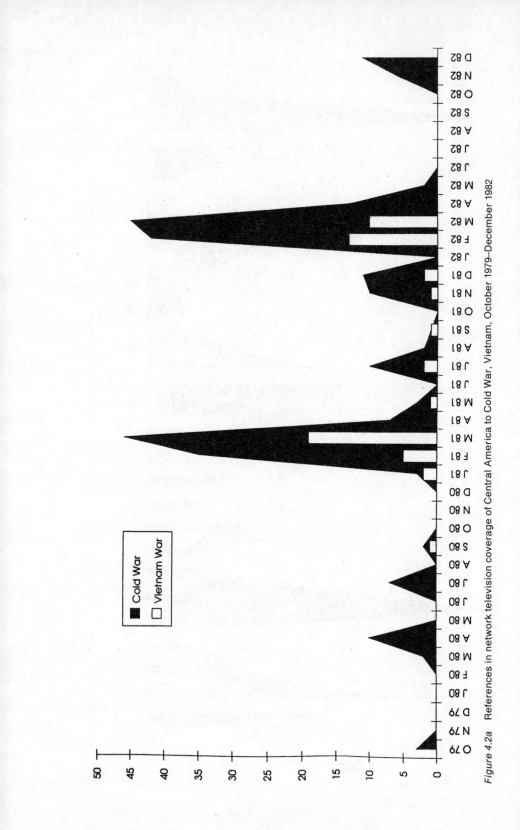

Figure 4.2a References in network television coverage of Central America to Cold War, Vietnam, October 1979–December 1982

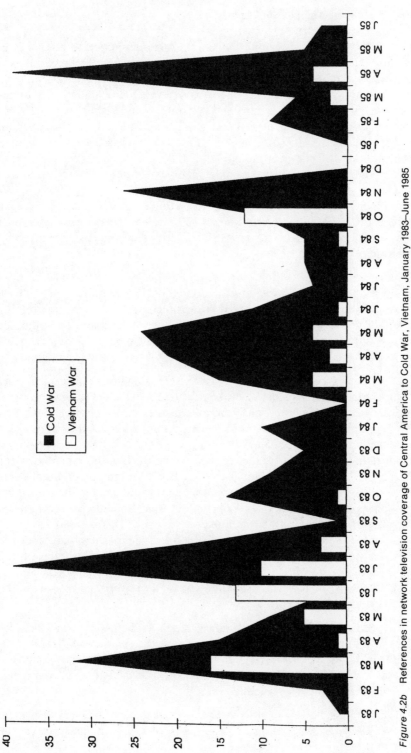

Figure 4.2b References in network television coverage of Central America to Cold War, Vietnam, January 1983–June 1985

The Reagan administration, for its part, was committed to reversing the ideological change we have explored. It sought to restore the Cold War consensus, at the expense of the human rights orientation of the Carter period. To accomplish this goal, the increase of American military aid to the Salvadoran regime was accompanied by a public relations campaign designed to change the emphasis of news coverage. The contents of the White Paper, for example, were leaked to the *New York Times* several weeks before its release, and, from early February through April 1981, there was a steady stream of official statements emphasizing Soviet involvement in the Central American conflict.

Journalists, most of whom were closer to the Carter than the Reagan administration's view, were personally skeptical of the Reagan position. A wire service bureau chief responsible for Central America coverage describes his reaction this way:

> When the administration came out with this White Paper all the news stories mentioned Communist intervention, Communist intervention. Nobody in Washington bothered to mention that this thing had been going on for years, that the guerrillas have been around for a long time, that the government itself in El Salvador . . . has been accused of human rights violations, and that is in large part why people are rebelling against it.[9]

Reporters in the field, who, unlike those in Washington, had been covering Central America on a regular basis, were most critical of the Reagan position. But the weakening of the Cold War consensus has been broad enough that they were by no means alone in their skepticism. *National Wire Watch*, for example, the newsletter of an association of 'wire editors' who select national and international stories for the regional press, criticized the wire services for 'heeding in lockstep fashion' 'the party-line from Washington on Communist infiltration.'[10] And yet, as both these comments note, and as the data show very dramatically for television coverage, it was 'Communist intervention, Communist intervention' that dominated the news. This is a classic case of 'news management,' and of the power of journalistic routines to override the personal judgements of most of the journalists themselves. It also suggests the depth of reporters' respect for political authority, even in the post-Vietnam, post-Watergate period. One television correspondent, trying to explain the success of news management, said:

> Anybody who'd been to Salvador as much as the people who normally cover it knew [the White Paper] was a pretty simplified view of the situation. But if the leader of the Western world makes that statement, it's policy almost. You've got to follow it up. . . . There's always a thing in your mind, 'Well, maybe there is something to it!'[11]

It wasn't long, however, until the plot began to thicken. The very week after the White Paper was released, as noted earlier, the administration was criticizing the press for giving the Central America issue 'too much visibility.' The reason was that a bitter debate quickly arose in Congress, centering both on the theme of human rights – which former Carter administration ambassador to El Salvador, Robert White, sharply criticized the administration for ignoring – and around a new theme that entered Central America coverage at this point: the analogy to Vietnam, whose emergence can be seen in Figure 4.2a. Interestingly, the analogy to Vietnam was raised first by the administration itself – on 24 February Reagan held a ceremony giving the Congressional Medal of Honor to an Hispanic Vietnam veteran, and taking the occasion to attack the 'Vietnam syndrome.' It was then taken up by Democrats in Congress, and finally by the media, with Walter Cronkite, for instance, opening one day's Central America coverage early in March with map of Vietnam behind him. The administration's policy in Central America had awakened deep divisions in American politics, and would not prove an easy issue on which to manage the news agenda.

If the release of the White Paper was a classic example of traditional news management, the period that followed was a classic example of another standard pattern in media–government relations, which we encountered in the preceding essay: when élite opposition surfaces, the administration at least partially loses control of the news agenda.[12] In part, what happens is simply that the news reflects the debate among 'newsworthy' actors. But the media's own behavior also normally becomes more active, often in part as a result of discussions within the profession about the need to be more critical of administration statements on a controversial issue, more sensitive to other points of view, and so on. At the end of February, television's mode of operation changed dramatically, from relatively passive reporting of official statements from Washington to an extraordinary effort to 'catch up' on the story. This is the period that produced the long background reports, culminating in *Central America in Revolt* the following winter, which broke so strongly with the standard Cold War model.

The erosion of the administration's ability to affect the framing of news in this period should not be exaggerated. Back in Washington the administration continued to stress the Cold War angle, and Cold War references continued to outweigh references both to human rights and to Vietnam. But the cracks were great enough to make the administration nervous. And public opinion data suggest it was right to be. After March 1981, polls never showed a majority of the public approving of Reagan's handling of El Salvador.[13]

In April 1981, the administration made a decision to 'low-key' the Central America issue.[14] Attention to the issue in Washington did drop off about that time, and Central America mainly faded from the television screens until the fall. At that point, a pattern very much like the pattern of the previous winter was repeated: a jump in references to Cold War themes, followed, with a slight lag, by jumps in Vietnam and, especially, human rights coverage. What happened was that the administration began once again making statements about Cuban and Soviet involvement in the region, as part of a new push for military aid to El Salvador. The new push for aid, coupled with the congressional debate that ensued, put Central America back on the news agenda, and the Hotel Camino Real in San Salvador began once again to fill up with journalists. This time press attention was heightened by elections in both El Salvador and Guatemala, and a coup in the latter, and some 700 American journalists eventually flocked to El Salvador.

And as before, as the coverage increased and its locus shifted from Washington to a joint focus on Washington and El Salvador, the coverage shifted away from an exclusive emphasis on Cold War themes. This was a period of heavy and very visible activity by El Salvador's death squads; and with hundreds of journalists on the scene, including several camera crews each for the networks, it is not surprising that coverage of the human rights issue shot up dramatically. Journalists were often skeptical of the upcoming Salvadoran election, stressing that it would not resolve the issues underlying the conflict there. The administration, of course, continued its efforts to frame the issue in Cold War terms, and was able to push Cold War themes a little above human rights themes for February and March, but all in all the first three months of 1982 were a difficult period for the administration – until 28 March, when the Salvadoran election was interpreted by most of the US media, and certainly by the three networks, as a dramatic victory for democracy.[15] We did not, unfortunately, measure this new 'fledgling democracy' frame, since it arose after the study was underway. Suffice it to say that it became extremely prominent following the 1982 election.

The election of 1982 may have been a public relations victory, but it did not solve the administration's political problems. It was in 1983 that the administration had the most difficulty controlling the news agenda.[16] As the numbers in Figures 4.1b and 4.2b show, the two 'problem' themes in public discourse about Central America – human rights and Vietnam – reached their highest levels in television coverage in 1983. A number of 1983 polls, incidentally, asked respondents directly whether they thought the conflicts in Central America were due primarily to Communist intervention or to poverty and/or human rights. All showed strong majorities saying poverty/human rights.[17]

The reason for the administration's troubles in 1983 is easy enough to understand within the framework already laid out: élite divisions increased in 1983. It was a year of intensified conflicts between the administration and Congress. And it was also a period when sharp divisions and differences of priority emerged within the administration. At the end of October 1982, Deane Hinton, the US ambassador in El Salvador, publicly attacked what he called a 'Mafia' in El Salvador that was carrying out attacks on innocent civilians. This is probably part of the reason that the budget cycle pattern of the previous two years was not repeated this time around. Before, attention to the human rights issue rose only *after* attention to Cold War themes. This time it rose earlier, and higher than attention to the themes the administration preferred to stress; but the administration itself – or a faction of it – was now acting to put human rights on the agenda. Hinton and Assistant Secretary of State for Inter-American Affairs Thomas Enders were both removed in May 1983 in a major shake-up of the administration's Central America team.

Congress, meanwhile, was also becoming increasingly restive, and the administration faced its toughest fight over renewed aid to the Salvadoran government early in 1983. No doubt this was due in large part to the midterm election of 1982, which shifted power toward the Democrats, and the generally low level of Reagan's popularity at this point. The congressional debate of March 1983 produced a substantial increase in references both to human rights and to Vietnam. The Vietnam theme also jumped in the summer, in response to the death of a US advisor in El Salvador ('The first casualty,' *Newsweek* ethnocentrically called it on its cover), the beginning of major military maneuvers, and the administration's request for 'covert' aid for the Contras. The dramatic jump in Cold War references in July and August 1983 resulted from US military maneuvers – which involved a confrontation with a Soviet ship early in August, and illustrate the ability of an administration to create events which change news frames – and from a public relations push by the administration, including a major speech by Reagan and the appointment of a blue-ribbon panel known as the Kissinger Commission.

The last major debate on aid to El Salvador during the Reagan administration took place at the beginning of 1984. By this time the administration had made the decision to come out publicly against the repression in El Salvador, and made many statements to this effect in the period leading up to the two-stage electoral showdown between José Napoleón Duarte, backed by the US, and his right-wing opponent Roberto D'Aubuisson in March and May. These elections, coupled with the debate in Congress, led to a high level of attention to the human rights issue early that year. After that conflict between the administration and Congress over El Salvador faded and attention shifted to Nicaragua and the issue of Contra aid; the peaks and valleys in the figures late in 1984 and in 1985 relate mainly to that debate, and carry us beyond the scope of the present essay.

Three points should be made in concluding this section:

1 There was a real political contest over the framing of the Central America story. This is not a case that can easily be assimilated to a model of the media that see them essentially as a tool of a unified ruling élite (Herman and Chomsky's 'propaganda model' is close to this view).[18]

2 On the other hand, the administration retained the predominant power to shape the news frame. This is suggested by the fact that Cold War themes outweighed human rights themes in thirty-seven of the fifty-three months of the study after the Reagan administration came to office (they outweighed Vietnam themes in all but three months). The importance of this finding is

underscored if we keep in mind that conditions for successful news management were highly unfavorable: political élites and the administration itself were divided, public opinion was generally unsympathetic to Reagan's policy, and realities in Central America were embarrassing, with the administration's allies killing tens of thousands of civilians in this period and leaving the bodies around the capital city where reporters could easily view them.

3 Finally, although there were important upsurges of unusual journalistic activity, and although the presence of journalists in Central America surely made a difference – it seems unlikely, in particular, that human rights would have become a public issue if they had not been present as witnesses – still the broad patterns in the framing of the story can be accounted for almost entirely by the evolution of policy and élite debate in Washington.

INERTIA OF THE IDEOLOGICAL SYSTEM

Ideological change is limited not only by journalistic routines, but also by the inertia of ideology itself. Ideological presuppositions become so central to the thought-process that they change only with difficulty. An ideological system, moreover, is complex and multi-leveled; the political impact of a change in one element may be blunted by the stability of others.

The Cold War ideology itself, although it had lost its monopoly even in this pre-Gorbachev period, retained a good deal of power throughout the Central America crisis, not only through the ability of the government to force Cold War themes to the forefront, but also through the media's habits of framing. To some degree, different 'factions' of the media may have chosen sides in the ideological conflict. *Time*, for example, reporting on an important Reagan speech in April 1983, took aim directly at what the Reagan administration called the 'Vietnam syndrome:'

> Out of fear at repeating that colossal misadventure, Americans have seized hold of its lessons, perhaps inaccurately, perhaps obsessively. There is a strong aversion to undertaking any commitment to shore up threatened pro-American regimes in the third world, no matter how strategically important they are, and a reluctance to believe that the countries of a region could topple like dominoes, no matter how compelling the evidence of spreading subversion.[19]

To a much greater extent, however, the Cold War ideology was probably reproduced through a less conscious process, employed by journalists not so much to make a political point as to 'package' the presentation of news in terms they assume the audience will find interesting and easy to understand. 'It's been one year since the fighting in Nicaragua ended,' said ABC's Hugh Downs, introducing a segment of the magazine program *20/20* on the Nicaraguan revolution. 'What is the U.S. doing to ensure that the new

Nicaragua turns out to be democratic instead of totalitarian? . . . The Cubans
are there and the Russians are coming. But where is the U.S. in Nicaragua's
future?'

Why the focus on the Cold War angle? 'We assume that most of the people
we are reaching have zero knowledge and zero interest in the subjects we
intend to cover,' explains Av Westin, who was then executive producer of
20/20:

> There has to be something that will relate the story to the basic concerns of
> the television viewer . . . . The simplest way is to tie it to American interests
> . . . . Central America is just South of our borders; Cuban interests and
> other dangerous forces are at work there. An understanding of the locale in
> terms of American national security makes it all the more important for the
> distracted viewer to pay attention to what is about to come up.[20]

Nevertheless, the weakening of Cold War ideology was clear, and I would
like to turn to two other points: first, the persistence of another aspect of
American political ideology which has maintained its strength and which may
limit the significance of the fragmentation of the Cold War consensus; and
second, the failure of a substantial alternative to the Cold War framework to
develop.

It will be useful here to step back for a moment and make clear how the
concept of hegemony applies to foreign affairs reporting, for this is a
somewhat complicated case. To say the media play a 'hegemonic' role is to say
that they contribute to the maintenance of consent for a system of power. The
relevant system of power here is the post-Second World War *pax Americana* –
the world capitalist system dominated both politically and economically by
the United States. The leading power in such a system has to maintain a
double hegemony: it has to maintain the consent both of subordinate nations
and of its own population. This domestic consent, which we are concerned
with here, also has two components. The public has to consent to the domestic
system of power – to recognize the legitimacy of foreign policy élites and the
institutions of their rule – and also to the international system itself. The Cold
War ideology was ideally suited to maintaining this double consent. American
dominance of the international system – and the need for domestic sacrifices to
maintain that dominance – were justified by the threat of a Soviet-dominated
world system; tight élite control of foreign policy was justified by the danger to
national security that could lie in any conflict.

As the Cold War ideology weakens, however, other ideological factors serve
to maintain consent. These are too numerous to outline exhaustively here. But
for one important example let us return to *Central America in Revolt*. In the
conclusion to that documentary, Bill Moyers made the following comment:
'My colleagues and I come back from Central America thinking it looks
different from up close than from afar, and different if you don't have an
ideology to promote or a policy to defend.' This seemingly insignificant

Table 4.2   Direction of statements presented about major political actors in television coverage of Central America

	Favorable (per cent)	Unfavorable (per cent)	Number
US administration	40.0	60.0	410
Salvadoran, Guatemalan, Honduran gov'ts	46.0	54.0	113
Right-wing opposition	22.9	77.1	35
Left-wing opposition	6.8	93.2	44
Nicaraguan government	17.9	82.1	112
Nicaraguan opposition	60.4	39.6	53

Note: comments counted here are those made by all actors appearing in the news.

remark expresses what is in fact one of the most important and pervasive elements of the value system of American journalism: a general distaste for political conflict and partisanship. It was an important underlying theme in *Central America in Revolt*, which presented *all* parties to the conflict in an essentially negative light. American officials were presented as dogmatic; their critics (who 'often sound as though no revolution ever goes sour') as simplistic. The rulers of Central America appeared as brutal and backward; their opponents as naive (the Catholic missionary) or power-hungry (the revolutionary). Only the journalists themselves, 'without an ideology to promote,' appeared to possess real wisdom.

The figures in Table 4.2 suggest that a similar tale can be told about the evening news throughout the Central America period. The table shows how many comments were presented supporting or criticizing the major actors in the story. For every actor except the Nicaraguan opposition more critical than supportive comments were shown.

As the example of *Central America in Revolt* suggests, distrust of political partisanship is an ideological principle that can cut both ways politically. But at the deepest level, its implications are conservative; it is at root a preference for order, and it affects most strongly the reporting of those who seek to challenge an established order. Its significance for the maintenance of consent in the field of foreign policy is twofold.

Distrust of partisanship means, first of all, that, even in periods when the media are not supportive of foreign policy élites, they tend to be at least equally unsupportive of any attempt to challenge established authorities. Indeed, the political opposition faces the special disadvantage that it has no choice but to embrace partisanship and to engage political passion, while élites can often fall back into a quiet 'technocratic' or 'statesmanlike' posture. (One reason the Reagan administration had difficulty 'managing' the news on El Salvador may be that it took a particularly 'partisan' stance initially, attacking the previous administration ideologically and declaring that it sought a basic change in the direction of US foreign policy.)

In their coverage of domestic opposition to US foreign policy, the media have changed little since the later (post-Tet offensive) period of the Vietnam War. Coverage of domestic opposition was generally negative, even during the period when the media were most critical of administration policy, often presented more as a threat to public order than as a political statement.[21] In the case of Central America, a look back at Table 4.1 will show that coverage of the domestic opposition outside of Congress was quite limited, with opposition activists making up about 2 per cent of those appearing on television (some of the 6 per cent classified under church and human rights representatives were also domestic opponents). One important consequence of this limited coverage of domestic opposition was that coherent statements of alternative visions of the world order and of US policy rarely appeared in the news.

Internationally, distrust of partisanship has equally conservative implications. Oppositional political movements in the Third World, especially in areas like Central America where class antagonisms are deep and bitter, necessarily involve levels of political passion quite unfamiliar to most North Americans. With a few exceptions, they appear in the media in a harshly negative light, whether or not they are presented in Cold War terms as agents of Communist aggression.

It is interesting here to consider El Salvador coverage in the period before the Reagan administration came to office and invoked the Cold War framework; this period might prove to prefigure coverage of such conflicts in a post-Cold War world. Journalists neither made much use of Cold War themes in this period, nor were they sympathetic toward the established socio-economic order in El Salvador. Yet the opposition to that order appeared in the news most of the time as carrier of *irrational* violence, a threat not to the old order but to *order in general*. Here are two examples:

[CBS, 13 February 1980, a report on the seizure by leftists of the Panamanian embassy and a government building]:
Walter Cronkite: Our Martha Teichner went to the education ministry . . . and found the militants fresh-faced youngsters who looked as if they were playing some guerrilla warfare game. But it's no game. . . .
    Teichner: Wherever these children go they hear the rhetoric and read the slogans that lead them into leftist groups . . . Luis is eleven years old. 'I saw the misery of the people,' he says. His words sound like propaganda. [One might imagine here what an 18-year-old GI sounded like explaining the war in Vietnam in 1965.]

[NBC, 1 April 1980, again a report on political violence]:
David Brinkley: In the tortured country of El Salvador the violence and killing continues every day, and it is random and senseless. It doesn't even have the cold clarity of one side killing those on the other, as Phil Bremen reports from San Salvador . . . .

Bremen [wrapping up]:   Before the violence, tourists came to see the ruins of an ancient civilization here. In the face of modern ruins, the United States is urging Salvadorans to bring some civilization to their politics.[22]

The violence was described most of the time as instigated by 'extremists' of both left and right (though the focus, as these examples suggest, was mainly on the left), with the US-backed government caught in the middle. More important than this specific political interpretation, though, is the vague but powerful impression of the 'senselessness' of political conflict conveyed by the whole series of images. The ideological deep structure of this coverage is well expressed by Bremen's conclusion. Revolution in the Third World does not appear here as a challenge by the Communist bloc to United States security; but the specter of Communist world conquest was replaced by the specter of world anarchy, the image of a bipolar struggle between democracy and totalitarianism, by the image of 'Fortress America,' an island of civilization in a sea of political barbarism. It is important here to place Central America coverage in the context of coverage of the Third World generally. In its focus on violence, and in its sporadic, fragmented quality, El Salvador coverage in this 1979–80 period, before Central America had become a major issue in the United States, was quite typical of Third World coverage;[23] El Salvador stories, in fact, were generally packaged in the news broadcast as part of a series of stories about political violence and terrorism in the Third World, often as a sequel to reports on the seizure of the American embassy in Iran – a fact which substantially enhanced the strength of the image of a world of anarchy (a similar example begins the following essay).

Second, it is significant that the nascent, alternative perspective on political conflict in the Third World that could be glimpsed in the early years of the debate over Central America policy never caught hold. What I have called here the 'human rights' framework, like most conceptual models, was a cluster of subframes. Besides the concern with human rights, it involved a notion of civil wars as something different from superpower confrontations, a concern with social inequality as a cause of political conflict, and desire to break with the history of 'Yankee imperialism.' Only the human rights component of the framework really had much influence on subsequent political discourse, however. This was probably in large part because it fit more easily the liberal 'deep structure' of American political ideology. This framework also lacked the simplicity of either the Cold War or fortress America world-images: it required journalists to go into considerable detail about unfamiliar societies, and lent itself much better to 90-minute documentaries (now unheard-of on commercial television) than to 2-minute news reports.

We did measure the use of some of the other components of this framework. We coded for references to the oligarchies that have traditionally ruled most of the states involved in the Central American conflict, for example, the so-called 'fourteen families' of El Salvador. These references ran about five to six a year from 1981 on. (Poverty, on the other hand, was mentioned very often in television coverage. But poverty is a relatively 'weak' political concept, compatible with many different frames in a way that references to structural inequality are not. Often poverty was associated with a 'backwardness' frame, which would certainly be worth further study.) We also coded for references to the history of US intervention in Central America. Background reports on the region occasionally, for instance, included newsreel footage of the Marines landing in Nicaragua to fight Sandino. These peaked in 1982 at six references, and thereafter declined.

One of the Reagan administration's most significant public relations successes was that it was able in effect to lower expectations about what constituted meaningful reform in El Salvador. When the debate began, there was significant attention to the social structure of El Salvador, and 'success' meant in part social reform; the land reform program was an important part of this. By 1985, 'reform' had come to be identified with three things: holding elections – the 'fledgling democracy' frame; curbing death squad activity; and prosecuting people responsible for murdering North Americans; social reform was no longer a criterion. Land reform basically dropped off television's agenda in 1984. In 1983, the year of greatest attention to land reform in television coverage, there were fifty references to that topic in the sample; there were twelve in 1984 and one in the first six months of 1985. So in a sense we were back to 1961, where the grievances of peasants were seen as perfectly irrelevant to the political definition of the story.

CONCLUSION

Gramsci developed the concept of hegemony in part to explain why revolutionary movements were unable to succeed in Europe in the 1910s and 1920s, despite the deep social and economic crisis of that period. The popularity of the concept with modern Marxism is based largely on its ability to explain the persistent political stability of western capitalism. But there is an intellectual danger associated with this use of the concept: the danger of assuming a priori that ideology and ideological institutions will perform their appointed hegemonic 'function.'[24] The most extreme example of this sort of functionalism is perhaps Louis Althusser's essay on 'Ideological state apparatuses:'[25]

> All ideological state apparatuses [for Althusser all cultural institutions are part of the 'state'] ... contribute to the same result: the reproduction of the relations of production .... Each of them contributes to this single result in the way proper to it .... [The] concert is dominated by a single score, occasionally disturbed by contradictions ... the score of the Ideology of the current ruling class.

Ideology appears here as a *deus ex machina*, standing above and regulating political conflict.

Ideological change of the sort we have explored here tends, from this perspective, to be interpreted as a means of restoring political equilibrium – evidence of the *strength*, not the weakness, of ideological hegemony. There is a good deal of truth to this interpretation. To the extent that the media abandoned the Cold War perspective in the wake of Vietnam, and adopted a more critical attitude toward official policy, they did so primarily in response to a growing division *within* the foreign policy establishment over how best to manage and preserve American power. And it is plausible that the ideological changes the media have undergone since Vietnam – now of course pushed into a new phase by the literal end of the Cold War – will prove to be an effective historical adaptation, incorporating the Vietnam experience and the loss of the Cold War adversary into the political culture without threatening the established order in any significant way.

But this outcome cannot be assumed a priori. The difficulty that foreign policy élites have managing public opinion in the absence of the Cold War consensus (one poll – taken during the spring of 1982 when coverage on the model of *Central America in Revolt* was particularly common – found 51 per cent saying they would support young men who refused to be drafted to fight in Central America)[26] may well have a profound affect on the conduct of American foreign policy and in the long run on the shape of the world system. Even the 'Fortress America' perspective seems ambiguous in its political implications, with a potential for isolationism as well as for jingoistic nationalism (we saw both these sides of that ideology during the Gulf crisis) or for the kind of liberal paternalism implicit in the wrap-up to the Brinkley/ Bremen story quoted above (pp. 77–8). No one planned the fragmentation of the Cold War consensus; if ideology is a symphony, it is a symphony without a conductor. And as for Althusser's 'composer,' Ideology with a capital 'I,' it is pure reification to imagine that it stands above the ironies of history.

Once we have set functionalist assumptions aside, however, the hegemonic process can clearly be seen at work, holding communication within limits relatively less threatening to the established order. Critiques of the concept of hegemony often fall into the trap of confronting only the most simplistic version of it. David Altheide, for instance, assumes that journalistic routines must be shown to 'negate any journalistic independence' and socialization to mold journalists into a 'uniform ideological shape' if the 'hegemonic' perspective is to be confirmed.[27] But this is to miss the entire intent of the concept of hegemony, as it has been articulated by Gramsci and others, which is precisely to explain how ideological boundaries can be maintained in modern capitalist societies *without* rigid control of political communication, which is obviously impossible in a liberal democratic political order.

It is always dangerous to speculate about the impact of the media on popular consciousness. But it seems most reasonable to assume that changes in foreign affairs coverage which began after the Vietnam War will have the effect of creating a sort of ideological vacuum, weakening established assumptions, shattering old myths, but leaving little of any symbolic power in their place. In the Gulf War, the administration attempted in a sense to jump the clock back to the Second World War, to an earlier conflict with a similar structure to that of the Cold War, and to portray it as a two-sided battle between good and evil. It is also possible that a new ideology, presumably a form of defensive nationalism, might develop out of the image of 'fortress America' in a hostile world, particularly if incidents like the Iranian hostage crisis were to become more common. But what seems most likely is an extended period of public confusion and uncertainty about world politics, and a passive, sometimes grudging consent to the decisions of the foreign policy establishment, so long as the costs of those decisions are not extremely high.

APPENDIX

Frames, as Todd Gitlin puts it, are 'persistent patterns of cognition, interpretation and presentation, of selection, emphasis and exclusion, by which symbol-handlers routinely organize discourse.'[28] It is very useful in analyzing the behavior of the media over the course of a developing political conflict to have content analysis data that document the ups and downs of major political frames. The problem is that framing is not easy to quantify. The cues that analysts typically look for to identify the framing of a story can be varied and subtle, and judgements about whether a particular frame is present or absent often are quite subjective. This is particularly true in a situation where a number of competing frames share the political space, and may be mixed together within a news story, as was often the case with Central America reporting. The analyst then faces the task not merely of coding a story in one category or the other, or judging the presence or absence of the frame, but determining whether one or the other frame is emphasized or privileged, which makes an already-subjective decision far more so. Nevertheless, framing can be roughly measured to produce useful data.

In measuring framing here, the primary unit of analysis was what I will call the reference. We did not attempt to code whole stories by their dominant frame – this seemed likely to lead to serious reliability problems – but instead broke them down into smaller units. Each reference within a story to the three major frames on which the study focused – the Cold War, human rights, and Vietnam frames – was coded. Two kinds of coding problems are involved in this kind of analysis. One has to do with unitizing – the problem of what constitutes one reference. What we tried to do was to code single, separable ideas within the story; usually one reference would correspond with one sentence of narrative within a transcript, though this was not invariably the case, in part because we worked from tapes, not transcripts. References by any speaker, journalist or not, were counted; so, for example, if a story included a soundbite of Alexander Haig saying that the Soviets had a 'hit list' for Central America, and later the journalist concluded by saying the US and the Soviets were squaring off in the region, this would be counted as two Cold War references. Visual references were also coded; so, for instance, when ABC in 1981 started using as its logo for Central America coverage a map of El Salvador with the US and Soviet flags on either side, this was coded as a Cold War reference. However, when simultaneous visual and verbal references were coordinated – which is usually the case – only one reference was coded.

The other problem is semiotic: it is the problem of determining what is to count as a reference to a particular frame. What we did here was to stay away from subtleties and try to code clear, explicit invocations of different frames. The Cold War frame was coded when the involvement of the Soviets or Cubans in Central America was mentioned (usually by name, but sometimes in phrases like 'outside forces'), or political actors were described as Communist or Marxist (not 'leftist'), or the conflict was described as one of east versus west. The human rights frame was coded when that phrase was used explicitly, as well as when references were made to 'repression' or 'oppression' or murder by the forces allied with the US. (Human rights issues of course changed their political meaning, and were treated differently, when they involved the Sandinista government in Nicaragua, falling more within the Cold War frame – these references were not included in our coding scheme. References to death squad activity were not coded unless they were linked to the government.) The Vietnam frame was also coded when the analogy between Vietnam and Central America was raised explicitly. This leaves out a lot of more subtle elements of news presentation that may be quite important. When, for example, a reporter tells us that the guerrillas in El Salvador 'infest' such and such a per cent of the countryside,[29] he certainly is using a formulation that can be traced to Cold War interpretations of revolution and guerrilla warfare (reporters would never have used this language in talking about the Contras, even though they were often very critical of the latter). But there are too many of these subtle cues, and too many questions at the margins about which should count and which shouldn't, to include them in content analysis. One hopes – and this is probably a reasonable assumption – that they correlate fairly well with more direct references to the major frames.

References were also coded by whether they were favorable or unfavorable or neutral to the administration position (for example, an assertion that Central America was indeed 'another Vietnam' would be coded as an 'unfavorable' reference to Vietnam, since the administration held that it was not). For the analysis reported here all references to each frame regardless of their valence were combined. (Most Cold War references were favorable to the administration position. Most human rights references were unfavorable. Vietnam references were more mixed, though they became mostly unfavorable in 1982.) Stories were coded by myself and by a political science graduate student who had done extensive work on media and politics. A subsample including sxty-five stories was coded by both of us, and reliability was very good.[30]

Following is the transcript of one story with its coding:

CW = Cold War, **HR** = human rights, **VN** = Vietnam, **+** = favorable (to administration position), **−** = unfavorable, **N** = neutral.

ABC *World News Tonight*, 2 March 1981

Frank Reynolds: The conflict in El Salvador is a civil war, but it is also more than that. **It has become in fact an East/West confrontation by proxy. [Video: map of El Salvador with US and Soviet flags.] [CW+]** Tonight a report on how and why this has happened from diplomatic correspondent Barrie Dunsmore.

Barrie Dunsmore: El Salvador is the place to draw the line. This was the decision in the first few days of the Reagan administration, **when it began to sift through the evidence of Communist interference in the Civil War in El Salvador. The captured documents released last week point to direct Cuban and indirect Soviet involvement in the arming of El Salvador's leftist insurgents. [CW+]** The U.S. has now countered with an increase in military assistance of 25 million dollars. This includes helicopters, machine guns, ammunition and surveillance equipment, and an additional 20 military advisors, bringing to 54 the number of American instructors teaching maintenance and combat techniques.

US spokesman William Dyess: U.S. personnel will not accompany Salvadoran units outside their garrison areas, nor will U.S. personnel participate in any combat operations.

Dunsmore: The decision to draw the line in El Salvador is designed to make several points. **Principally, it's to put the Russians on notice that their practice of using proxies such as Cuba will be challenged, especially in this hemisphere. [CW+]** In a way, El Salvador is an unlikely place to draw the line. A pitifully poor country of four and a half million, it has been torn apart for more than a year by a civil war in which some 12,000 people have been killed. Government troops, in an apparent effort to show their need for U.S. arms, today patrolled using 1898 German Mausers, although even without new equipment the current fighting is at a stalemate. **The modern day domino theory is that Cuba currently is a strong influence in Nicaragua. If El Salvador is subverted, Honduras and Guatemala will be next, making Mexico very vulnerable. [Video: countries on map turn red.] [CW+]** This is not a policy without risks. **Vietnam may not be an accurate comparison, but having made a stand, it's hard to see where you stop if the other side doesn't. [VNN] Additionally, the security forces in El Salvador are very repressive. [Video: body being loaded on truck.] And by aligning itself with that group, the U.S. may inadvertently be reviving the slogan, down with Yankee Imperialism. [HR−]** Former U.S. Ambassador Robert White, who was fired by the new administration, certainly feels that more guns for the military is not the answer.

White: **The security forces in El Salvador have been responsible for the deaths of thousands and thousands of young people, and they've executed them just on the mere suspicion that they are leftists or sympathize with the leftists. [HR—]**

Dunsmore: Latin America's Social Democrats, meeting in Panama, are proposing a mediation effort headed by former West German chancellor Willy Brandt. Most of America's allies would be very happy to see some kind of political solution. Reagan's people are not against a political solution, but they're not pushing one either. **And it's very clear that the Reagan administration sees El Salvador as the first test of wills with the Communists, and one it's most eager to win. [CWN]**

Total scores: CW – 5, HR – 2, VN – 1.

NOTES

* Assistance with the content analysis was provided by Wendy Prentice and Ana Cobian. The study was funded in part by the Committee on Research of the University of California, San Diego, and the William Joiner Center for the Study of War and Social Consequences. An earlier version appeared in D. L. Paletz (ed.), *Political Communication: Approaches, Studies, Assessments*, Norwood, NJ, Ablex, 1987, and another was presented at the annual meeting of the American Political Science Association, San Francisco, 1990. See also D. Hallin, 'The media go to war – from Vietnam to El Salvador,' *NACLA Report on the Americas*, July/August 1983, vol. 17. Thanks to Wendy Prentice who was the principal coder for the study, to Bruce Jones for help with the figures, and to Marjorie Miller for her hospitality and help in San Salvador and Managua.

1 For example, J. E. Masow and A. Arana, 'Operation El Salvador,' *Columbia Journalism Review*, 1981, vol. 20, pp. 52–8.
2 P. Anderson, 'The antinomies of Antonio Gramsci,' *New Left Review*, 1976–7, vol. 100, pp. 5–78; T. Gitlin, *The Whole World Is Watching: Mass Media in the Making and Unmaking of the New Left*, Berkeley, Calif., University of California Press, 1980; A. Gramsci, *Selections from the Prison Notebooks*, New York, International Publishers, 1971; S. Hall, 'Culture, the media and the "ideological effect," ' in J. Curran, M. Gurevitch, and J. Woollacott (eds), *Mass Communication and Society*, Beverly Hills, Calif., Sage, 1979; R. Williams, *Marxism and Literature*, Oxford, Oxford University Press, 1977.
3 One network evening news broadcast was selected randomly for each day during this period, Saturdays excluded. The sample contains 917 stories.
4 B. Cohen, *The Press and Foreign Policy*, Princeton, NJ, Princeton University Press, 1963.
5 *New York Times*, 18 February 1962, p. IV4.
6 Ideological changes are only part of the explanation for the difference between the two wars. Physical access to the NLF was virtually impossible for American reporters in Vietnam; in El Salvador access to the guerrillas was relatively easy.
7 *One-Dimensional Man*, Boston, Mass., Beacon Press, 1964, p. 87.
8 L. Schultz, *Human Rights and United States Policy toward Latin America*, Princeton, NJ, Princeton University Press, 1981.
9 Interview, Juan Tamayo, UPI, Mexico City, 15 July 1981.

10 *National Wire Watch*, 30 April 1981, no. 35, p. 2. A survey of editorial comment in thirty-five newspapers around the United States found that most rejected the Cold War interpretation of the Central American crisis. See M. E. Leary, 'U.S. press shines harsh light on Reagan's Salvador policy,' Pacific News Service, 27 March 1981.

11 Interview, Ike Seamans, NBC, Miami, 31 July 1981.

12 See D. C. Hallin, *The 'Uncensored War': The Media and Vietnam*, New York, Oxford University Press, 1986; M. Kern, P. W. Levering, and R. B. Levering, *The Kennedy Crises: The Press, the Presidency and Foreign Policy*, Chapel Hill, NC, University of North Carolina Press, 1983; and B. L. Nacos, *The Press, Presidents and Crises*, New York, Columbia University Press, 1990.

13 W. M. Leogrande, 'Central America and the polls,' Washington Office on Latin America, 1987.

14 Quoted in S. Blumenthal, 'Marketing the president,' *New York Times Magazine*, 13 September 1981, p. 43.

15 J. Spence, 'The great Salvador election blitz,' *NACLA Report on the Americas*, July/August 1983; R. Bonner, *Weakness and Deceit: U.S. Policy and El Salvador*, New York, Times Books, 1984, ch. 15; E. S. Herman and N. Chomsky, *Manufacturing Consent: The Political Economy of the Mass Media*, New York, Pantheon, 1988; E. S. Herman and F. Broadhead, *Demonstration Elections: U.S.-Staged Elections in the Dominican Republic, Vietnam, and El Salvador*, Boston, Mass., South End Press, 1984.

16 There were important counter-currents in this year, including a good many stories that focused on growing efficiency in the Salvadoran military. But the volume of attention to human rights themes leads me to conclude that on balance it was not a particularly good year for the administration. For an argument that the media were beginning to 'go soft' on El Salvador in that year, see M. Massing, 'About-face on El Salvador,' *Columbia Journalism Review*, November/December 1983, vol. 22, pp. 42–9.

17 Leogrande, op. cit., table 19.

18 Op. cit.

19 W. Isaacson, 'Harsh facts, hard choices,' *Time*, 9 May 1983, p. 21.

20 A. Westin, *Newswatch: How TV Decides the News*, New York, Simon & Schuster, 1982, p. 199.

21 Gitlin, op. cit.; Hallin, op. cit.

22 The assertion that the violence in El Salvador didn't have 'the cold clarity of one side killing those on the other' referred primarily to the assassination of Archbishop Romero, which Bremen presented as something that could have been done either by the right (Romero was a strong human rights advocate, and just before his assasination had argued that soldiers sometimes had a duty to disobey orders), or by the left, 'knowing it would be blamed on the right.' In December, however, after the American nuns were killed, Bremen reported, 'In the struggle for power both left and right burn, kidnap, and kill. But only the right has targeted the clergy' (NBC, 4 December 1980) – a good example of the power of the dominant news frame to affect the reporting of particular events.

23 P. H. Dahlgren with S. Chakrapani, 'The Third World on TV news: western ways of seeing the "Other," in W. C. Adams (ed.), *Television Coverage of International Affairs*, Norwood, NJ, Ablex, 1982; W. Q. Morales, 'Revolutions, earthquakes and Latin America: the networks look at Allende's Chile and Somoza's Nicaragua,' in ibid.; S. Peterson, 'International news selection by the élite press: a case study,' *Public Opinion Quarterly*, 1981, vol. 45, pp. 143–63.

24 For Gramsci the concept of hegemony was also used in a more dynamic way, to discuss the 'war of position' between forces contending for leadership, in which

each tries to shape political culture.

25 L. Althusser, 'Ideology and ideological state apparatuses,' in *idem, Lenin and Philosophy and Other Essays*, New York, Monthly Review Press, 1971.

26 D. Shribman, 'Poll finds that fewer than half in U.S. back Latin policy,' *New York Times*, 29 April 1984, p. 1.

27 D. L. Altheide, 'Media hegemony: a failure of a perspective,' *Public Opinion Quarterly*, 1984, vol. 48, pp. 479–81.

28 Op. cit., p. 7. See also G. Tuchman, *Making News*, New York, Free Press, 1978; S. Hall, 'Encoding and decoding in the television discourse,' Centre for Contemporary Cultural Studies, University of Birmingham, 1973; R. M. Entman, 'Framing U.S. coverage of international news: contrasts in narratives of the KAL and Iran Air incidents,' *Journal of Communication*, 1991, vol. 41, pp. 6–27. Gitlin adapts the concept from E. Goffman, *Frame Analysis: An Essay on the Organization of Experience*, New York, Harper & Row, 1974. It is also used by linguists; see the discussions of frame semantics in G. Lakoff, *Women, Fire and Dangerous Things: What Categories Reveal About the Mind*, Chicago, Ill., University of Chicago Press, 1987. The concept of frame is also closely related to that of schema, which has been applied to political communication by S. Iyengar and D. Kinder, especially in *News That Matters*, Chicago, Ill., University of Chicago Press, 1987; and also by D. A. Graber, *Processing the News: How People Tame the Information Tide*, New York, Longman, 1988.

29 For example, Jack Smith, ABC, 14 February 1982.

30 Combining positive, negative and neutral references, the correlation between the two human rights codings is $\gamma = 0.95$; for Cold War references $\gamma = 0.99$. Gamma is used here because the variables have skewed marginals, with large numbers of cases having 0 references. Measures of association can be misleading as indicators of reliability, but these are high enough that they do not seem problematic.

Chapter 5

'We Keep America on Top of the World'
TV news in the age of Reagan*

The *CBS Evening News* for 20 June 1985 began with the words and image of Allyn Conwell, an American held hostage in Beirut: 'I am speaking on behalf of my fellow forty hostages, who have elected me as their spokesman to make a brief press conference to advise our families, friends, and loved ones of our welfare . . . .' Dan Rather then cut in to introduce the day's events:

> For the first time in a week, the first look at and word from some of the passenger hostages from TWA flight 847 in Beirut.
> And in El Salvador, the bodies of six Americans gunned down by leftist rebels, a grim reminder that terrorism is not exclusive to the Middle East.
> Good evening, this is the Western Edition of the *CBS Evening News*, Dan Rather reporting.
> New assurances in Beirut today, assurances from one of the American hostages that all thirty-seven of the passengers still captive from that hijacked jetliner are still safe. This on the seventh day of the hijacking ordeal. Welcome news to the families of the hostages.
> But it was news of a different, more tragic kind from El Salvador, where thirteen people, four of them U.S. Marines, two of them U.S. civilians, were killed in a guerrilla attack.

The broadcast closed with a report on the funeral of the Navy diver killed by the hijackers in Beirut, and the reactions of the families of the Americans killed in El Salvador. Here is Rather's introduction to the closing report, and the close of Bruce Morton's narration.

Video	*Audio*
Still of sailor in uniform, in inset behind Rather.	On this seventh day of the hijacking of the TWA plane, they buried the young hostage brutally beaten and then murdered by terrorists. But
Drawing of American flag at half staff, in inset.	as the killing of Americans in El Salvador reminds us, that death proved to be

preamble, the title page written in blood to a volume of terrorist violence against the United States.

The Marine Corps hymn says, 'We'll fight our country's battles, on the land and on the sea.' But these young men did not die fighting battles, fighting an enemy in a war they knew about. More and more American servicemen are going peacefully about their peaceful rounds and being murdered for it. [then a pause, while video continues] Bruce Morton, CBS News, Arlington.

Bugler plays taps (sound continues under narration). Still of American flag. Camera zooms out slowly to show huge flag hanging above flag-draped coffin and honor guard. Stills of Marines in uniform, alternating with stills of Arlington funeral.

Putting a piece of the lead story before the anchor's introduction is television's equivalent of a banner headline – and this was, of course, no ordinary day for television news. But if not typical, the *CBS Evening News* on day seven of the TWA hijacking crisis was archetypical, and represents well the contradictory character of television news today.

TV news, for one thing, is both journalism and show business, a key political institution as well as a seller of detergent and breakfast cereal. In the mid-1960s, television took its place alongside the wire services, the major daily newspapers, and the news magazines as an integral part of the fourth estate. Like the press, television news was accepted as a kind of quasi-constitutional branch of the American political system. 'Press' conferences – whether Ronald Reagan's or Nabih Berri's – became televised events. Network journalists were granted their seats on Air Force One and in the front row of presidential briefings. And those journalists identified with and accepted the 'professional' standards of their print colleagues. Television reporters interact with other journalists every day, with their fellow employees in the entertainment division of the network, virtually never.

Yet TV news is also entertainment, carried on in an intensely competitive commercial environment. It is, as Rather's metaphor of the 'title page written in blood' suggests, at least as much a teller of stories as a provider of political information and commentary. The combination of entertainment and journalism is not something television invented. It goes back at least to the first commercial mass media, the penny papers of the 1830s. But television is its premier practitioner today. When an event like the hostage crisis comes along – full of characters that the audience can identify with, villains they can hate, a world political context that elevates the whole story to a realm larger than everyday life, and suspense over the outcome that keeps the audience coming back night after night – television can rarely resist making the news a melodrama. (Ratings at CBS, which profited most from the hostage crisis, jumped 11 per cent during the early days of the crisis.)[1]

The political consequences of this mix of journalism and show business are complex. Consider the issue of presidential authority. Conservatives, as we have seen, have long argued that the media are hostile to established political authority, or at least serve unwittingly to undermine it. There are many versions of the argument: some, for example, focusing on the ideology of the 'liberal intelligentsia;' some on the hunger of a dramatic medium for controversy and conflict. Most consider television the worst offender.

And, indeed, much of what appeared on CBS news on day seven was potentially damaging to the Reagan administration. Hostage Conwell delivered an articulate statement calling on all the politicians involved to do what was necessary to 'let innocent and free people go home,' including those held by Israel – calling on the administration in effect to do precisely what it was refusing to do, to negotiate. The administration called the 'parading of hostages before TV cameras' a 'senseless exploitation,' but the networks were not about to turn the cameras away from one of the best characters in the story. Nor were they about to ignore the relatives of seven Americans held in Beirut before the hijacking, who in interviews the same day criticized the administration, some of them bitterly, for lack of attention to the fate of their loved ones. White House correspondent Lesley Stahl, meanwhile, pointed out that the administration's actions did not fully match its rhetoric. '[A]s if to underscore the limitations involved,' she reported, right after a tough statement by presidential press secretary Larry Speakes, 'all Mr. Reagan was able to announce was a new study on terrorism and more military aid to El Salvador.' The potential was there for the administration to appear insensitive to the fate of the 'little guy,' or incompetent, or both. In any case, it was clear that the flow of information and the news agenda was in important ways out of its control.

There was, however, another side to television's presentation of presidential authority. Rather, for instance, introduced Stahl's White House report this way: 'This has been one of the most turbulent weeks for our country in a long time. And, suddenly, President Reagan and his fellow Americans find themselves under attack from different sides in a war against faceless enemies.' Stahl wrapped up in this fashion: 'White House officials see a pattern of terrorism which they believe may be an attempt to test the will of President Reagan and the American people.'

American journalists in the post-Watergate, post-Vietnam era are deeply ambivalent about political authority. They often treat the president as a self-serving politician, something which was extremely rare, particularly on television, fifteen or twenty years ago. Yet the president also appears in television's political dramas as the brave marshal who suffers with the town's citizens and rides out to defend the town from the bad men. In the end, for all the controversy over television's portrayal of the hostage crisis, the net effect on this president was about what it usually is in the immediate aftermath of an event that gets defined as an international crisis:[2] Reagan's popularity jumped five points between the June and July Gallup polls.

TV news is widely believed to be the most powerful force in journalism, and often condemned for its political influence. The TWA hijacking was precisely the kind of event that has led to this perception. The whole episode seemed largely a performance staged for the media. Again, this is nothing television has invented. Politics has always been to a large degree a matter of orchestrating performances in order to project images. Machiavelli's *The Prince* is in part a manual on image-making. If television didn't invent image politics, however, it is the primary stage on which it takes place in the modern world.

Television is clearly in some sense an actor on the political stage as well. It doesn't merely transmit to the public information about what is going on. One of the things that is most distinctive about TV news is the extent to which it is an ideological medium, providing not just information or entertainment, but 'packages for consciousness'[3] – frameworks for interpreting and cues for reacting to social and political reality. If one looks closely at the CBS broadcast of 20 June 1985, it was clearly full of complexity and contradiction, but at another level it had a simplicity and unity, a single interpretation of the meaning of the news event. The broadcast returned again and again to a single theme: Americans under attack.

The network news was an active arbiter of political meaning during the Beirut hostage crisis, but the nature of the theme and the imagery it emphasized bring into focus the paradox of television's power. Here were the supposedly liberal media, indeed the notoriously liberal Dan Rather and CBS (this, at least, was their reputation at the time), emphasizing not the 'Vietnam syndrome' or any such thing (the theme of the day's broadcast, after all, could have been 'military intervention in civil wars doesn't pay'), but the nationalism and the military-oriented patriotism of Ronald Reagan. They were blowing with the prevailing political wind. And it should come as no surprise that for all the hostage press conferences and live television interviews with their captors, viewers blamed the crisis on the same roster of enemies conservatives were urging television to assail. Respondents in one CBS poll, for instance, focused on Greek airport security (48 per cent saying it was 'a lot' to blame for the crisis), Iran (42 per cent), and Nabih Berri, the man most often said to have manipulated television (46 per cent). More than twice as many (24 per cent) thought the Soviet Union bore 'a lot' of blame as thought US policy did (11 per cent). Twenty per cent named Israel.[4]

POPULISM AND THE NEWS

News is pervasive in the modern television schedule, beginning with early morning news followed by 2 hours of morning news, continuing with the local news, also now 2 hours long in many areas, then the flagship network evening news shows (a rather small part of the news line-up), prime-time news magazines, late local news, and finally *Nightline* and late-night news. For those who want something more or a little different, there are *The MacNeil–Lehrer Newshour*, CNN, and other cable news services. In my own television market of San Diego, setting aside PBS, CNN, independent stations, documentaries, and magazines, one can watch 8 hours of news on any weekday.

Each of these forms of news is distinctive in certain ways, and it is impossible to do justice to all of them here. I shall focus on two forms which lie toward opposite ends of the continuum that connects TV news to the worlds of entertainment and journalism it often uncomfortably straddles: morning news, which is first of all entertainment, and network evening news, which is journalism set within an entertainment medium.

To grasp either form, it is important to grasp the complex implications of the *populism* of TV news. Populism is of course a central part of American political culture: at least since the age of Andrew Jackson, politicians, the press, and popular culture have paid obeisance to the wisdom of the People, often contrasting it with the corruption and selfishness of those who hold power. This strain in American culture, to be sure, coexists and interacts with other very different ones, including a reverence for 'leadership' and order that was greatly strengthened by the development of the Cold War doctrine of 'national security.' But its power is great enough to have left a distinctive mark on American journalism: in few countries, for example, would the news have focused on ordinary citizens caught up in political events the way American television focused on the Beirut hostages. The fact that CBS began its broadcast on day seven of the hostage crisis with Allyn Conwell rather than Ronald Reagan, the State Department, or Congress, is strong testimony to the populism of TV news. The populism of American culture affects journalism at all levels, but among the major media it affects television particularly strongly. This is so because of the intensely competitive nature of the television industry, in which the three networks compete head-to-head for a mass national audience. Television worries about pleasing and entertaining the ordinary citizen in a way that the *New York Times* does not.

The political consequences of television's populism are complex, and often, in fact, anti-democratic. At times, it causes the news to spill beyond the bounds of official discourse, as it did in the reporting of Allyn Conwell's news conference. At other times, it causes the news to avoid controversies that seem likely to offend the mass audience, or to jump on the bandwagon of what seems a safe and appealing majority sentiment. Sometimes it manifests itself in 'anti-establishment' themes; television loves nothing more than a story about a 'little guy' who stands up to the 'powers that be.' Sometimes it serves as a resource to the power broker who knows how to play the populist hero. The success of Ronald Reagan in shaping the tone of television ironically owed much to television's populism, because Reagan played the populist hero particularly well, and because television was both fearful of crossing his popular appeal to restore American greatness and irresistibly tempted to adopt that appeal as its own.

HEROES AND FREAKS OF EVERYDAY LIFE: MORNING NEWS AS ENTERTAINMENT

Television has a number of different modes, different forms of presentation that work well on the medium: action, usually involving vehicles or gross body movements – fights, car crashes, and the like; collage – the rapidly succeeding images of the modern commercial being the classic example; irony – achieved through the juxtaposition of contrasting statements or images ('I don't know of anybody being oppressed,' said an American businessman in Guatemala, interviewed by Ed Rabel for *Central America in Revolt*, the CBS documentary discussed at length in Chapter 4. 'I think this is just something that some reporters have thought up.' Cut to visuals of Guatemala's shanty towns, and a murdered reformer.) Finally, television loves intimacy of a certain kind – carried on at just enough social distance that it is all right for a third person to listen in. This is the mode of morning news. Friendly and interesting people have conversations with other friendly and interesting people, and the viewer is invited to 'join them.' From time to time, other friendly people fill the viewer in on matters of public interest – weather, sports, and the news.

Good Morning America is produced by ABC's entertainment division; NBC's *Today* and the *CBS Morning News* were produced in the mid-1980s by the news divisions (the CBS morning show was taken away from the news division in July 1986). But all three morning news shows are entertainment first and journalism second. In 1985, for example, during the May rating sweeps, Bryant Gumbel, Jane Pauley, and NBC's *Today* traveled around the country on an Amtrak train. It was no doubt a difficult and expensive technical feat, and it had little journalistic purpose. But it produced exceptionally good morning television. It meant, for one thing, that there would be plenty of little crises that would enhance the aura of informality so important to the intimacy of morning news. In Memphis, for instance, it rained intermittently, forcing Jane and Bryant to explain apologetically that the show might be a little chaotic – just as 'real' hosts often have to do. Putting the show on the road also added a new twist to the symbolic participation of the audience. People could actually come down to the railroad stop to greet *Today* and be seen on the air; this they did, cheering and waving signs as fans do at a football game when the cameras point at them. The relation of television to its audience involves a kind of mutual flattery, which, as we shall see, is important on many levels.

Aside from the rain and the presence of the audience, though, the *Today* show was not unusual during the Amtrak trip. From Memphis, one hour-long segment included the following stories: a feature on people who had lived on boats in the Mississippi; an interview with Tennessee Senators Albert Gore Jr and Sr; a story on the tourist industry centered on Elvis Presley's birthplace; a story on Memphis race relations; and an appearance by singer Jerry Lee Lewis.

As entertainment, the morning news deals relatively little with the political conflicts which are the stock-in-trade of front pages and the evening news. Typically, unless some unusual political event is going on, each 1-hour segment will contain one feature on a political topic. In this case, it was the race relations story (the story on the Albert Gores, father and son, was a human interest, not a political, story). The balance of the items will be 'soft' feature stories of one sort or another. Even the 'hard news' bulletins, which typically take up about 10 minutes of each hour, focus fairly heavily on certain kinds of stories considered to be good material for entertainment television. During May and June 1985, the stories that received special emphasis included the Frustaci septuplets (the lead story the day *Today* was in Memphis), the 'Walker spy family,' the trial of the socialite and accused wife-murderer Claus von Bulow, a cyclone in Bangladesh, the introduction of the Reagan tax reform plan, and of course the TWA hijacking.

What is it that these stories have in common? Each is in some way about everyday life. The tax reform story belongs to a familiar special category. It is 'news you can use,' like the consumer and medical reporting that occupies a large niche on the local news. The morning news, like much other television coverage, emphasized not the tax plan's impact on economic growth or social equality or priorities, but 'what it will mean to you.'

The rest of the stories are about perversions, exaltations, interruptions, or crises of everyday life. The birth of seven children to one family is not an everyday event; if it were, it wouldn't have the fascination that makes it news. But it is a twist on something that is an everyday event. People can imagine what it is like for an ordinary person to go into the hospital and suddenly have seven sick babies, just as they can imagine what it must be like to be flying home on an airliner and suddenly be taken hostage. Most of these stories are positive. (The 'tabloid' news shows – like *A Current Affair* and *Hard Copy*, which have developed since 1985 – have a similar agenda in many ways, but with a *negative* inflection.) Most are about heroes of everyday life – people who, though they seem ordinary and easy to identify with, either deal gracefully with an extraordinary crisis or rise above the usual boredom of life, like the people who lived on the Mississippi, or a man who appeared in the second hour of *Today* in Memphis pursuing a dream of restoring the steam engine. In this category also is the celebrity, whose life, which we as 'friends' are privileged to share, is like our own projected on to a higher plane.

The Walker and von Bulow families, on the other hand, are freaks of everyday life – a seemingly normal American family which begins to spy for the Soviets; a marriage gone awry like so many others, but a fabulous marriage gone fabulously and grotesquely awry. Many stories combine images of heroism with the fascination of the freak show. The story of the Frustaci septuplets combines the courage of the family, which occupies the foreground, with the freakishness of a multiple birth. Another of the great morning news stories of 1985 also falls into this category – the story of Cathleen Webb, who recanted the testimony that had put her former boyfriend, Gary Dotson, in prison for rape, both of them subsequently appearing together on all the morning shows. A particularly clear example appeared on the local news in New York in July 1985 when WABC ran a series on rare diseases. The emphasis was on how people coped with illnesses that made parts of life most of us take for granted extremely difficult; in this sense, those who appeared were clearly heroes. But at the same time, each of the two episodes I saw was about diseases that produced gross physical deformities, including the 'elephant man' disease.

The morning news does do some political stories, and it is interesting to consider what happens when it brings political issues into the intimacy of its small circle of friends. At times, the result is much more substantial coverage than would normally be found on the evening news. In 1981, for example, when Ground Zero Week was organized to publicize the danger of nuclear war, arms control advocates were much happier with the coverage they got on the morning than the evening news. Why should this be? The morning news, for one thing, is much slower-paced than the evening news, with its tight editing and 10-second soundbites (whose origin and meaning will be explored at length in Chapter 7). One can express a stripped-down feeling or attitude in 10 seconds, but it is difficult to make an argument. It is also difficult to step outside of conventional modes of thought: to frame an issue in a way that is unfamiliar to the audience requires time for explanation. It might be added that the 10-second soundbite seems likely to promote a particularly passive relation of the audience to the news: it is necessarily prepackaged thought, 'like a cartoon bubble,' in the words of David Marash, a maverick local anchor with a reputation for bucking the powerful trend in recent years toward faster-paced evening news broadcasts.[5] Compared with the evening news, the 5 minutes of unedited conversation permitted by the talk-show format of the morning news seems a luxurious opportunity to discuss issues in depth.

Because it is not primarily journalism, moreover, the morning news is not bound by a number of journalistic conventions that made it difficult for arms control advocates to put the nuclear issue on the national agenda in the 1980s. 'Serious' journalism is primarily concerned with issues being debated in Washington. This is not to say that TV news at any level is concerned exclusively with the affairs of Washington officials. The concern of television with ordinary people and ordinary life spills over to the evening news as well. This is one of the things that is distinctive about American TV news compared with that of other countries. (About a third of those who appear on American TV news are citizens without official position. In Italy, as we will see in Chapter 6, virtually all are officials of government, political parties, or other organized groups.) Still, the ordinary citizen is brought into the evening news primarily to react to certain official policies, or else to appear in human interest stories, which are included in the evening news to 'lighten it up.' Washington controls the agenda for political reporting, and it is relatively difficult for a movement pushing an issue not on that agenda – as arms control was not in 1981 – to get itself taken seriously as 'hard news.'

For the morning news, on the other hand, Ground Zero's very lack of Washington roots made it excellent material. Few things are as deadly to the intimate format of morning news as interviews with the likes of Caspar Weinberger and George Schultz (Reagan's Secretaries of Defense and State). This is not to say that no Washington officials appeared. The morning news enters a mixed mode when it deals with an issue like arms control, and many standard conventions of journalism apply. On the final day of Ground Zero Week, for instance, *CBS Morning News* set up a debate between Richard Perle, Assistant Secretary of Defense, and Sidney Drell, a physicist supporting the freeze movement.

What made Ground Zero a good story, though, and paved the way for the concluding discussion of arms control policy, was the fact that it emerged from a grass-roots movement concerned with an issue that anyone could relate to on some level. The people behind Ground Zero were precisely the sort who normally appear on the morning news: articulate and upscale – it was largely a movement of the professional middle class – yet also ordinary people for whom politics was only a sideline. In a way, such a story fit perfectly the formula of crises and perversions of everyday life. People tend to think of nuclear war, after all, as something like a natural disaster, which is one of the major types of human interest story – think of the way it was later presented in the ABC film *The Day After*, as an unexplained event that disrupted the lives of ordinary people. So along with the debate about policy, *CBS Morning News* also included a segment on 'living with fear,' which included interviews with high school students about how they felt growing up in a nuclear world, and with bomb-shelter developers who described the features of underground living (balanced, it might be added, by a statement from a psychiatrist, another articulate non-official voice, who made the case that a nuclear war was not survivable).

'Serious' journalism, as we saw in Chapter 2, tends to treat politics from a technical or strategic perspective, rather than as a discussion of social values: it asks 'Who is winning?,' not 'Who is right?' or 'What should we do?' So when the evening news covered Ground Zero, it focused not on the argument the movement was making about nuclear war and nuclear policy, but on the question of whether the movement would be politically effective; CBS, for example, interviewed California pollster Mervin Field on that subject. On the morning news, on the other hand, in part simply because the anti-nuclear advocates were part of a live conversation, they had many opportunities to emphasize their own central issue, 'the urgency, the determination,' as Drell put it, 'to get back to the negotiating table.' An entertainment medium cannot pose as an authority the way an information medium can, but must enter into dialogue with the public, represented in the case of the morning news by the guests. So the morning news is in some ways more open than the evening news even in the coverage of politics.

But consider the following story from ABC's *Good Morning America*. On 23 May 1985, Joan Lunden interviewed Sylvester Stallone about *Rambo*, the 'action-adventure' film in which Stallone plays a Vietnam veteran on a crusade to rescue Americans still held captive, killing plenty of Vietnamese in the process. Here is part of the interview:

Lunden: And Sylvester Stallone is joining us from Los Angeles. Good morning. Gee, I love those simple drawing-room comedies. This thing is action-packed! How *hard* was it to make a movie like this?

Stallone: This was probably the most difficult film . . . . Because of the heat, the inherent dangers of the stunts . . . and the terrain – people were always coming across tarantulas in the bushes, or coral snakes, or whatever.

Lunden: You go through, I know, a pretty rigorous training period before each film. But you went through the most grueling, rigorous training for this one. How long and what was it like?

Stallone: I wanted him to look like the terrain, hard and cut up but very inflexible, almost like a piece of machinery.

Lunden: I think you succeeded on that one. [Then speaking more quickly.] It's getting good reviews. Now the only thing is, is that the movie does maintain of course that the Vietnamese still have POWs, American POWs. And a few critics have said that that 'exploits the emotions of relatives whose families are still listed as missing in action.' What do you *say* to that criticism?

Stallone: What we're trying to show is . . . they are there. From all the data that has been compiled from the people that have been working with the film, which is from very reliable sources, there are men there. So I think a dramatization to show this only helps put the spotlight on a very darkened area . . . .

Lunden: So it's more than an action-adventure film. It's a statement.

The conversation then put politics aside and moved on to a more typical celebrity interview 'issue,' the question of whether Stallone was 'stuck in a rut' with the image of a 'larger-than-life hero.'

Rambo was among the most popular films of 1985. It was also a political phenomenon whose significance went well beyond the dubious claim that American prisoners were still alive in Vietnam. It belonged to a genre of Vietnam revenge stories which has long had powerful appeal to the *Soldier of Fortune* crowd, but with *Rambo* broke into the mainstream of American popular culture. The response was powerful – audiences often cheered with Rambo and chanted 'USA, USA.' And the 'stab in the back' mentality was chillingly similar to that of Germany in the early 1930s, not only in its aggressive nationalism, but in the particular kind of vigilante spirit it portrayed: in the end, Rambo turns his violence on the 'wimp' civilian who betrayed him, while a chorus of faceless 'little men' cheers, and the colonel, the one authority figure who has always respected Rambo, looks on understandingly. Rambo, moreover, is a strange kind of hero whose only mode of expression is violence. He is, as the colonel says, a killing 'machine.' Stallone has been described as the new John Wayne, but he is in fact a significant break from the John Wayne image: the machismo of John Wayne was always bound by a sense of connection to a human culture – usually symbolized by the nuclear family Wayne could not be part of – and an idealized vision of political order. Rambo's violence was profoundly antisocial.

The United States was never so far gone that the implications of *Rambo* escaped the notice of at least some critics. (*Variety*, reporting on gross returns at New York theaters one week, described *Rambo* as the 'all-American on-screen war machine manipulating the masses for $450,000.') But to have raised this kind of issue on the morning news would have disrupted its friendly atmosphere. Stories on popular culture fall unequivocally in the entertainment mode of the morning news. In the celebrity interviews, the morning news avoids controversy in the same way, and for largely the same reasons, that casual acquaintances avoid it when they are trying to make conversation. As entertainment, television is a consensual medium. It focuses on what people are assumed to share. Even the reporting of Ground Zero was not really an exception. Nuclear war was good material for the morning news in part because it was at one level a consensual issue. Everyone is against nuclear war; Bill Kurtis was even able to get Richard Perle and Sidney Drell to agree on that. But Vietnam remains far too touchy an issue to bring into a story that is intended essentially as diversion from the cares of the world.

THE EVENING NEWS: JOURNALISM ON AN ENTERTAINMENT MEDIUM

The evening news as we know it today began in September 1963 when CBS and NBC expanded their news broadcasts from 15 minutes to half an hour (ABC followed in 1967). The quiz show scandal of 1959 had tarnished the networks' public image, and an activist chairman of the FCC, Newton Minow, had called television a 'vast wasteland,' warning that the license renewal process would cease to be treated as a formality. In this atmosphere, the expanded evening news, along with a new commitment to live public affairs programming and documentaries, gave the networks a claim to be something more than a high-tech way of selling detergent. It made them a part of the fourth estate, or as modern journalism is sometimes called, the 'fourth branch of government.' It associated them with the prestige of the state; each of the new half-hour shows was inaugurated with an interview with President Kennedy. At the same time, reflecting the ambivalent political heritage of American journalism, it associated them with the tradition of the press as a defender of the public *against* the state – and hence an institution protected by the First Amendment against government interference.

The news was initially seen as a 'loss leader' whose function was more to restore prestige than to make money. As a result, the news divisions were largely freed from the commercial considerations that dominate most television production, while television journalists came to enjoy a degree of professional autonomy not so different from that of their counterparts in the 'prestige' press. A network news ethic developed of giving the public 'what it needed' more than 'what it wanted.'

Despite its ambitions, however, television journalism was very primitive in this era. This was most evident in Washington reporting, which makes up the bulk of 'hard news' coverage. Even in the late 1960s, most television reports from Washington consisted of little more than unedited film of official speeches and press conferences, introduced by the anchor and followed by his commentary, which usually summarized and reiterated what officials had said in public. The major print media, by contrast, were much more active in the gathering and presentation of news: Washington coverage in the 'prestige press' made use of a variety of sources (albeit still official), many of them unnamed, which the journalist would put together to reveal 'the real story' which was presumed to lie behind the surface of official proceedings. By the mid-1970s, as Vietnam and then Watergate opened the gap between official statements and the 'real story' wider and wider, television journalism began to catch up with the more active and sophisticated journalism of the 'prestige press.'

But if television reached journalistic puberty sometime around 1970, it also became more commercial. By the end of the 1960s, the evening news shows were already making small profits, and in 1968, in an augury of dramatic developments to come, *60 Minutes* arrived on the scene, and soon began to gather large audiences. *60 Minutes* was television's original contribution to the increasingly active journalism of the era. It also rocketed to the top of the ratings charts by 1969, putting the entire CBS news division into the black for the first time. And then in the early 1970s, local television, for which news had become far and away the primary source of profits, entered an intense competition for ratings that would bring all the tools of commercial television, from graphics-generators to market research, into the news business.

All of this began to catch up with the network evening news in the mid-1970s. One important event was ABC's 1977 appointment of Roone Arledge to head its news division. Switching from ABC Sports in defiance of a tradition of promoting news division heads from within the news division, Arledge turned ABC News from an also-ran into a serious ratings competitor of NBC and CBS. The news divisions entered a new period of intense competition, still in progress, during which the old barriers isolating news from commercial television have progressively weakened.

That television shows the duality between news and entertainment more sharply than other news media has to do with the structure of the television industry. In the newspaper business, the tension between entertainment and journalism was sharpest in the days depicted in *Citizen Kane* and *The Front Page*, when urban newspapers competed head-to-head for readership. Today, most papers have monopolies, or nearly so, in their primary markets; in other cases, New York for instance, where a number of papers compete in the same urban area, the market is stratified by class.

But in the television business, the three networks compete head-to-head for the same national market, and in each major urban area at least three television stations fight for the advertising dollars. Television consumers, moreover, are volatile. They are like the newspaper reader of years ago, who bought the paper on the newsstand rather than by subscription, and might buy one paper today and another tomorrow depending on the headlines. The audience for an evening news show can fluctuate considerably from day to day, and even from minute to minute – the more so with the advent of the remote control. And though the news is not a major money-maker compared with prime time, the financial consequences of fluctuating ratings are considerable. In the early 1980s, when ABC News made its run at the other networks, a slide in ratings for the *CBS Evening News* from a 27 to 24 per cent share of the audience cut the value of a 30-second spot on the show by as much as $10,000.[6] Add to this the fact that the evening news is an integral part of the 'audience flow' that channels people into the network's prime-time programming, and it is clear that the networks have strong incentives to act aggressively to maximize the audience for the evening news. The result has been a significant convergence of news toward the conventions of television entertainment, with news broadcasts becoming faster-paced, more visual, and with greater emphasis on the kinds of stories – usually, like morning news stories, those with a human interest angle – the audience is assumed to enjoy watching.

THE POWER OF TELEVISION

The networks' very success at creating a form of news that would have both the prestige of élite journalism and the mass appeal of television has produced new problems for them. In the early 1960s, they were criticized for their lack of concern with public issues. Today, they face the opposite criticism: television news is widely seen as a dangerously powerful political institution. In part, this is because of the size and national scope of television's audience. The networks introduced the first daily news coverage to reach a broad national audience (the *Wall Street Journal* and the *Christian Science Monitor* have long had national circulations, but their readerships are smaller and more specialized). Even with the advent of *USA Today* and the national edition of the *New York Times*, they have by far the largest daily exposures.

Television, moreover, presents the news differently than print media do, in ways that have led many to argue that it has greater impact on its audience than other kinds of news. Television is personal: the news is brought to us not by anonymous writers but by individuals selected in no small part for a persona that combines authority with likability. It is well known that polls once showed Walter Cronkite to be the most 'trusted' man in America. Television is also visual; people may feel they are 'seeing it for themselves' on television.[7] And television is more 'interpretive' or 'thematic:' unlike most newspaper reports, television stories tend to be tightly organized around a particular 'story-line' or interpretation.

Many of the claims made today about the power of television are so sweeping (the cover of Barbara Matusow's book *The Evening Stars*,[8] for instance, says of the anchors, 'They influence our opinions more than any politician – and can do so with the mere flicker of an eyebrow') that it is worth introducing a note of caution. The main evidence for television's pre-eminent power is a set of polls conducted by the Roper Organization which showed, as of 1984, that 64 per cent of the public said they got most of their news from television, while only 40 per cent named newspapers, and many fewer radio or magazines (people could name more than one medium). According to the same polls, most people said they found TV more believable. But this, as Lawrence Lichty has pointed out, simply shows that most people *think* they get most of their news from TV.[9] Whether they really do is another matter; on any given day, only half as many people – about a third of the population – watch any TV news, national or local, as read a newspaper. A similar percentage of the public, about a third, reads *Time, Newsweek*, or *U.S. News & World Report*. A quarter read *Readers' Digest*. It is one of the ironies of the CBS–Westmoreland libel case that more people read *TV Guide*'s attack on *The Uncounted Enemy: A Vietnam Deception* than saw the documentary itself. The circulation of *TV Guide* at the time was 17 million; the audience for the documentary was about 8 million.

As for the impact of TV on those who do watch it, it is clear that it can be substantial. It was once the standard view of academic media researchers that the mass media did not have much impact on people's opinions. But this view has been discredited in recent years as researchers have become more sophisticated about *how* the media might influence public opinion. The researchers of the 1950s were interested primarily in propaganda; that is, direct efforts to change people's political opinions. Modern media research is concerned with more indirect forms of influence. Thus Iyengar and Kinder, whose work has been decisive in putting the 'limited effects hypothesis' of the 1950s to rest, found that the emphasis in television broadcasts on different issues affected not only people's assessments of the importance of the issues (the 'agenda-setting effect') but their evaluation of presidential performance as well.[10] At the same time, though, there is no real confirming evidence that television affects people's opinions more than print. And it clearly often happens that people reject what they hear and see on the news. At the Democratic Convention in 1968, Walter Cronkite not only flickered his eyebrow but called the Chicago police 'thugs.' Surveys, nonetheless, showed that the public sided with the police.[11]

Nobody can say for sure how powerful television actually is, but television does present the news in a way that may make it particularly important as a carrier of ideology and social values. The crucial thing here is the unified, thematic nature of television presentation. A newspaper story, particularly a 'hard news' story about a political event, is traditionally organized in the form of an 'inverted pyramid.' The 'who, what, when, where' is given in the lead paragraph, and the article then moves on to fill in details, reactions, and background, theoretically moving from the most to the least important facts, on the assumption that most readers will not get to the end of the story. A certain 'angle' or point of view will of course guide the sifting of 'important' from 'unimportant' facts, and this will usually be expressed at least implicitly in the lead paragraphs. After that, though, a story will often strike out in a number of different directions; the theme of the lead paragraphs need not carry through the entire piece.

But television has a very different relation to its audience than the newspaper. A newspaper reader can browse at will from story to story; television must 'carry the audience along' from the beginning of each story to the end and on to the next. So a television story is more like a circle than a pyramid. It introduces its central theme at the beginning, develops it throughout the story, though perhaps with twists and turns dictated by problems of balance or ideological tensions the journalist may consciously or unconsciously be trying to resolve, and returns to it in a closing line that 'wraps the story up.' This is often true not only of the individual story but of 'segments' – groups of stories placed together between two commercials – and even of the news broadcast as a whole. This of course was the case with the *CBS Evening News* on the day of the hostage press conference and the guerrilla attack in El Salvador. In the newspapers, the stories from Lebanon and El Salvador shared the front page, but were reported with little reference to one another, except in quotations from administration officials, who sought to connect them. On television they were treated as part of the same story (with the result that the El Salvador story, which a year or so earlier might have been framed as 'deepening American involvement in El Salvador's guerrilla war,' became instead 'America held hostage'). And the newspaper had nothing like the refrain that again and again hammered home the theme of the CBS broadcast: 'For President Reagan and all Americans, one more tough situation . . . one of the most turbulent weeks for our country . . . volume of terrorist violence against the United States . . . American servicemen going peacefully about their peaceful rounds and being murdered for it.'

TELEVISION AND POLITICAL AUTHORITY

Television is no mere headline service. It plays a special role in assigning ideological meaning to political events. But what kind of ideology does it promote? Television's ideology, to summarize very roughly, descends from the liberalism of the Progressive era. It is reformist, and stands ready to expose violations of ideals of fair play, equal opportunity, and prosperity. It is also populist in the sense that it is suspicious of power and those who seek it, and will often praise the wisdom of the 'common man' against the cynicism of the 'politician.' But reformism and populism coexist with a strong belief in order, consensus, moderation, leadership, and the basic soundness of American institutions and benevolence of American world leadership. Here I would like to return to one facet of this 'reformist conservatism' already touched upon in this essay – the ambivalent attitude of television journalism toward political authority.

The conservative claim that television journalists 'view with special suspicion whatever political leaders and organizations seem most powerful at the moment'[12] does have a grain of truth. Since the mid-1960s, influenced by Vietnam and Watergate, American journalism has become more 'adversarial' – more inclined to question political authority. The change has been particularly dramatic in the case of television, though this is in part because television news started out with a much more deferential attitude toward government officials than comparable national media. This change has many dimensions, a number of which we will explore in Chapters 7 and 9. One of the most striking, certainly, is a habit of pointing out the political motivations of a statement or a 'photo opportunity.' ' President Reagan's visit to the German military cemetery in Bitburg now is called by many the greatest blunder of his administration,' reported Dan Rather in 1985. 'Before leaving West Germany today, Mr. Reagan tried to deflect some of the criticism leveled at him by criticizing the Soviets.' A year and a half earlier, in November 1983, NBC's Chris Wallace, summing up a report on a Reagan trip to South Korea, said, 'Any trip a president makes is political, and officials traveling with Mr. Reagan were clearly delighted with pictures of him on the front lines. At one point, an aide motioned to the president to move more into the sunlight.' Television journalists didn't do this in 1965 or 1970.

But this is only half the story. Chris Wallace, for instance, continued his remarks on Reagan's Korea trip this way:

Still, it was clear that Mr. Reagan was genuinely moved by what he saw here today – the choir of orphans, young American soldiers ready to fight far from home. It's safe to assume Mr. Reagan will be speaking and thinking of this place for a long time.

The president is the prime character in television's personalized presentation of politics, and even setting aside the fear of crossing a popular president, a fear which journalists share with members of Congress and other political figures, TV has the same interest in presenting him sympathetically as in presenting Sylvester Stallone that way. What Wallace does here is to separate 'Reagan the person' from 'Reagan the politician,' and protect the former from the negative image of the political role. This, of course, is precisely what politicians have tried to do since Vietnam, Watergate, and the rest deflated the more patriarchal image of authority that prevailed in the 1950s and 1960s: to project an image of personal sincerity and effectiveness while being a 'regular guy' in contrast to a 'Washington politician.' Jimmy Carter tried to do this and failed; Reagan succeeded. It is an image that works well on television for someone who can play the part, the more so as TV news drifts toward a more entertainment-style format.

Does this mean, then, that television recognizes only celebrity, rather than authority in the traditional sense? Not really. Television's cynicism about politicians – it is really not television's exclusively, but part of American culture – coexists with a strong belief in leadership and the importance of public support for it. A good illustration can be found in an ABC 'Status Report' on the May 1985 bombing by a police helicopter that burned to the ground a city block in Philadelphia. Here are excerpts from that story, reported by Richard Threlkeld:

Threlkeld: For the cradle of independence, William Penn's City of Brotherly Love, this seemed terribly out of place. Combat on the streets. A police helicopter drops a bomb – *a bomb* – on a house full of men, women, and children . . . . There was outrage here.

Angry citizen: How do you justify a bombing in public? Is this a war zone or is this Beirut? What's up, man?

Threlkeld: And a lot of Tuesday and Wednesday morning quarter-backing from outsiders who saw these pictures. [New York mayor Koch appears, here in the role of politician rather than leader.]

In some other cities we can think of, perhaps including Mayor Koch's New York, that awful sequence of events might have started a riot . . . .

That didn't happen here in Philadelphia. Quite the opposite . . . .

Yesterday, the city's black clergy prayed for the mayor. The polls indicate most Philadelphians actually endorse what he did, although not the tragic, unintended result.

Half the explanation lies in the people the police were trying to evict . . . members of MOVE, a tiny, bizarre cult whose members wear Rastafarian

hairdos and have all changed their name to 'Africa.' . . . Police moved in
after days of negotiation failed and people in the house started shooting . . . .

Despite what happened and all the unanswered questions, people have
been uncommonly forgiving of Wilson Goode, the mayor . . . .

The mayor has promised that all the homeless will have brand new homes
by Christmas. And in the meantime, the whole city, black and white, has
pitched in to help . . . . America's fifth largest city is suddenly behaving with
all the good-neighborliness of a little town . . . .

An event like the Philadelphia bombing, as Threlkeld conveys in setting the
scene, is potentially damaging to the society's self-image ('for the cradle of
independence . . . a bomb . . . . What's up, man?'). What television tends to do in
a case like this, far from focusing on 'controversy and violence,' is to
emphasize unity and the restoration of normality, and to reassure the viewers
that nothing is fundamentally wrong. Populism means that the restoration of
normality will be attributed in part to community self-help. But we are
reassured as well that government institutions are responding to the crisis;
Peter Jennings introduced the story by reporting that officials from various
agencies were touring the area and had promised aid. The mayor appears not
as a politician but as a symbol of the unity of the community. (The fact that
Goode is black, of course, makes him a particularly important symbol in a
crisis that raises the specter of a renewal of black–white conflict.) The causes of
the conflict, meanwhile, Threlkeld pushes outside the mainstream of society,
on to the 'tiny bizarre cult.' Threlkeld calls MOVE 'half the explanation.' But
whatever the other half is – a sense of hopelessness in parts of the black
community, the machismo of American culture that leads to escalation once
confrontation begins, failure of city officials to deal with the crisis sooner or to
think out the consequences of their tactics – Threlkeld says nothing about it.

Those who believe a show-business medium inevitably tends to emphasize
conflict rather than harmony should think about what television entertainment is actually like. There is conflict, of course; drama can't exist without
conflict. But the portrayal of conflict by no means always casts established
institutions or authorities in a bad light. Most of television's conflict is of good
against evil, evil being located outside the mainstream of society – in 'faceless
enemies' and 'bizarre cults.' Here the message is often precisely the necessity of
order and authority. When conflicts take place within the community of major
characters – the community we are expected to identify with – it is normally
resolved in the course of an episode or two, proving the strength of that
community and the legitimacy of the family-like relations within it, including
authority relations.

A television drama is like certain dreams: it enacts a fear and provides an
idealized resolution of it. TV news often has this character as well. It is more in
its journalistic than its show-business mode that television focuses on
controversy. A paper like the *New York Times* or the *Washington Post*,
dealing with an event like the Philadelphia bombing, tends to focus on issues,

that is, things that people disagree about. This is true not because they are 'anti-establishment,' but because their kind of journalism is oriented toward policy-makers or people who follow politics closely, and who are assumed to be interested in *problems* which require action or decision. But as a medium oriented largely toward a huge and politically inactive mass public, television is more inclined to be consensual.

A POPULIST MEDIUM IN THE AGE OF REAGAN

Ronald Reagan was often seen as having nearly unlimited power to manipulate the media, but this was never really accurate.[13] Television was not going to call Reagan a liar or a militarist or a right-wing ideologue, of course. It wasn't going to call his policy in Central America imperialistic, or his domestic policy systematically class-biased. It wasn't even likely – with the exception of an occasional appearance on *Nightline* – to throw in such a view for the sake of 'balance.' The rules of 'objectivity' require the television journalist, like any American journalist, to stick to narrower issues which do not bring the legitimacy of the state into question. Do the budget numbers add up? Can the Salvadoran government beat the guerrillas? Will Congress buy the proposal? By historical standards, though, coverage of Reagan was probably no softer than coverage of any post-Watergate president; indeed, it was often my impression during these years that journalists were at pains to demonstrate that the 'Great Communicator' did not have them in his pocket. Rather's and Stahl's comments on the aftermath of Bitburg were certainly as barbed as anything Jimmy Carter suffered from the media, and they were not really exceptional.

If television was not consistently deferential to Reagan or his specific policies, however, *Reaganism* was another matter. And this is closely tied to the populism of TV news. By 'Reaganism' I don't mean so much ideological conservatism, though it is probably true Reagan's success and the disarray of the Democratic party shifted the center of gravity in American politics to the right, carrying all of American journalism with them to some extent – since 'balance' requires that the journalist straddle this center of gravity. Nobody in the mainstream of American politics was about to deliver a ringing endorsement of the public sector, for example (this is really still true today), so aside from an occasional piece on the op-ed page, no such view was going to get into the news.

But the element of Ronald Reagan's politics that most dramatically affected television was something less openly ideological: it was the 'America Is Back,' 'We're Number One' nationalism that exhibited such deep appeal for the mass public. In a sense, television itself may have done a good deal to lay the groundwork for this political current, above all through its daily coverage of the Iran hostage crisis ('America Held Hostage, Day 276') and its presentation of that event as a national humiliation. The public and media reaction could be seen most strongly in another great media event – the invasion of Grenada. During the first day or two, television treated Grenada as it would treat a tax plan or budget proposal – with a neutral tone and a modest amount of skepticism of the administration's rationale. But as the positive public reaction mounted, television's emphasis quickly shifted away from political issues to the patriotic celebration – medical students kissing the ground, soldiers coming home to a heroes' welcome, and the like. The public, moreover, not only cheered for the invasion of Grenada, but, according to a number of polls, endorsed Reagan's decision to keep the press from covering it. A year later, after a campaign that stressed the restoration of national pride, the 'Great Communicator' was overwhelmingly re-elected. After that, television scrambled to get on the right side of the 'new patriotism.' Deference to authority was less the cause here than the effect: what television really fears is being out of step with a strong movement of public opinion.

The period following Grenada and Reagan's re-election was characterized by increasing stridency in coverage of consensus enemies – terrorists and the more traditional Cold War enemies. The same day Rather and Stahl said Reagan was attacking the Soviet Union to deflect criticism from himself, for instance, CBS also had a story on the memory of the Second World War in the Soviet Union. The story itself was ideologically ambiguous, representing the Soviet mood as paranoiac, but at the same time treating with some respect the psychological impact of 20 million deaths. But Rather's introduction was as heavy-handed as anything his counterparts in the Soviet Union could dish up: 'The militaristic and totalitarian Communist party that rules modern Russia constantly emphasizes its version of the war as a lesson for its people and a lesson for others.' (What it was about the Soviet 'version' of the Second World War he considered false, Rather did not say.) The rules of 'objectivity' have never applied to 'militaristic Communists' any more than to 'faceless enemies' or 'bizarre cults' (which belong to the sphere of deviance introduced in Chapter 3); but this kind of colorful prose had for the most part faded out in the mid-1960s. Its function here seems to have been to balance the liberal skepticism of the Bitburg story with a bow to the spirit of the new Cold War. And this was just the beginning: as 1985 progressed and the Reagan– Gorbachev summit approached, the news, like every other part of television, was increasingly filled with Cold War rhetoric and imagery.

The most important way television 'balanced' its liberal image, though, was to adopt the imagery of Reagan's principal campaign theme: 'America Is Back.' One particularly interesting example occurred on CBS the day after the broadcast discussed at the beginning of this essay. Most of the news that day, of course, was about the Beirut hostage crisis. Near the end of the broadcast was a rather nervous piece of self-analysis, a story by Bob Simon recalling the press conference the day before – at which the hostages and the Amal militia had lectured journalists to behave in a civilized manner – and detailing various criticisms of the role of the media in the hostage crisis. Then came a 'tease bumper' (one of the new techniques the networks have used to liven up the evening news) announcing the closing story. The tease showed the TWA plane on the ground in Beirut, and in an inset – cowboys on the range; the title was 'Song of America.' The story that followed bore remarkable resemblance to the Reagan film at the Republican convention that CBS and ABC had declined to televise the previous summer: it began with a soft-focus shot of a crew rowing down a river at sunrise, and then moved on to the Statue of Liberty surrounded by scaffolding and a series of shots of Americans going happily about their everyday life, concluding with a cowboy who reflected, 'There's a lot to be said for the freedom that's involved in this lifestyle, and realizing that there's people like [the hostages] that don't have that opportunity, it stays on your mind.' The theme was that America was strong despite the hostage crisis – morally strong, that is, in the sense of the City on a Hill, not strong in the sense that its immense political and economic power was unchallenged, an emphasis which would have given the story a very different slant. 'There is a lot of concern in the country this week,' Bruce Morton concluded. 'But there is strength and order too.'

Earlier the same month, on 3 June 1985, NBC reported on the aftermath of a tornado that hit Newton Falls, Ohio. The story focused on the way the community pulled together to help those in need; and in this respect it was a very standard story. There is nothing new or unusual about upbeat news on television, though it may be particularly common in periods when television has been under political attack. ('Happy news' began appearing on the local news not long after Vice-President Spiro Agnew's 1969 assault on the media.) The story of how neighbors pull together at a time of crisis is one of the most common genres of good news. But in this case, there was a twist: community spirit became transformed into nationalism. The last line of the story was supplied by a resident who said, 'Everybody's interested in helping. And I say that's what makes America great. There's no country in the world like the United States.' Then a shot of an American flag standing amid the rubble.

The response people in television generally give when asked about the impact of Reagan is familiar. 'Reagan has brightened the national mood; I don't think there's any question about that,' said Bruce Morton in an interview for this essay. 'And I think that clearly is reflected in the news coverage. As it should be: we're supposed to be kind of a mirror of what's going on.' But the notion of 'mirroring' hardly does justice to stories like Morton's or the NBC story from Newton Falls, which was reported by Jack Reynolds. Mirrors do not make strategic use of the romanticizing technique of soft focus. Television has not only mirrored but *identified itself* with this element of the popular mood. Morton's story, as its title indicates, was a song, a paean, not a mere report. So was Reynolds', closing not with a correspondent's wrap-up but with the views of the patriotic resident, reinforced with a symbolic visual. In each of these stories, television was in a sense doing what the morning news does in a less political way, with its folksy celebration of everyday life, and what Ronald Reagan did with such powerful political effect: flattering the public.

To say that television responds to or even flatters the public mood is not necessarily to say that it gives a *voice* to the ordinary American. The hostage crisis is a good example. The hostages and their families were clearly the stars of television's drama. Their lives became immensely important. They were elevated to heroic proportions. But their role on television was primarily symbolic, and to the extent that they began to become participants in political discussion, rather than symbols of American courage, this made television people quite nervous; even as the hostages were being lauded as heroes, quite a bit of commentary was devoted to explaining them away ('the Stockholm syndrome') and counteracting some comments that were proving politically uncomfortable.

The American public mood, like any 'public mood,' is complex. Why does television choose to 'mirror' the spirit of 'We're Number One?' Surely there are a number of reasons, not least of which is that television people, like other Americans, sincerely believed in the image of America Reagan invoked. But this kind of reporting is also very useful for television. In a way, Dan Rather is as much a politician as Ronald Reagan. He goes before the public every day to appeal for 'votes.' And just as politicians have often found that it is more effective to wrap oneself in the flag and praise the wisdom of the People than to get involved in controversial political issues, so in recent years has television.

And what's wrong with 'feeling good?' The danger is easy to see if we keep in mind the fact that the emphasis on the moral strength of America has been combined both with escalating rhetoric against consensus enemies and with an image of America as a nation under siege. In this context, the celebration of the new American 'optimism' (it could, of course, be called 'complacency' or 'chauvinism' just as easily) produced a strong trend toward a more black-and-white view of the world, partly reversing a shift toward more nuanced reporting that resulted from the movements and crises of the 1960s.

This can be seen in the reporting of the Beirut hostage crisis, which is worth one last look. Despite all the furor about television becoming a hostage and an instrument of the terrorists, the most powerful theme in television coverage was the simple contrast between evil terrorists and good Americans going about their apolitical lives. This theme dominated coverage in the early days of the crisis, faded a little as reporters focused on the negotiations with Amal and the conditions of the hostages, and then returned with a vengeance – in part, no doubt, as a response to criticism of the networks for their slippage from the earlier theme – at the end of the crisis. The night the hostages were released, Dan Rather closed the live CBS special with his own summation of the event, which contrasted 'profiles in cowardice' (the terrorists) and 'profiles in courage' (the Americans). Conservatives lamented television's focus on the hostages, arguing in effect that it made it more difficult for the administration to treat them as expendable. And so it did. But personalizing the hostage crisis in the way television did also fed conservative rhetoric about the singular evil of terrorism.

There was, of course, evil here. The Americans were indeed innocent victims of political violence; and it is one of the strengths of television that it can convey a powerful sense of the human costs of terrorism – as it can the costs of war or recession or of apartheid in South Africa. But in two important ways, television's populist portrayal of the meaning of terrorism in Beirut, as in a number of other incidents, has been highly distorted. It is, in the first place, highly selective. There are, after all, tens of thousands of innocent victims of political violence in the world in any given year, only a tiny proportion of them American – and only a tiny proportion of them mentioned at all on television. Even the seven Salvadorans killed along with the six Americans in the attack that coincided with the TWA hijacking were hardly mentioned.

What sends television into a mode of high human concern and moral indignation – and here we come to the second way television's portrayal of terrorism is distorted – is not political violence against innocent human beings, not even necessarily violence against Americans (a number have died in political violence in Central America without this sort of attention), but the fact that this particular violence was seen as directed against *America* itself. As with Iran, the story in Beirut was not 'people held hostage,' not even 'Americans held hostage,' but (as ABC titled its half-hour nightly special on the Iran hostage crisis, which eventually became *Nightline*) 'America held hostage.' This is not to say that there is anything insincere about television's concern with the hostages and their families; what does happen, however, is that human concern is adapted to the service of political symbolism. The hostages were symbolic of America. The hostages were innocent victims of political violence. So it appears, in television's personalized portrayal of terrorism, that America is an innocent victim of political violence.[14]

But at the political level, it is not clear that the language of innocent victims, of uncomplicated good and unadulterated evil, of courage and cowardice, is appropriate. Directly and indirectly, American policy has taken its share of innocent victims in the Middle East, as it has in Central America and many other places. The terrorists hardly have a monopoly on the killing of innocents. Terrorism, moreover, does not come out of nowhere – nor is it a result simply of the fanaticism or 'cowardice' of certain individuals. It has political roots; and, again, American policy-makers certainly bear some share of the responsibility. (Never in the course of the Beirut hostage crisis did I hear a television journalist mention the decision of the Reagan administration to use US forces in Lebanon, initially brought in as peacekeepers, to intervene against Shiite forces in Lebanon's civil war.) But all of this complexity is pushed into the background once the story has been defined in terms of violence against the symbolic American everyman; to mention it comes to seem morally insensitive and unpatriotic.

In 1985, CBS was promoting its news broadcast with the slogan 'We Keep America on Top of the World.' Perhaps the *double entendre* was sheer coincidence; perhaps it was intended to capitalize on the 'new patriotism.' But it expresses a disturbing truth about television news in the age of Reagan: the news in important ways shifted back toward the days when journalism was the strident ideological arm of Cold War foreign policy, presenting the world as a great and simple battleground between good and evil, with America as the unique embodiment of good. One would think the nation would have learned over the course of forty years of Cold War the dangers of this kind of perspective, which include not only the risk of war, both 'limited' and cataclysmic, but also damage to democracy and complacency about festering problems within the United States. In the age of Reagan, however, television showed strong signs of repressing this history.

EPILOGUE

This essay was written in 1985. Since then television news has continued to converge into the general culture of entertainment television. The impetus comes from two directions, a push and a pull. The push arises from the increasing economic pressure the networks face as competition has eroded their ratings. The pull comes from the proliferation of new forms of 'reality-based programming.' That term itself, of course, is symbolic of the change under way: television news is increasingly seen as a subgenre of television programming, rather than as a branch of journalism. The most dramatic, and most disturbing, development in the years since 1985 is the growth of the 'tabloid' news shows (whose significance is discussed at a bit more length – though far from exhaustively – in the final essay of this book). Already their agenda and techniques have had considerable impact both on the network news divisions and on local TV news, which is important both for its wide audience and the fact that it is now the main training ground for television journalists. Thus the network 'magazine shows,' *48 Hours*, for instance, are full of sex crimes and the like, and a local TV report may retrace the steps of a murder victim using a hand-held camera. The latter technique suggests one key element of the tabloid style: the push to cancel critical distance, to plunge viewer and 'journalist' into the emotion of the moment.

Since 1985, too, we have witnessed the supreme example of 'populist' TV news, an example that shows particularly well its often ironic political consequences and the dangers it can pose to the integrity of the public sphere. To back up just a moment here, the flag-waving journalism that so struck me in 1984 and 1985, faded from the news late in 1986, as a Republican setback in the congressional elections of that year and then the Iran–Contra affair took the glow off the age of Reagan. Then it came back with a vengeance in the Gulf War. How that happened is of course a complex story. But an important part of that story has to do with the desire of television journalists to be at one with the people, to share and celebrate their feelings; increasingly, I think, TV news people feel (I say 'feel' deliberately; I doubt that this is conscious) that it is more important to be *loved* than to be *believed*.

What happened with television coverage of the Gulf War is well illustrated by a CBS story early in the crisis. Rather had gone to Saudia Arabia – anchors, like presidents, need to be seen as personally involved; he began one broadcast like this:

> This is the CBS Evening News, Dan Rather reporting with the First Tactical Air Wing of the United States Air force in Saudia Arabia. Good Evening. These are the warplanes and these are the fighting men and women who are the heart of the U.S. military buildup in the area. We'll show it to you up close and from the inside on tonight's broadcast.

Later in the show, making the transition from a Pentagon report on the military build-up to his own story on the pilots, he said, 'All these troop movements are in support of the men who fly the missions. We spent the day with them.'

'Up close and personal' was the formula Roone Arledge had employed successfully at ABC Sports in the 1970s, before moving to news. And this is the formula modern TV news uses when it can. When the Gulf War actually started, the emphasis was heavily on 'the fighting men and women' and on their families back home. This, of course, meant that it would inevitably be celebratory and lacking in critical distance: the war was identified with the soldiers and their families; to question it was to question them; even to remain dispassionate was to insult their feelings.[15] (Notice the reversal of political ends and means in Rather's comments: the administration's political policy is presented as 'in support of the men who fly the missions,' rather than the other way around.) If the United States had gotten bogged down in an indecisive war in the Middle East, and morale among the soldiers and families had eroded, 'up close and personal' coverage would eventually have begun to cut the other way. But in the context of a short, successful war, it meant that the public sphere essentially collapsed into the state.

NOTES

* Thanks to Todd Gitlin and Tom Engelhardt for comments on this essay.
1 J. Loftus, 'Are TV webs hostage in Beirut?,' *Variety*, 26 June 1985, pp. 1, 81.
2 I am referring to the 'rally-round-the-flag effect.' R. Brody, *Assessing the President: The Media, Elite Opinion and Public Support*, Stanford, Calif., Stanford University Press, 1991.
3 T. Gitlin, 'Spotlights and shadows – TV news,' *Cultural Correspondence*, 1977, vol. 4, pp. 3–12.
4 CBS News Poll, 18 June 1985.
5 Interview, New York, 1 July 1985.
6 S. Beddell, 'The upstart and the big boys head for a showdown,' *TV Guide*, 6 February 1982, pp. 5–8.

7 Cf. W. Stott's discussion of the credibility of radio in *Documentary Expression and Thirties America*, Chicago, Ill., University of Chicago Press, 1973.

8 New York, Ballantine, 1983.

9 'Video versus print,' *Wilson Quarterly*, 1982, vol. 6, no. 5, pp. 49–57.

10 *News that Matters*, Chicago, Ill., University of Chicago Press, 1987.

11 J. P. Robinson, 'Public reaction to political protest: Chicago, 1968,' *Public Opinion Quarterly*, 1970, vol. 34, pp. 1–9.

12 Austin Ranney, *Channels of Power: The Impact of Television on American Politics*, New York, Basic Books, 1983.

13 The best statement of this view of Reagan and the media is M. Herstgaard, *On Bended Knee: The Press and the Reagan Presidency*, New York, Farrar Straus Giroux, 1988. It seems to me, though, that Herstgaard fell into the trap of taking the boasting of Reagan's aides – particularly Michael Deaver – at face value, rather than looking at the coverage to see if they were really as good at manipulating the media as they claimed.

14 See also B. A. Dobkin, 'Paper tigers and video postcards: the rhetorical dimensions of narrative form in ABC news coverage of terrorism,' *Western Journal of Communication*, 1992, vol. 56, pp. 143–60.

15 This argument is developed in much greater length in D. C. Hallin and T. Gitlin, 'Prowess and community: the Gulf War as popular culture and as television drama,' paper presented at the Annual Meeting of the International Communication Association, Miami, Florida, 21–5 May 1992. A version of this paper will appear in W. L. Bennett and D. L. Paletz (eds), *The Mass Media, Public Opinion and the Politics of the Gulf War*, Chicago, Ill., University of Chicago Press, forthcoming.

Chapter 6

Speaking of the president

Political structure and representational form in US and Italian television news*

The metaphor of the mirror has always attracted observers of the media, just as it once attracted theorists of language.[1] It has been used in many ways, both simple and sophisticated. Media people themselves often describe the news as a more or less literal reflection of 'the course of events,' a conception particularly useful for warding off political criticism.[2] Others have likened the news image to the images of a fun-house mirror, distorted by such factors as the organizational structure of the media, but still essentially reflective. And many have described the media as mirrors not so much of 'reality' as of culture, or politics, or social structure, reflecting in their standards of judgement the cultural or social framework or the political balance of forces in their society.[3]

The metaphor is true enough in certain ways. But just as language is not really separate from the 'world' it 'pictures,'[4] the media do not stand apart from the social processes reflected in the contents of the news. Just as language is embedded in the 'forms of life' in which we use it, constituted by and helping to constitute those forms, the media are an integral part of political and social life. Their function, as we understand it in modern liberal societies, is primarily to provide a running, day-to-day *representation* of the life of the community. But *how* they do this, the form of representation they employ, varies greatly, shaped by the structure of those very political and social processes that they attempt in one way or another to 'reflect' and by their own role in those processes. And there is every reason to believe that these forms of representation, in their turn, profoundly affect the conduct of politics and the character of social interaction.

This essay compares the presentation of news in two liberal democracies. It is a study of television coverage in the United States and Italy during President Reagan's trip to Europe in June 1982. There are many reasons one might expect television news to differ between these two countries. The two political systems are of course very different. The American system is presidential, the Italian parliamentary. The United States has two political parties, loose in ideology and organization; Italy has many parties with much tighter organization and clear ideological orientations. The United States is a world power with military and political interests around the globe; Italy is not.

The media themselves, moreover, are very differently organized in the two countries. American television networks are owned by private corporations and operated for profit. The main nationwide broadcasting company in Italy, Radiotelevisione Italiana or RAI, is state-owned, directed by a board elected by parliament. RAI does broadcast advertisements, but most of its income is provided by subscription fees paid by television viewers; in 1980 66 per cent of RAI's revenues from broadcasting and related activities came from subscription fees, which were paid in that year by 73 per cent of Italy's households, 28 per cent from advertising.[5] Of the three channels operated by RAI, two, the ones we will be concerned with here (TG1 and TG2), have partisan and ideological attachments. One is pro-Catholic, employing managers and journalists close to the Christian Democratic party; the other is secular, and close to the parties of the non-Communist left. The third is essentially a cultural channel, focusing on regional matters. After thirty years of uncontested monopoly for the state-owned company, recent legislation now allows the existence of private and commercial networks. But these networks were still barred at the time of our study from broadcasting news simultaneously over the entire nation; the first commercial competition to RAI's news broadcasts began in January 1993.[6] Local news is of little importance in Italy, either on public or private television. The news broadcasts of TG1 and TG2, which are 30 and 45 minutes in length, respectively, without commercial interruptions, are watched by over half of the Italian population each night, TG1 by 15 million Italians and TG2 by 5 million.

We will show how these differences affect not only the *content* of television news, in the sense of the kinds of political actors and activities that are covered, but also the *form of representation*, the conventions of narrative employed. We will argue that it is in these differing forms of representation that the differing conceptions of politics in the two societies are most profoundly embodied. And we will try to spell out tentatively some of the political consequences that seem likely to flow from them. As Michael Schudson has written:

> The power of the media lies not only (and not even primarily) in its power to declare things to be true, but in its power to provide the forms in which the declarations appear. News in a newspaper or on television has a relationship to the real world not only in content but in form: that is, in the way the world is incorporated into unquestioned and unnoticed conventions of narration, and then transfigured, no longer a subject for discussion but a premise for any conversation at all.[7]

The news in the United States and Italy reflects the differences between the two political systems, emphasizing different institutions and actors. But that is not all. The 'pictures' of political life provided by the media of the two societies, first of all, present to their respective audiences differing conceptions of what politics is about: even as mirrors of political life the media are active constructors of meaning. The media of the two countries, moreover, not only mirror the forms of political life of their respective societies, but *embody* them. Because they are embedded in such different political contexts, the media themselves play very different roles: reporting the news in Italy is not the same kind of activity as reporting the news in the United States. Political structure thus comes to be embodied in certain ways of speaking about politics, conventions of communication that in their turn profoundly affect the possibilities for political discourse in the society.

This study is based on an analysis of ten Italian and fifteen American news broadcasts – all the major network evening news coverage from the week of 7–11 June 1982. This is, of course, a limited amount of material; we intend this analysis as an illustration of a certain approach to the study of news, not as a comprehensive survey of either Italian or American television coverage.[8] Any cross-national comparison of news faces the problem that news will vary not only because of different conventions of reporting which we are interested in here, but also because the domestic political context is different and the international context of different relevance. But the week we have chosen is a relatively good one for comparison. It was dominated by three international events of great importance to both countries: President Reagan's trip to Europe, which included a stop in Rome to meet with Italian President Pertini and with the Pope, the Israeli invasion of Lebanon, which had just begun, and the war in the Falkland Islands, which was approaching its final stages. (Italy, incidentally, has a special interest in Argentina, which has many citizens of Italian descent, including Leopoldo Galtieri, who was president during the Falklands War.) Domestically both countries were involved in elections of roughly comparable importance. In the United States primary elections were held in many states on 8 June. In Italy, on 6 June, elections were held for some city and county councils. The Italian elections were of slight significance in themselves, but were regarded as an important indicator of the strength of the various parties; a large part of the news on 7 June was devoted to the results and the reactions of the various parties to them.

CONTENT: NEWS AS MIRROR, MIRROR AS FRAME

The news does, of course, mirror in its content the political structure of the society. Figure 6.1 summarizes the major subjects and political actors covered by American and Italian television during Reagan's trip to Europe. Two differences are particularly important.

American television, in the first place, gave far more coverage to foreign politics during this week of war than Italian television: foreign politics occupied 60 per cent of the coverage in the US, 30 per cent in Italy. This is not, certainly, a typical figure for foreign coverage on American television. It is a good illustration of the often-observed fact that the American media cover

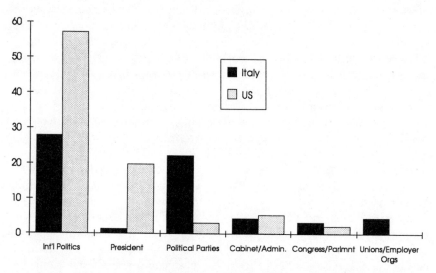

Figure 6.1   Per cent of television time devoted to selected subjects and actors in
US and Italian news broadcasts

foreign politics when US interests are at stake. Foreign politics is defined for
purposes of this analysis as the internal politics of foreign countries and
relations among them, and does not include relations of Italy or the United
States with other countries. Reagan's trip is therefore considered a domestic
rather than a foreign story for American news. But it nevertheless provided the
occasion for an unusual number of stories about European politics. And of
course the United States was deeply involved in the diplomacy that
surrounded both the Falklands War and the war in Lebanon, with the
consequence again that coverage of these areas was exceptionally high.
Nevertheless, estimates of the *average* level of foreign coverage in American
TV news range from about 30 to 37 per cent, still larger than the figure for
Italian news during this period of international tension.[9]

The second difference has to do with the political actors who appear in the
news. The prime actor in American coverage is the president; in Italian, the
political party. Nearly 20 per cent of American coverage concerned President
Reagan; Italian television devoted less than 2 per cent of its time to President
Pertini, and an additional 4 per cent to the government of Prime Minister
Spadolini. Twenty-two per cent of Italian news, on the other hand, was
devoted to the parties, compared with about 3 per cent of American news.

These differences are neither surprising nor difficult to explain (nor,
incidentally, are they peculiar to this time period, when the American
president was abroad, though this certainly heightens the president's visibility
on the American news).[10] The President of the Republic is in fact a minor
figure in Italian politics, and even the prime minister and his cabinet are
transient creatures of shifting coalitions: Italy had had forty-four

governments in thirty-eight years at the time this was written. What is constant and powerful in Italian politics is the party. In the United States by contrast the party rarely acts as a unit except – and then to a limited extent – in support of a presidential campaign. As for the difference in foreign coverage, it is an excellent illustration of the version of the mirror theory that holds that news reflects culture and social structures. American and Italian news reflect world politics differently; they do not show the same picture of the world. But their differences of emphasis 'mirror' real differences in the role the two countries play in international affairs. The United States has much more extensive international involvements than Italy.

But though they are in a sense obvious, these differences in news content are not without significance for the political culture of the two societies. Even in mirroring society the media frame it: they reflect back to society not just events, not unmediated reality, but a particular *conception* of politics embodied in that society's political life. This becomes clear if we look at the differences of emphasis in domestic coverage in a slightly different way. The attention in American news is devoted primarily to the institutional and administrative spheres: it deals with the executive branch of government, with those actors, the president and other administration officials, who stand at the head of governing institutions. The emphasis in Italy, on the other hand, is on the *political* sphere. Italian news devotes the greatest part of its attention not to official governing institutions but to the process of political and ideological debate and the actors who participate in that process. If we compare coverage of the institutions of government, on the one hand (including the presidency, the cabinet, the courts, public administration, local government, and the police), and those of political debate on the other (Congress/Parliament, the parties, and, finally, unions and employers' organizations – which received 4.5 per cent of Italian coverage, none in the US), US coverage includes 27 per cent devoted to the institutional sphere and 5 per cent to the political. For Italy the figures are 16 per cent institutional and 31 per cent political. (Nearly half of Italian coverage of governing institutions concerned the police and lower courts, and their battle with the Red Brigades.)

So politics appears in American news as government, in Italian as debate and party activity. Politics also tends to appear in American news, because of the focus on international politics, as an affair of the nation as a unit; in Italy it appears as a matter of conflict among social and political groups within the nation. The particular emphases reported here are of course affected by the context: they would have been somewhat different if we had chosen a different period of time, a time for example when President Reagan had been fighting with Congress over the budget rather than traveling abroad. But given the context of this week, in many ways closely comparable for the two societies, US and Italian journalists made very different sets of choices. The Italians focused heavily on the local elections held on 6 June; American journalists chose largely to ignore the 8 June primaries, and to focus instead on foreign politics and the president's trip to Europe. These choices reflect the political priorities of United States and Italy; at the same time they are an important part of the process by which those priorities are maintained as an ideological framework.

FORMS OF REPRESENTATION

'In comparison to newspaper news,' Paul Weaver has written,

> television news is far more coherently organized and tightly unified, and this is true of the individual . . . story as well as of the . . . news aggregate . . . . [T]he TV news program tends to present a single unified interpretation of the day's events *as a whole* . . . .[11]

The reason for this difference, Weaver argues, is that television news is organized in time rather than space. The television audience must therefore be carried along by the narrative. It is not free, like the newspaper audience, to browse at will from story to story, and cannot be allowed to stray; its attention must be maintained continuously. A definite theme or story-line is thus essential.

And, indeed, television news in the United States is characterized by its thematic, unified presentation. But the imperative lies in the institution and its social role, not in the technology *per se*. Italian television shows none of the thematic unity that characterizes its American counterpart. Here are the anchors' introductions to two news broadcasts, one Italian and one American:

> RAI TG1, 7 June, Valentini: Lebanon, the Falklands. From our headlines you already know about the disquieting development of the situation in the Middle East and about the growth of military activity in the archipelago contested by England and Argentina. These, surely, have been the subjects most discussed during the Roman talks that Reagan, after the visit to the Pope, has had at the Quirinale with President Pertini and at Palazzo Chigi with Prime Minister Spadolini. The presence of Reagan in Rome constitutes, with the two serious international events going on just now, one of the outstanding events of this day, together with the results, that so far we know only partially, of the elections for the city councils of about eighty municipalities, which indicate, up to now, a likely victory of the Socialist Party and of the other secular parties. But let's see what is going on in Lebanon.

> ABC *World News Tonight*, 7 June, Frank Reynolds: Good evening. If this had been almost any other day it would, indeed, be big news that the President of the United States is at Windsor Castle, seat of the British monarchy, especially since Mr. Reagan came here right after a visit to the

seat of the Papacy and a meeting with Pope John Paul. They talked, the president and the Pope, of peace; and we'll have a full report later. But this has really been another day of war, so we begin the broadcast, tonight, with the latest on the latest war, the one in the Middle East. Up the road in London, at our foreign desk, here is Peter Jennings.

The Italian broadcast begins with a list of headlines; the day's events are interpreted by the journalist only in the sense that certain ones are listed as especially important. The American broadcast begins with a frame: it opens with a set of contrasting images – war on the one hand, peace, authority, tradition, religion, on the other – which places all the day's events within a sort of cosmology, giving them both coherence as part of a single story and meaning as part of a moral order.

To a large extent, the unity of American news broadcasts during this week was achieved by organizing them around the central figure of the president. NBC's 7 June report is an excellent example. Tom Brokaw, one of NBC's two 'anchors' (the terminology is significant: they are not just announcers), was traveling with the president in Europe. Anchoring the international portion of the broadcast from No. 10 Downing Street, he wrapped up each international segment of the broadcast, and the broadcast as a whole, by bringing it into relation to the president's trip: 'and tomorrow, when President Reagan will come here to No. 10 Downing Street, that war [in the Falklands] will be the major subject of attention.' The broadcast was thus provided both with a central actor, the president, and a central setting, No. 10 Downing Street. On subsequent days, international events continued to be tied together by an emphasis on their relation to the president's trip. This is an unusually high level of unity even for an American news broadcast; the journalists made a special effort to integrate the news during this week, due probably both to the unusual complexity of international news and to the availability, in the president's trip, of a compelling organizational device. But the *tendency* to unify is typical of American news. Av Westin, once executive producer of ABC *World News Tonight*, writes:

> Stories . . . should be combined into a logical progression that threads its way through the day's news. The audience ought to be guided through the news so that it doesn't have to make sharp twists and turns to follow and understand what is going on. My preference is to divide the lineup into segments. In each segment, a narrative of sorts is fashioned, weaving together stories that relate to one another.[12]

An Italian news broadcast, in contrast, has little internal logic, and never has a central theme, setting, or actor.

At the level of the individual news report, the same contrast of representational form can be seen once again. The American report is both 'story-like' and interpretive; it is constructed to convey a certain under-standing of events. The Italian report could be called 'referential.' It does not offer meaning within itself, but refers the viewer elsewhere: it provides a review, a list, of the interpretations offered by political actors outside of journalism. Here again are two examples:

RAI TG1, 7 June 1982 [following a report giving election returns]: What do the political forces say about the results we have heard so far, even though they are only partial? One finds, of course, great satisfaction on the socialist and secular side with the good returns for these parties. As for the Christian Democrats, they underline the satisfying results they got in an administrative election in which, generally, the DC never achieves as good a position as in a political or general election . . . . But now we have to wait and see what will be the effect of these results on the general political situation because, although it is true that this has been a minor race, it comes just before an important discussion among the parties of the majority.

Meanwhile, a comment from Craxi, Secretary of the PSI [Socialist] . . . .

From the point of view of the PSDI [Social Democratic], this election confirms that . . . .

From the Republicans, there is a statement of Del Pennino that . . . .

The judgement of Zanone, Secretary of the PLI [Liberal] is that . . . .

From the Communist side, Cossuta observes that . . . .

Finally there is a statement of Almirante of MSI [Fascist]. Almirante says that . . . .

These are the comments that have been delivered so far.

NBC, 11 June 1982, Roger Mudd: In an effort to act responsibly and pass a budget, any budget, House Democrats and Republicans joined forces today and passed, 219 to 206, the Republican version of the budget. Lisa Meyers reports.

Lisa Meyers: . . . More than 18 billion would be cut from domestic spending, most of it programs for the poor . . . . Majority leader Jim Wright likened it to the practice of medieval bleeders.

Wright: And if the patient does not respond to the first bleeding and indeed gets worse, just bleed him some more.

Meyers: Until the very end, it was questionable whether the House could muster the courage to pass anything.

Representative: I suggest to you the country won't go to hell without a budget.

Meyers: But leaders of both parties argued otherwise . . . .

Minority leader Robert Michels: If the bipartisan substitute goes down we all go down . . . .

Meyers: Wright pleaded for every member to vote for something.

> Wright: To do otherwise, to vote against both, would be a craven cop-out and a retreat from responsibility.
>
> Meyers: This budget must still be reconciled with the one which passed the Senate . . . . Then the House will have to wrestle with a compromise budget, a prospect which excites no one.

The Italian report, like most of RAI's political reporting, is divided into a three-part structure: announcement of event, interpretations of the parties, and (though this part may often be omitted) interpretation of the journalist. The order of presentation varies, but most reports on domestic politics contain these three elements. The journalist's interpretation (in this case, marked by the phrase 'We must wait to see') is always easily recognizable, and in fact is frequently marked off by a phrase that identifies it as interpretation: 'How can we interpret this?,' 'What does it mean?,' or simply, 'In other words.'[13]

The NBC report, on the other hand, has no such divided structure, nor are the journalists' interpretations separated either from the reporting of the event or from the reporting of the views of party representatives. The structure of the report is a *narrative* structure, though of course a simple one: it sets the scene and describes the stakes, builds to a moment of crisis ('until the very end, it was questionable whether the House could muster the courage'), achieves a resolution, and closes by setting the stage for the next 'episode.' And embedded in the narrative there is a political interpretation: Congress moved so slowly on the budget that in the end any budget was better than none; it is to be hoped that there won't be any squabbling that will delay final passage any further. It is the journalist, as narrator, who controls the interpretation of reality. The statements of the political actors do not stand independently, as they do in the Italian report, but are woven by the journalist into her story.

The difference in the role of interpretation and framing is the most important difference in representational form between US and Italian news, but it is by no means the only one. We will summarize here three other important differences. For reasons we will explore in the following section, all of the representational conventions discussed here are closely related.

Use of visual images

The conventions of Italian TV news are essentially, to return to Weaver's distinction between print and television journalism, print conventions. Not only does Italian television not employ the conventions of unified, thematic presentation that mark American TV news, it also makes little use of the visual characteristics of the TV medium. A good deal of the Italian news report is simply read by the announcer, without any accompanying visual images. And film is used primarily as background to the verbal narrative. It is generally unedited, often of poor visual quality, and often only loosely related to the meaning of the report. The film that accompanied RAI's reports on Reagan's visit with the Pope was filled most of the time with unidentified people milling about on the periphery of the event; reports from Moscow and Washington were narrated over street scenes. Film in Italian television is referential rather than rhetorical; it *shows* the scene but most of the time has nothing to *say* about the event. In American television it is different. Film, and increasingly other visual images ('graphics'), are central to the semantic structure of the story. They are primarily symbolic: American television uses film not so much to show Windsor Castle or Beirut or the president and the Pope, as to *represent* tradition, war, diplomacy.[14]

The role of the 'common man'

Television news in the United States devotes a good deal of attention to the private citizen. This tendency was somewhat less marked than usual during the week of our study because of the focus on international politics; it is especially in stories on domestic economics and public policy that American journalists are so fond of investigating the impact of events on 'common' men and women. Nevertheless, nearly a third, approximately forty-eight of 150 people who appeared on US television news during this week were 'non-official' – civilians in Lebanon, families of British soldiers in the Falklands, arms control protesters and other civilians in Germany, and so on.[15] Italian television, on the other hand, is almost exclusively concerned with the institutionalized public sphere. Rarely does anyone appear on Italian television news who does not represent an organized participant in the political process.

Relation to audience

Television journalists in the United States rarely speak in the first person; they used it only a handful of times during the week of our study. Italian newscasters use the first person routinely. US and Italian newscasters, moreover, mean different things when they do use the first person. To an American newscaster, 'we' means the news organization: 'Up the road in London, at our foreign desk . . . .' When an Italian newscaster says 'we,' on the other hand, he means himself and the audience: 'Let's see what is going on in Lebanon.' (This usage, incidently, is sincere: the Italian announcer has in fact not yet seen the report from Lebanon, and will therefore be just as much informed by it as the audience.) The television journalist in the United States, in other words, will not normally 'cross the screen' to put himself 'on the side' of the audience in relation to events (former CBS commentator Bill Moyers is an exception here), while the Italian announcer routinely moves back and forth across that invisible boundary.

POLITICAL STRUCTURE AND REPRESENTATIONAL FORM

The most obvious explanation for this pattern of differences is that American TV news is commercial and Italian is not. American television sells the attention of a mass public to advertisers; its most fundamental task as a business is to generate and maintain that attention. The news divisions of American networks are by no means their major money-makers, and to some degree they are exempted from the commercial imperatives that dominate other forms of programming. But the exemption is limited: although it has lower ratings than any other major form of programming, news can by highly profitable, and its profits depend directly on audience size. *CBS Evening News*, for instance, had profits of $28 million in 1980.[16] The slide in the network's ratings in the late 1970s and early 1980s, described in the previous chapter (p. 99), lowered the price of a 30-second advertising spot on the *Evening News* by as much as $10,000.[17] With about 8 minutes of commercials in a 30- minute broadcast, this would add up to a revenue loss of roughly $160,000 a night. In order to keep its hold on the audience, American TV news adopts a set of conventions that serve to involve the viewer emotionally. The form it employs is essentially cinematic, combining visual imagery with narrative structure.[18]

For Italian television, by contrast, ratings are not a pressing concern. RAI has a relatively stable base of revenue in the subscription fees that provide nearly two-thirds of its income from broadcasting. As for the 28 per cent of that income that is dependent on advertising, this too has until very recently been quite stable. Before 1983, when competition from commercial television intensified, the demand for RAI's legally limited amount of advertising time exceeded the supply by a considerable margin. The national news broadcasts are still protected from commercial competition. Budgetary allocations, finally, are made to RAI's three channels from a common revenue pool, and are not directly related to audience size. The economic structure that ties the budget of an American news program closely to the size of its audience is thus not present in Italian television. Italian TV news, of course, faces organizational constraints of its own, which in part account for its particular conventions of reporting. Italian news is political rather than commercial, and political in a certain way. While the primary constituency for American television is the advertiser (and therefore the consuming public), the constituency for Italian television is the political party system (and the public as political observers or participants). Italian TV news is essentially a utility maintained by the parties to inform the public about their views and activities. Hence the characteristic disjointed, non-narrative structure of the Italian news report: announcement of event, statements of the parties, journalist's interpretation.

But the distinction between a commercial and a political news organization is not by itself an adequate explanation for the differences between the American and Italian systems. In fact, the contrast between US and Italian TV news in some ways *reverses* the contrast most commonly drawn between the commercial journalism of America and the political journalism of Europe. The rise of commercial mass media that began in the United States with the penny press of the 1830s was associated, as we saw in Chapter 2, with a shift away from the active political role the newspaper had played in the late eighteenth and early nineteenth centuries. As the commercial press developed, newspapers became both more entertainment-oriented and more committed to the ideal of a professional, politically neutral 'objective' journalism. Many European countries, fearing quite reasonably that commercialization would destroy the newspaper as an active participant in political debate, subsidize the party press.[19] But when one compares American and Italian TV news, it is the American news that is the more active, that puts forth political interpretations and, as we shall see, that often plays a critical role *vis-à-vis* political authority, while Italian news is much more neutral, passing on in dry 'objective' style the official statements of established parties.

Why should this be? The answer seems to lie in the differing structure of the public sphere in the two societies: it is, in a sense, empty in the United States, while in Italy it is filled to overflowing, and solidly, even rigidly institutionalized. And this profoundly affects the role that journalism plays in the two societies. Political interpretation is provided in Italy by the institutions that have traditionally dominated the modern public sphere – political parties, unions and industrial associations, and parts of the print media, many of which are oriented toward political commentary rather than news coverage in the American sense. There is no need, therefore, for the television journalist to play an active interpretive role – and no reason for the parties, having control over the state broadcasting company, to allow journalism to usurp their function as arbiters of political meaning.[20]

In the United States, on the other hand, the institutions of the public sphere are weak. Newspapers have for the most part abandoned their earlier role as vehicles for the expression of political opinion.[21] The parties are entrepreneurial parties in the sense of Schumpeter and Downs, loose coalitions organized not for the purpose of expressing unified ideologies but for competing for political office.[22] And unions and other private organizations function for the most part as interest groups, pressing particular demands, often behind the scenes, rather than attempting to mobilize public opinion around general ideological perspectives. There is thus a kind of vacuum in the American political system, an absence of the institutions which in liberal democracies have traditionally performed the function of interpreting political events. That vacuum is filled primarily by two institutions (which exist in a close, though not always comfortable relation to one another): the presidency,[23] and journalism. Journalism is thus the primary institution of the American public sphere: it is the major institution outside of the state which performs the function of providing political interpretation and critique.

No wonder, then, that journalism in the United States has developed into an institution that is both more active and more autonomous than Italian journalism. It is, in fact, somewhat artificial to say that journalism exists at all as a single, recognizable institution in Italy. Italy has two journalisms, and neither of them has the autonomy of function, organization, and ideology that American journalism has. Many of the print media in Italy are oriented toward providing political commentary, a function that they share with the other institutions of political debate. And if print journalism in Italy shares the functions of the political parties, television journalism serves them. The Italian television journalist is, both in training and in terms of actual power relations, a party functionary. The journalist is trained in the party apparatus, and can be transferred by the party if his or her work displeases its leadership. American journalism, by contrast, has developed into a separate political institution, with a set of functions and an ideology that are more or less its own. American journalists are not only free of direct political control, their political loyalty is primarily to journalism itself rather than to any distinct political tendencies. They see themselves, and are socialized, as members of an autonomous profession of journalism.

It is important to note, as Schudson has pointed out, that the idea of a profession of journalism developed in the United States primarily during the Progressive era, a period when party organizations were losing both influence and respect, and 'good government' was contrasted with bad – that is, partisan – politics, when, in short, the traditional institutions of the public sphere were on the decline.[24] And it was simultaneous with the rise of the professional ideal that American journalism began not only to tell stories, something it had done since the rise of the penny papers, but to understand its function in terms of providing expert commentary on political affairs. A second significant increase in the interpretive activity of American journalism occurred, as we shall see in the following essay, during the late 1960s and early 1970s, again, a period when political parties were losing influence, and this time also a period when the presidency, which has shared with journalism the function of political interpretation, was losing credibility as well.[25]

So the unified, thematic character of the American news report results not only from the imperatives of commercialism, but also from the central role journalism plays in the American political system. In the absence of other institutions, it falls upon journalism to play the active role of giving meaning and structure to the events of public life. Together these two characteristics of American journalism account for its particular conventions of representation, as contrasted with Italian news: the greater tendency to frame and interpret, the use of narrative structures, the more extensive use of visual images, and their integration into the semantic structure of the story. The journalist plays a more active social role in the United States than in Italy in two senses, both as a link in the chain of economic communication – an entertainer and salesman – and as a provider of political meaning. And American journalism is an active creator of 'publicity' in two corresponding senses: it generates the public attention, the mass audience, which makes possible the communication of commercial images, and it opens up an arena for the discussion of political affairs. And because journalism as an institution plays a more active social role in the United States, the journalist plays a more active role in the presentation of news, working over the raw material of political information and giving it form both as entertainment and as comment on the meaning of events.

The greater centrality of journalism as an institution in the United States also explains what at first might seem a paradox in the contrasting relations of American and Italian journalists to their audiences. In a sense, American TV news seems populist in its style, compared with Italian. As we have seen, American television covers the 'common person' much more; Italian television focuses almost exclusively on political officials. Italian news also tends to be presented at a relatively sophisticated level of discourse, making routine use of political jargon accessible only to those familiar with political affairs. At the same time, however, we have seen that Italian journalists are in a sense more familiar with their audiences than American, establishing relationships with them both by 'crossing the screen' through a use of the first person that includes the audience, and through the use of performatives[26] that disclose directly to the audience the journalist's role in the presentation of the report. American journalists, by contrast, normally stand apart from the audience.[27]

How are we to make sense of these seemingly contradictory patterns? The answer lies in the fact that American journalists are public figures in a sense that Italian journalists are not. Because of the special role they play as interpreters of reality, American journalists must present a persona of authority that will legitimate the power they obviously possess. This they do in a number of ways – the identity of American journalism, because it plays multiple roles, is complex – two of which are particularly important here. First, they present themselves as *professionals*, who, because of their training in certain methods and rules of conduct, are competent to make judgements that no one outside the profession is competent to make. Second, they present themselves as, and in a certain sense, are in fact, *representatives of the public*. Journalism in the United States is (as many newspapers call themselves) a sort of 'tribune of the people:' in the absence of other institutions that could represent the interests of the public against those of the state, journalism fills that role. It is a role that on the one hand endows journalists with authority, setting them apart from the public at large and requiring them to act in a manner that confirms their public status,[28] and on the other hand – particularly given an individualist political culture which places a high value on the wisdom of the 'common person' – requires them frequently to adopt a populist stance, to act as advocates for the interests and perspectives of the ordinary citizen.

Because they have so little power, in contrast, the Italian newscasters have neither much need for authority, nor much opportunity to take upon themselves the role of representing anyone. The parties and other institutions of the public sphere perform the role of representing the citizen *vis-à-vis* state power, as well as the role of interpretation. The journalists are merely public servants whose task it is to transmit information to those concerned with politics. They speak to the public as people who have specific information to pass on, but no authority either to represent them or to interpret for them the meaning of that information. It should be added that the commercial nature of American television news also pushes the journalist in a populist direction, requiring a presentation accessible to the widest possible audience. The Italian journalist is not so constrained, and speaks to an audience assumed to be familiar with political language and issues.

WHAT DOES IT MEAN?

The implications of these two forms of journalism are too numerous and too complex for us to give a full account of them here. We will close, however, by noting tentatively several that seem to us particularly important.

Because of the differing forms of representation of the two media systems, first of all, certain types of political action and certain types of actors 'come across' much better in each system, and this has important implications for the nature of both political authority and political debate. A narrative requires a hero: the conventions of American TV news therefore place a premium on individual political leadership.[29] Both in the underlying message they convey about the nature of politics and in the conditions they create for effective communication, these conventions would seem to favor the centralized political authority of the presidency. Their implications for presidential power may, however, be complex. The image of the president in American news coverage results as much from the needs of journalism as from the real nature of presidential power: there is no guarantee that the president can live up to the role in which he is cast. The imperative of creating an image of heroic leadership may be more a liability than an asset to American presidents in a period of economic decline and political confusion.

As for political debate, the narrative conventions of American journalism make it very difficult for abstract political ideas to be dealt with, and focus attention instead, as has often been observed, on contest: the clash of presidential contenders, the test of wills between the president and congressional leaders.[30] For Italian news, on the other hand, it is precisely the process of ideological debate that dominates the news, and the actions of political leaders appear as secondary to that debate. Italian TV news therefore seems likely to reinforce the prevailing pattern of Italian politics: a strong and stable party system, weak and unstable central government.

There is, at the same time, another wrinkle to the differing relations of US and Italian TV news to political authority. Italian TV news rests content with the reporting of official statements, both from government and from the parties, and rarely provides any information or perspective beyond the bounds of official discourse. American TV journalism, on the other hand, is more active than Italian not only in the presentation of news, through framing, interpretation, and the creation of narrative, but also in the gathering of information. The American journalist not only interprets a story but much of the time investigates it: he or she takes a camera to the scene in search of visual images, interviews the people affected by a policy or a conflict, seeks out sources within a political bureaucracy that can give more information than was contained in the official statement. The news thus spills out beyond the bounds of official discourse.

This last characteristic of American journalism, combined with the observation that the search for heroes may, in the end, make it more rather than less difficult for a president to maintain his authority, has prompted many observers to describe the American media as a force generally destructive of political authority, as we saw in Chapter 3. And indeed, compared with Italian TV news, American TV much more often plays a critical role. This was evident in the week of Reagan's trip to Europe: despite the intense focus on presidential diplomacy, the news that week was by no means consistently favorable in its portrayal of the president. It was, in fact, a major theme of the news that week that the president's trip was largely a 'media event,' calculated to enhance Mr Reagan's image both at home and abroad.

But the relation of American journalism to political authority is in fact intensely ambivalent and very unstable. We noted above two ways the American media legitimate the enormous power they possess as, in a sense, substitutes for the traditional institutions of political debate: by presenting themselves as professionals, standing above political ideology, and by presenting themselves as representatives of the 'common person.' There is also another way they legitimate their power: by identifying themselves with the authority of the state. When the journalist turns to official sources for legitimation,[31] the unified form of the American news story takes on a new meaning: the journalist will now take the frame provided by government officials and organize a story in which the official interpretation appears as the only interpretation possible. American journalism is thus at times a much more active critic of political authority, and at times a much more active instrument of it, than Italian journalism, which tends to maintain a constant, respectful distance.[32] The public sphere in the United States is thus more volatile than that of Italy. For all the shifting of governments in Italy, the public sphere remains more or less static. Year after year the news reflects the same spectrum of ideological positions. In the United States, on the other hand, the public sphere can expand and contract within fairly large bounds, depending on the relation between the media and the state: it can, in periods when the media identify closely with the state, virtually collapse into the latter, so that the official interpretation of events dominates political discussion almost entirely, or it can expand to the point that political authorities spend most of their time trying to seize control over the elusive process through which political events are given meaning and public opinion formed.

There is, finally, much about the form of television journalism in both societies that is destructive of the ideal of a politically active public. American TV news is politically exclusive in two senses. It is exclusive, first of all, in the sense that it presents the interpretation of political events as belonging to a sphere that includes the journalists themselves and other political élites, but does not include the audience. This message is implicit in the treatment of the television screen as an impenetrable barrier. In Italy, political thinking is assumed to take place on both sides of the screen, which represents only a line between those who have current information and those who don't yet have it. In the United States politics takes place only behind the screen, and members of the public can become a part of it only to the extent that they are represented there by the journalists.

And television journalism in the United States is exclusive in the second sense that it offers only a single interpretation of events, an interpretation, moreover, that is presented as though it were embedded in the events themselves and therefore not subject to question.[33] While Italian news offers a series of alternative interpretations (including the journalist's), clearly marked out as interpretations, the interpretation in an American news report is built into the narrative itself, both in its verbal and visual components. This is true even in the case of the very typical story for American television that balances a statement from one political actor with an opposing statement from another. In such a case, there is generally a higher-order interpretation that the journalist employs to frame the other two; the ultimate message, in fact, will often be the fecklessness of political debate. This characteristic of the news report results at least in part from the awkward political position that American journalism occupies. It is an institution endowed with enormous and very visible power as the central 'producer' of political meaning, but at the same time has little solid basis of legitimacy. The institution deals with this problem in part by concealing its power (from itself as well as the public – it is largely an unconscious process) through adherence to the professional norms of objectivity. The practices of 'objective journalism' in effect require that the meaning of the story be made to appear as though it emerged from the facts themselves, without the journalist's intervention.[34]

In certain ways, Italian news is more open than American: it treats the audience as participant in the political process; it also presents a range of alternative interpretations of any event, clearly marked as interpretations. In another way, however, Italian news is more closed: political discussion remains strictly within the bounds of discourse defined by the party system. The news provides little independent interpretation or information. It also speaks, as we have seen, in a language accessible only to those with a relatively high level of political sophistication: the addressee of Italian news is the party activist. And because of the lack of framing, events appear in Italian news in an extremely fragmented form,[35] with the consequence, once again, that it is accessible only to those viewers with sufficient political sophistication to place it within a context of their own. American television, in contrast, through the simplicity and apparent unity of its narrative form, strives to make the news accessible to the entire public, albeit in a way that assigns to the public a passive role in the construction of meaning.

NOTES

*   Co-authored with Paolo Mancini. Data for this article are drawn from research funded by a grant from RAI – Radiotelevisione Italiana, Verifica Programmi Trasmessi. We would like to thank Herbert Kitschelt and Michael Schudson, as well as the editors and reviewers for *Theory and Society*, for their comments on drafts of this article, and Helene Keyssar for guidance through the literature on cinema.
1   We are thinking primarily of the early Wittgenstein, *Tractatus Logico-Philosophicus*, Atlantic Highlands, NJ, Humanities Press, 1974.
2   E. J. Epstein, *News From Nowhere*, New York, Vintage, 1974, pp. 13–15.
3   Gaye Tuchman discusses this version of the mirror theory in *Making News*, New York, Free Press, 1978, pp. 182–3.
4   L. Wittgenstein, *Philosophical Investigations*, New York, Macmillan, 1958.
5   Relazione e Bilancio 1980, Roma: RAI-Radio-Televisione Italiana, 1981.
6   P. Mancini, 'Old and new contradictions in Italian journalism,' *Journal of Communication*, 1992, vol. 42, no. 3, pp. 42–7.
7   'The politics of narrative form: the emergence of news conventions in print and television,' *Deadalus*, 1982, vol. 111, no. 4, p. 98.
8   A review of the literature on comparative analysis of the media can be found in J. G. Blumler and M. Gurevitch, 'Towards a comparative framework for political communication research,' in S. H. Chaffee (ed.), *Political Communication: Issues and Strategies for Research*, Beverly Hills, Calif., Sage, 1975; and, more recently, J. G. Blumler, J. M. McLeod, and K. E. Rosengren, *Comparatively Speaking: Communication and Culture Across Space and Time*, Newbury Park, Calif., Sage, 1992.
9   Note that Reagan's trip was considered a domestic story for US news, but a foreign story for Italian news, except when Reagan was in Italy. Figures for international coverage on US TV are from J. F. Larson, 'International affairs coverage on U.S. evening network news,' in W. C. Adams (ed.), *Television Coverage of International Affairs*, Norwood, NJ, Ablex, 1982, table 2.2; and R. Frank, *Message Dimensions of Television News*, Lexington, Mass., Lexington Books, 1973. The average level of foreign coverage in Italy is about 20 per cent, according to *Le notizie dei telegiornali*, RAI Verfica Programmi Trasmessi no. 41, Roma, 1982.
10 On the centrality of the president in US news see H. Gans, *Deciding What's News*, New York, Pantheon, 1979, p. 9.
11 P. Weaver, 'Newspaper news and television news,' in D. Cater and R. Adler (eds.), *Television as a Social Force*, New York, Praeger, 1975, pp. 84–5. M. Esslin makes a related argument: 'in essence a dramatic medium, television from the beginning has been compelled by the special requirements of its nature – its own inner logic – to put its emphasis on material with a dramatic, emotional, personalized content.' *The Age of Television*, San Francisco, Calif., W. H. Freeman, 1982, p. 61.
12 A. Westin, *Newswatch: How TV Decides the News*, New York, Simon & Schuster, 1982, p. 66.
13 P. Mancini, 'Prescriptive doing in television news reporting,' paper presented at the International Sociological Association, Mexico City, 1982.
14 On the symbolic functions of television images see W. Gibson, 'Network news:

elements of a theory,' *Social Text*, 1980, vol. 3, pp. 88–111.

15 The figure is approximate because some people are hard to classify – lower-level civil servants, for example.

16 L. Lichty, 'Video versus print,' *Wilson Quarterly*, 1982, vol. 6, no. 5, p. 57.

17 S. Bedell, 'The upstart and the big boys head for a showdown,' *TV Guide*, 6 February 1982.

18 See S. Sperry, 'Television news as narrative,' in R. Adler (ed.), *Understanding Television: Essays on Television as a Social and Cultural Force*, New York, Praeger, 1981. The parallels between US television news and cinema, or, to be precise, western narrative cinema, are too complex to be developed fully here. They include a linear narrative form into which all elements, both visual and verbal, are integrated (see N. Burch, *To the Distant Observer*, Berkeley, Calif., University of California Press, 1979), and that is 'illusionistic,' which purports, that is, to allow us to view reality 'just as it is,' and a related claim to provide the audience with an intimate relation to its 'characters,' without, however, requiring the viewer to step out of the purely private role of viewing what unfolds (see S. Cavell, *The World Viewed*, New York, Viking Press, 1971; H. Keyssar, *Robert Altman's America*, New York, Oxford University Press, 1991).

19 A. Smith (ed.), *Newspapers and Democracy*, Cambridge, Mass., MIT Press, 1980.

20 See G. Bechelloni (a cura di), *Il mestiere di giornalista*, Napoli, Liguori, 1982.

21 The newspaper – in case this is confusing – continues to be central to the American public sphere, but the form of its activity changes from that of expressing explicit political opinion to that of providing authoritative information and interpretation. Most of what we say here about the political role of American TV news (and a good deal of what we say about forms of representation) applies to newspapers as well as television.

22 J. A. Shumpeter, *Capitalism, Socialism and Democracy*, New York, Harper & Row, 1950; A. Downs, *An Economic Theory of Democracy*, New York, Harper & Row, 1957.

23 On the US president as arbiter of political meaning see R. Neustadt, *Presidential Power: The Politics of Leadership with Reflections on Johnson and Nixon*, New York, Wiley, 1976, pp. 167–73.

24 Schudson, op. cit.

25 P. Weaver, 'The new journalism and the old – thoughts after Watergate,' *Public Interest*, 1974, vol. 35, pp. 167–73; A. Smith, *Goodbye Gutenberg*, New York, Oxford University Press, 1980.

26 A 'performative' is an utterance the purpose of which is to perform some social action, in this case to establish the bounds of the authority the speaker claims in making the statement that follows. See J. L. Austin, *How to Do Things with Words*, New York, Oxford University Press, 1962.

27 This is changing, however, as TV news moves more in the direction of the morning news model outlined in the preceding essay.

28 In this sense there is an interesting parallel between the American journalist's relation to the 'public,' that is to the private citizens who make up its audience, and the pre-bourgeois relationship Habermas calls 'representational publicity:'

> In itself the status of manorial lord . . . was neutral in relation to the criteria of 'public' and 'private'; but its incumbent represented it publicly. He displayed himself, presented himself as an embodiment of some sort of 'higher power.' . . . [T]he relationship of the laity to the priesthood illustrates how the 'surroundings' were part and parcel of the publicity of representation (from which they were nevertheless excluded) – those surroundings were private in the sense in which the private soldier was excluded from representation and from military honor, even though he had to be 'part.'

(J. Habermas, *The Structural Transformation of the Public Sphere: An Inquiry into a Category of Bourgeois Society*, Cambridge, Mass., MIT Press, 1989, pp. 7, 8–9)

29 See Sperry, op. cit.; and P. Weaver, 'Is television news biased,' *Public Interest*, 1972, vol. 26.

30 See, for example, T. Patterson and R. McClure, *The Unseeing Eye*, New York, Putnam, 1976.

31 See, for instance, L. Sigal, *Reporters and Officials*, Lexington, Mass., D. C. Heath, 1973.

32 There are occasions – particularly when the parties are united in identifying a threat to the existing political order – when the Italian newscaster also acts as a representative of the official perspective. This is true, most notably, in coverage of terrorist activities.

33 This argument needs to be qualified a bit. In *form*, an American television report is organized as though it had a unified message. But that formal unity is often an illusion: it is often possible to identify conflicting or at least disjointed frames, coexisting within the same news story. During the week of our study, for example, many reports were divided in their framing of Reagan's trip, accepting its symbolism at one moment at face value, yet presenting it in the next moment as image-making. One CBS report thus began with film of the ceremony that accompanied the president's visit to London, coupled with the statement that 'President Reagan today became a part of British history,' and ended with a discussion of the image the president hoped to convey on American television by associating himself with the symbolism of the British monarchy. These conflicting frames were not integrated into any coherent larger framework – at the same time, however, they were not acknowledged as different interpretations, and the story proceeded from one to the other as though no shift in point of view had taken place.

34 G. Tuchman, 'Objectivity as a strategic ritual: an examination of newsmen's notions of objectivity,' *American Journal of Sociology*, 1972, vol. 77.

35 F. Rositi, *Informazione e complessità sociale*, Bari, DeDonato, 1978. Italian political life can be seen as both static and fragmented: the same ideological conflicts persist year in and year out. And Italian TV news reflects both these characteristics, the first in the lack of unifying frames, the second in its tendency to remain rigidly within the established bounds of debate. American TV news is certainly fragmented in its own way, particularly if one looks at it over time. But each story and broadcast is presented in such a way that it seems to the audience to have some unity of meaning (see note 33 above). The media of both societies can thus be seen as reflecting different forms of a common malaise, an inability to achieve a working consensus on basic social perspectives through political debate. In Italy this leads to a fragmentation of perspectives, in the US to the imposition of an illusory unity.

Chapter 7

Soundbite news

Television coverage of elections, 1968–88*

In the twenty years from 1968 to 1988 television became increasingly central to the conduct of presidential campaigns. At the same time the nature and style of television news changed dramatically. The change is complex. But one simple index provides an excellent way to begin understanding it: the length of the average soundbite. The term comes originally from radio (where it is also known as an 'actuality'), and refers to a film or tape segment, within a news story, showing someone speaking.

The length of the average soundbite has been shrinking – from more than 40 seconds in 1968 to less than 10 seconds in the 1980s, as Table 7.1 shows.[1] It has become common in recent years, as political commentators have discovered the soundbite, to hear people decry the '20-second bite.' In fact in 1988 only 4 per cent of soundbites in the sample were that long. Twenty years before, nearly a quarter of all soundbites were a minute or longer, and it was not unusual to hear a major political figure speak for more than 2 minutes. These data are based on a sample of twenty weekday evening news broadcasts from each presidential election year from 1972 through 1984, and twenty-five from the two end points of the study, 1968 and 1988. The broadcasts were taken from September and October of each year, the three networks were sampled with equal probability, and all presidential election coverage in these broadcasts was coded.

TWO EXAMPLES

A couple of examples will help to illustrate the significance of this change: partial transcripts of two sets of TV news stories, one from 1968 and one from 1988, each reasonably representative of the campaign journalism of its era. The first is from the *CBS Evening News*, 8 October 1968:

> Walter Cronkite: Hubert Humphrey said today that the nuclear age calls for new forms of diplomacy, and he suggested regular summit meetings with the Soviet Union. He made his proposal to a meeting of the nation's newspaper editors and publishers in Washington.
> Humphrey: [Speaks for 1 minute 26 seconds.]

Table 7.1   Average soundbites in television coverage of elections, 1968–88, in seconds

Year	Average soundbite	95% confidence interval, ±
1968	43.1	6.8
1972	25.2	3.7
1976	18.2	2.1
1980	12.2	1.5
1984	9.9	1.0
1988	8.9	0.7

Significance tests for differences of means (one-tailed tests with separate variance estimates):

	T-value	Probability
1984–8	1.67	0.048
1980–4	2.50	0.007
1976–80	4.58	<0.001
1972–6	3.23	<0.001
1968–72	4.59	<0.001

Cronkite [over video of press conference]:   Humphrey was asked about the battered state of the Democratic party.

Humphrey: [Speaks 49 seconds.]

Cronkite: Last Thursday, when he became George Wallace's running mate, retired General Curtis LeMay characterized nuclear weapons as, quote, 'just another weapon in the arsenal.' He made clear he did not advocate their use in Vietnam. But in his words, 'I think there are many occasions when it would be most efficient to use nuclear weapons.' Today at a news conference in Los Angeles, the subject came up again.

LeMay: [Speaks for 1 minute 29 seconds, including an exchange with a reporter at his press conference.]

Cronkite: Campaigning in Connecticut today, George Wallace appealed at one stop for, quote, 'the support of people of all races and colors.' And at another stop he attacked the 1968 open housing law. In Wallace's words, 'when both parties joined together to destroy the adage that your home is your castle, they're not fit to run this country.'

Cronkite [following commercial break]:   Sources close to Richard Nixon say he believes that George Wallace reached his peak last week and will decline in strength. Today Nixon stepped up his attacks on the third party candidate. Bill Plante has that story in Michigan.

Plante [over video of Nixon striding through crowd to the podium]:   In Flint, Nixon made the same appeal as he did last week in the South, because the threat is the same, George Wallace. Several local unions here have endorsed Wallace. He divides the state enough so that Nixon and Humphrey are running almost even. Therefore Nixon's tactic is to convince the voters that a vote for him is the only real vote for change.

Nixon: [Speaks for 32 seconds.]

Plante [over video of Nixon shaking hands with exuberant children]:   Earlier Nixon brought his motorcade to a sort of scheduled unscheduled stop at the Michigan State School for the Deaf, where he told the youngsters of his aunt Olive, a missionary, though afflicted by deafness, and encouraged them. The Dean interpreted his remarks.

Nixon: When a person may not be able to hear, then he develops other qualities. Qualities of the heart. Qualities of understanding that people who may be able to hear do not develop to the same extent. It shows you that in the world in which you will be living, that your country needs you, and that what you learn here in this school will give each of you a chance to render wonderful service to this country [44 seconds.]

Here the report ended, and Cronkite went on to a story from Capitol Hill. Now let's jump forward twenty years. Here is ABC's election coverage for 4 October 1988:

Peter Jennings: Ever since the first presidential debate turned out to be pretty much of a draw, Dukakis' campaign staff has been seeking new ways to get at Vice President Bush. Here's ABC's Sam Donaldson.

Donaldson [over video of Dukakis rally]:   The Dukakis game plan has three parts. First an increasingly strident stump attack on George Bush's record by the candidate himself. Here's today's version.

Dukakis: He was asked to head up a task force on international terrorism. What happened? Mission failed. When he was asked to lead the war on drugs, we all know what happened. The mission has failed.

Donaldson: To be sure, Dukakis still talks about his own solutions to national problems.

Dukakis [talking to workers in a factory]:   I wanna make sure that every working family in this nation's got basic health insurance. You have it here, its terrific.

Donaldson: But more and more his stump speech is aimed at cutting Bush down.

Dukakis [in factory]:   They asked Bush about it; he said, well, we're going to help the unemployed buy into Medicaid. Tell me what that means. You're unemployed, you haven't got any money, George. Can't buy into anything.

Donaldson [over video from Dukakis TV ad]:   Part two of the strategy is to run television ads aimed at undercutting Bush's own attacks on Dukakis. Actors play the part of cynical Bush advisors who try to hoodwink the voters.

'Cynical Bush advisor:'   How long do you expect to get away with this furlough thing?

Second advisor: Hey Bernie, how long till the election? [Laughter.]

Voice-over announcer [over graphics]:   They'd like to sell you a package. Wouldn't you rather choose a President?

Donaldson [over video of Bush/Dukakis debate, then Quayle, then Bentsen]:   Part three of the strategy is to show up better in the televised debates. In this Wednesday's, Bentsen versus Quayle, the Dukakis camp is counting on Bentsen to look like the heavyweight.

Campaign Chairman Paul Brountas: He knows the issues, and I expect he will do a very good job.

Donaldson: This strategy, they believe, will produce a winner.

Advisor Francis O'Brien: We are making steady progress, and again, its all the pieces fitting together.

Donaldson [to camera]:   The themes of this campaign have turned out to be more negative than positive. But the Dukakis people believe they can still win that way. If they can't help you like their man more, they believe they can help you like his opponent less. Sam Donaldson, ABC news, Toledo.

A report on the Bush campaign followed. A few excerpts from it should suffice.

Barry Serafin: Under criticism even from some Republican party elders for not talking enough about issues, and seeking to blunt Democratic charges of callousness, Bush unveiled a new proposal called YES, Youth Engaged in Service, aimed at enlisting wealthy kids to help poor ones.

Bush: The end result, I hope, is that citizen service will become a real and living part of every young American's life.

Serafin: But by the second stop of the day . . . the vice president was back to the tried and true, the one-liners that in California, for example, have helped him erase a double-digit deficit in the polls. On crime:

Bush: I support our law enforcement community.

Serafin: On education:

Bush: I will be the education President.

Serafin: And another familiar refrain:

Bush: Read my lips: No new taxes!

SOUNDBITES AND MEDIATION

The average soundbite in the 1968 report is 60 seconds; in the 1988 report (counting the excerpt from the Dukakis ad as one soundbite), 8.5 seconds. But this merely reflects a more fundamental change in the structure of the news story and the role of the journalist in putting it together: modern TV news is

Table 7.2   Appearances by experts in television coverage of elections, 1968–88

1968	1972	1976	1980	1984	1988
1	0	4	4	8	37

much more mediated than the TV news of the 1960s and early 1970s. During the earlier period the journalist's role as a communicator was relatively passive. Frequently he or she did little more than set the scene for the candidate or other newsmaker whose speech would dominate the report. This may seem surprising to journalists who lived through these years, and remember them as a time when top television correspondents had enormous prestige and often considerable freedom to interpret or to comment on the news. And it is true that more active forms of television journalism did exist. Formal commentaries, for example, were a regular part of the news, while today they are rare. Long analytic pieces also sometimes appeared as part of election coverage, usually 'handicapping' the 'horse race' in a particular state (for example, 'Ohio has so and so many electoral votes, it's a key state this year for reasons X and Y,' etc.).

But day in and day out most television journalism, like the CBS report quoted above, was dominated more by the words of candidates and officials than by those of journalists. One should notice that Cronkite not only introduces long, uninterrupted soundbites from speeches and press conferences, but also spends much of his time quoting the candidates. This too is typical of the journalism of these years, which is studded with phrases like, 'in Wallace's words,' and 'the President said.'

The television journalist of the 1980s displays a sharply different attitude toward the words of candidates and other newsmakers. Today those words, rather than simply being reproduced and transmitted to the audience, are treated as raw material to be taken apart, combined with other sounds and images, and reintegrated into a new narrative. Not only are speeches and other statements chopped into brief soundbites, but visuals, including both film and graphics, are used much more extensively. Greater use is made of outside material, information brought in at the initiative of the journalists rather than offered by the candidates, and intended to put the statements and actions of the latter into perspective. The use of experts to comment on the campaign, for example, is a very recent development, as shown in Table 7.2.

Material from different settings is also combined more frequently. One striking example of this – and in general of the mediated form of modern TV news – is a CBS story on Bush's vice-presidential campaign (28 September 1984) in which correspondent David Dow illustrated a point about Bush's strategy by having the vice-president say a single sentence made up from five 1-second soundbites taken from speeches in different cities. This shifts the focus

Table 7.3   Soundbites as percentage of television time devoted to election coverage, 1968–88

1968	1972	1976	1980	1984	1988
17.6	11.9	11.4	7.4	6.3	5.7

from what Bush himself is saying, to what the journalist is saying about the Bush campaign. The sample also contained two stories in which the journalist (in both cases Bruce Morton of CBS) did little content analyses of candidates' statements, saying how often and for what purposes they used particular phrases and illustrating the analysis with video clips, for example (29 October 1980), three clips of Jimmy Carter uttering the fragment 'in the Oval Office.'

Finally, the journalist in contemporary American television news generally imposes on all these elements the unity of a clear story-line. The difference between Donaldson's 1988 Dukakis story and Plante's Nixon story illustrates this well. Donaldson's report has a single organizing theme that runs from beginning to end: Dukakis' three part 'game plan.' Plante does some interpretation of Nixon's strategy, but his report does not have a consistent unifying theme. Notice that it simply ends with Nixon speaking: the correspondent doesn't 'wrap' the story up. About 12 per cent of film reports in 1968 ended without closing lines by the correspondent; no such story appeared in the sample after 1976. These numbers only hint at the change, though, since closing lines in the earlier years didn't always sum the story up the way they usually do today. Some, for instance, simply told where the candidate would appear next. The metaphor of 'wrapping up' a story is quite apt: a modern television news story is tightly 'packaged' in a way that its predecessors normally were not.

This packaging means that the modern news story is much more journalist-centered than its predecessor: the journalist, not the candidate or other 'newsmaker' (a term which seems increasingly inadequate as the making of news has become more interactive), is the primary communicator. Table 7.3 shows the percentage of election coverage in each year taken up by soundbites – or to put it another way, the percentage of time someone other than the journalist is speaking. There are, not surprisingly, more soundbites in a modern TV news story, even though they are shorter. But even when you add them together, there is a significant decline over the years in the time taken up by soundbites.[2] If the figures for the earlier years seem small – about 18 per cent of TV time in 1968 was taken up by soundbites – one should remember that much of the journalists' reporting was also closely tied to the candidate's words, as when Cronkite quotes Wallace and LeMay. In any case the trend over time is clear and dramatic, with soundbites taking up about a third as much time in 1988 as they did twenty years earlier.

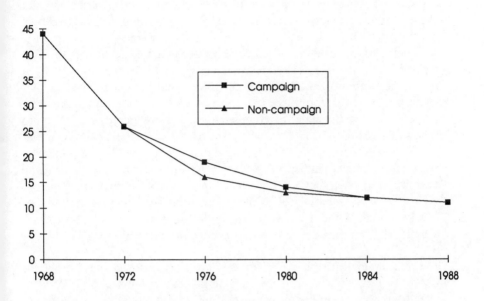

Figure 7.1 Average soundbites in campaign and non-campaign stories, 1968–88

WHY THE CHANGE?

The change in campaign coverage is part of a broader change in television journalism. In an effort to find out whether campaign stories differed in their structure from other television stories, eight of the sample broadcasts used in this study for each of the years from 1972 through 1984 were analyzed in full, campaign and non-campaign stories alike. Figure 7.1 shows the results: the trend is essentially the same for campaign and non-campaign stories.[3] This, incidentally, suggests that soundbite lengths probably would not have been much different if the study had focused on a different part of the campaign, say on the primary season. Soundbite lengths are part of the general style of TV news.

Technology

Three kinds of explanations for this change are plausible, and it is probably impossible completely to disentangle their separate contributions. The first has to do with the technical evolution of the television medium – not only technology in the narrow sense, but the evolution of technical culture more broadly, of television 'know-how,' and a television aesthetic. There were, of course, many new machines developed that made it easier to produce highly complex modern news stories, including graphics generators, electronic editing units, and telecommunications technologies that made it easy and cheap to transport video images. Beyond this, it simply took television people – who after all in the early days were trained in radio and in print – considerable time to develop a sense of how to communicate through this new medium. Looking back at the television news of 1960s and early 1970s, a period increasingly lionized today as the golden age of the medium, much of it seems not only more 'primitive' in the sense that it is technically simpler than modern TV news, but really less competent – dull, disorganized, and difficult to follow. This is certainly not to say that the particular television aesthetic that has since been developed is the only one that could have been. But in some sense it is probably right to say that television journalists are better at using the medium today than they were in 1968. Much of this technical development was presumably internal to TV news; but diffusion from other parts of television also played a role. Av Westin, for instance, writes of borrowing techniques from the commercial as executive producer of the ABC evening news in 1969.[4]

But technological explanations for political and cultural changes rarely can stand by themselves, even if we understand technology broadly. We have already seen, in the preceding essay, that in Italy, in a different political and economic context, the technology of television is used quite differently for delivering news. The data for this study yield one more piece of evidence that a purely technological explanation for the 10-second soundbite is inadequate. The change in soundbite length is much greater for certain types of people than for others: there is a big difference between élites and non- élites. In 1968, the average soundbite for candidates and other élites was 48.9 seconds, for ordinary voters it was 13.6. By 1988 the gap had narrowed to 8.9 seconds for élites and 4.2 for voters. Non-campaign coverage shows the same declining gap between élites and non-élites. The film editors of 1968 could produce short soundbites easily enough if this was wanted. But it was apparently not considered appropriate or necessary when reporting on a presidential candidate's press conference.

Politics

A second factor was the weakening of political consensus and authority in the years of Vietnam and Watergate, which pushed all of American journalism in the direction of more active reporting. At the beginning of the 1960s, American journalism in general, print or broadcast, was relatively 'un-mediated' in the sense that statements of government officials and other major political actors were for the most part reported at face value, with relatively little questioning or interpretation by the journalist. This was the main operational meaning of 'objective journalism.' As political divisions widened in the 1960s and 1970s, however, and as the 'credibility gap' over Vietnam was followed by Watergate, the old forms of reporting no longer seemed adequate.

The problem is illustrated well by one event early in the Vietnam War which is interesting enough to merit a brief digression. It occurred during the 'Buddhist crisis' of 1963. A bitter debate was going on within the Kennedy administration over support for the government of South Vietnamese president Ngo Dinh Diem, whose authoritarian government was facing a serious political crisis. The policy conflict was severe enough that the administration did not have a unified 'line' on many events. The most dramatic case was a raid on political foes in Saigon pagodas, carried out by the South Vietnamese government near the end of August. The US embassy in Saigon attributed the raids, correctly, to Diem and his brother Ngo Dinh Nhu; the State Department in Washington absolved Diem and blamed the South Vietnamese army. This left the press with two 'objective' dispatches, each quoting high government sources, giving exactly opposed accounts of the event. The *New York Times* ran the two stories side by side on the front page (23 August 1963) with a little note apologizing to the readers for the fact that they contradicted one another. This was obviously an awkward way to handle the problem, and there was much discussion at the time about how ridiculous the *Times* looked, not being able to get events in Vietnam straight. In the years that followed, journalists would increasingly deal with this sort of problem by taking official statements as a surface below which lay some deeper reality – in this case the policy conflict within the administration. In order to do this, of course, they had to become more active in reporting the news: since no single source could be taken as authoritative, the journalists came to feel that adequate reporting required them to provide their own synthesis and interpretation. Television was slower than other major media to move toward more analytic journalism.[5] But eventually it did so, and as it did the sort of report that consisted of little more than a 2-minute excerpt from a speech or press conference became increasingly rare.

Elections were important in their own right to the change in journalism. NBC's John Chancellor, who heard some of the results of this study at a 1990 conference, responded by saying, 'I think that the politicians started it' – started, that is, the soundbites and the packaging.[6] And there is much truth to this. The journalists were responding to election campaigns increasingly packaged for television, with a heavy reliance on pacing and visual imagery. The Nixon campaigns of 1968 and 1972 were especially significant. In 1968, for example, the Nixon campaign hired Roger Ailes, formerly a producer of the *Mike Douglas Show*, to create a series of 1-hour television shows directed at the voters of particular states. These shows were built around television 'production values' of a sort that television journalists had barely begun to consider – including considerable concern with the length of Nixon's answers to questions posed by the selected panels of voters, which Ailes carefully measured.[7] Journalists were excluded from the 'set' during these shows, and this sort of adversary relation between campaigns and the press was often characteristic of the new, television-oriented form of campaigning, as it was of television-oriented politics in general.[8] Television made it possible for candidates to reach the voters without the mediation of journalists. This is reflected in the data in a decline in the number of campaign reports in which press conferences played a prominent role, from fourteen such stories in 1968 to two in 1988.

Following the 1968 and 1972 campaigns journalists often sounded alarms about the danger that the media would be manipulated by image-making candidates. This anxiety was particularly strong among television journalists, who were correctly perceived as the main 'targets' of modern image-making. Sig Mickelson, an executive of CBS news, wrote following the 1972 campaign:

> Television news has acquired skills, experience, remarkable electronic machinery, and sophistication. But there seems to be no place or way to use them. The political managers seem to have learned more. They discovered the methods required to bend news reports to their own ends and to take the leadership themselves. They have the momentum. It now remains to be seen whether the broadcasters can recover the initiative.[9]

The manipulation of television and the need for journalists to be less passive was also a major theme of Timothy Crouse's influential book on the 1972 campaign, *The Boys on the Bus*.[10]

As television journalists became increasingly wary of being manipulated, they responded by taking a more adversarial stance toward the candidates, dissecting their statements, as Donaldson and Serafin do in the 1988 stories quoted above, and debunking their image-making strategies. (A good index of the increasing preoccupation of journalists with the packaging of candidate images is the appearance of the word 'handlers' to refer to campaign aides; it first began to appear in the sample in 1980, and quickly became a standard part of the journalists' vocabulary.) The more interpretive reporting of 1980s campaign coverage is largely preoccupied with this debunking enterprise.

One result is that election coverage has become increasingly negative in tone. Robinson and Sheehan found in a study of CBS coverage of the 1980 campaign that stories negative toward the candidates were about twice as common as positive ones.[11] Following their analysis, we coded stories as positive, negative, ambiguous (or mixed) in the predominant tone of their commentary. The results, presented in Table 7.4, show that the negative tone developed simultaneously with the 10-second soundbite: in 1968 positive and negative stories were about equally frequent; from 1980 on, however, negative stories clearly predominated.[12] The numbers here are small, mainly because most television stories remain neutral in tone (a fact which should remind us not to exaggerate the extent to which journalists have become more active and adversarial). But the trend over time is clearly strong.

Table 7.4   Evaluative tone of campaign stories, 1968–88

	Positive	Negative	Ambiguous	Neutral
1968	5	6	12	35
	(8.6%)	(10.3)	(20.7)	(60.3)
1972	1	1	1	49
	(1.9)	(1.9)	(1.9)	(94.2)
1976	1	3	3	49
	(1.8)	(5.4)	(5.4)	(87.5)
1980	0	5	6	53
	(0.0)	(7.8)	(9.4)	(82.8)
1984	1	5	5	33
	(2.3)	(11.4)	(11.4)	(75.0)
1988	1	16	13	32
	(1.6)	(25.8)	(21.0)	(51.6)

A few examples will give a sense of the changed tone. NBC's Herbert Kaplow closed a report on Nixon, who was to give a campaign address on violence at the recent Chicago Democratic Convention later that evening, by saying simply, 'It may be one of his most important campaign utterances, touching on that important issue we label "law and order." '[13] And Morton Dean of CBS introduced one Humphrey soundbite by saying, 'From a man who has heard much chatter and noise lately, [came] this call for reason' (12 September 1968). (Humphrey went on to chide peace demonstrators in the audience, saying, 'you don't have to go to the university to learn how to chant "peace," ' and then to give assurances he would do his utmost to bring peace to Southeast Asia. But he said nothing about how he would do this. Dean did not mention his failure to do so.) Contrast these with Bruce Morton on 13 September 1988:

> Biff! Bang! Powie! It's not a bird; its not a plane; it's presidential candidate Michael Dukakis in an M1 tank, as staff and reporters whoop it up. In the trade of politics it's called a visual . . . . If your candidate is seen in the polls as weak on defense, put him in a tank.

Economics

We do not yet, however, have a full explanation for the coming of the 10-second soundbite. Television journalists might have moved toward a more active form of journalism without adopting the staccato pace of the modern broadcast. Much Watergate coverage combined relatively long soundbites with active analysis by the journalists. But another major change was taking place in television news in the early 1970s, a change in the economics of the industry.

The network news divisions were losing the special status they had enjoyed in their early days as 'loss leaders' (see Chapter 5). The change started in local news. By the early 1970s, local stations had discovered that news could make a great deal of money; indeed, by the end of the decade it was common for a local station to make 60 per cent of its profit from news.[14] The local television industry is intensely competitive, with at least three stations competing head to head in most markets, and it is not surprising that this was a period of considerable innovation in the structure of news programs as stations battled for ratings. Consultants were brought in to recommend more effective ways of maintaining audience attention. And their recommendations typically pointed in the direction of a more tightly structured and fast-paced presentation of the news. Though there are no systematic data on the lengths of soundbites in local TV news in this period, it is likely that it was the local stations that led the way in shortening them.[15]

The same forces began to impinge on the network news divisions in a serious way in the middle of the 1970s. In 1977, ABC began a successful effort to make its news division competitive with those of CBS and NBC, increasing the number of contenders in the ratings game from two to three. This was followed in the 1980s by increased competition from cable and from independent stations, which along with other economic forces have squeezed the networks economically. Increased competition, moreover, came at a time when broadcasting was being substantially deregulated, decreasing the political pressure that had once motivated the development of news divisions insulated from ratings criteria. In this environment the barriers separating news from commercial television have been significantly eroded, and network TV journalists have felt increasing pressure to accommodate the same kind of production values that apply to local news and to the rest of television.[16]

THE POLITICAL MEANING OF SOUNDBITE NEWS

These forces have converged to produce the modern style of TV news. The modern television journalist is expected to be more active both as a political analyst and as a television producer, and the 10-second soundbite emerges out of this conjunction. And as the complexity of its origins suggests, its implications for the quality of political journalism and ultimately for the quality of the nation's political discourse are not simple.

In many ways modern TV news is much better journalism than it was twenty years ago. It is, first of all, often more interesting to watch; there is certainly nothing wrong with television people learning to use the medium more effectively. It is also more serious journalism in several ways. Media critics pressed the networks to be less passive, to tell the public more about the candidates' image-making strategies. The networks have done so, and this is surely an advance. Modern campaigning is based on refined, often manipulative techniques of image-making and news management, and the public needs to know how these techniques work. The more active modern form of TV news also involves certain kinds of serious issue coverage that did not exist in

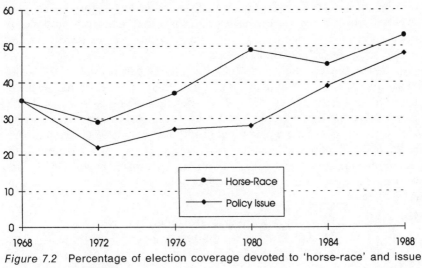

Figure 7.2   Percentage of election coverage devoted to 'horse-race' and issue
coverage

the earlier years. For many years critics have been decrying the predominance
in election coverage of the 'horse-race' story over issue-oriented reporting.
Horse-race themes do indeed dominate. This is one of the most consistent
findings of research on election coverage,[17] and we shall discuss its significance
in a moment. But the trend over time is more complex than might be expected.
Figure 7.2 shows the percentage of time the networks devoted to policy issues
during each year of the study, contrasted with the percentage devoted to
horse-race coverage, defined here as reporting which focuses on the campaign
as a contest, including discussion of polls, 'momentum,' and campaign
strategy.[18]

The numbers in Figure 7.2 add to more than 100 per cent in 1988 because
issue and horse-race coverage can be overlapping, as in the now typical case
when a candidate's statement on a policy issue is shown as an illustration of his
or her 'game plan.' Also, the fact that the sum of the two types of coverage
increases over the years reflects the more highly structured, thematic nature of
contemporary TV news: more and more of the news is fit into the standard
journalistic frames.

In 1968 policy issues and horse-race themes were 'running neck 'n neck.' In
the 1970s increased mediation by the journalist seems to have reduced issue
coverage, as reporters directed attention in their own framing of the story
toward the horse-race angle, with its increased focus on campaign strategy.[19]

In the 1980s, however, a counter-tendency appears to have developed. Just
as early in the 1970s journalists were often criticized – and criticized
themselves – for failing to focus on the candidates' image-making strategies,
later they were taken to task for failing to deal with issues. And this criticism
too seems to have produced significant change, with the percentage of issue

coverage turning back up. (For the media critic the history of election coverage is heartening – there is clear evidence that journalists respond to criticism eventually – and also a bit sobering, as changed coverage often has consequences the critics did not foresee.)

Increased issue coverage in the 1980s is in large part a result of two new, highly mediated forms of reporting. First, there are occasional lengthy, analytical stories on the candidates' positions on major issue areas. These often involve the use of issue experts outside the two campaigns, who first began appearing in the sample in significant numbers in 1984. Second, there are what could be called 'truth squad stories,' assessing the accuracy of candidates' statements. Here, for example, are excerpts from an NBC report on one Bush–Dukakis debate in 1988, reported by Jim Wooten (26 September):

> Bush: The Governor raised taxes five different times.
> Wooten: The Governor also cut taxes 8 times, and people in 33 states pay a greater percentage of their income in taxes than citizens of Massachusetts.
> On defense, Bush offered to cancel three weapons systems that had already been eliminated. Dukakis suggested that Bush himself was once sympathetic to a nuclear freeze. He wasn't. He simply said it shouldn't be a partisan issue.

To create this story, NBC put a platoon of researchers to work the night after the debate to check every statement of fact made by the candidates. It may be that television still doesn't do this nearly as often as it should. A recent study of the 1988 election, for instance, found that out of 125 occasions when the networks ran clips of candidates' television ads, less than 8 per cent of the time did they comment on the accuracy of the claims the ads made.[20] Still, the networks do this sort of thing far more today than they did in the past.

And yet there is a great deal that is disturbing in the mediated style of modern campaign reporting. First and simplest, it is disturbing that the public never has a chance to hear a candidate – or anyone else – speak for more than about 20 seconds. Showing humans speaking is something television does very effectively. Some of the long soundbites in early television news were very dull, to be sure; many could have been cut in half with little loss, and many no doubt could have been eliminated altogether. It's hard to see what viewers gain by hearing Richard Nixon ramble for 43 seconds about his Aunt Olive. But often it was extremely interesting – or so it seems to me looking back from twenty years later – to hear a politician, or even once in a while a community leader or ordinary voter, speak an entire paragraph. One had a feeling of understanding something of the person's character and the logic of his or her argument that a 10-second soundbite can never provide. One also had a feeling of being able to judge for oneself that the modern 'wrap-up' denies. That feeling may have been false for the average viewer, given the limited background information the old style of journalism provided. But analysis and background information can be provided without shortening soundbites to 10 seconds and less.

One of the most striking differences between TV news twenty years ago and today is the overall pace. Stories are slightly shorter now – film reports in the sample averaged 178 seconds in 1968 and 147 seconds in 1988, and the trend over time was statistically significant. At the same time, far more is packed into them, with their many visuals and short soundbites and their rapid-fire editing. Often in 1968 or 1972 a soundbite would be followed by 2 or 3 seconds of silence before the correspondent started talking. One 1972 story had 15 seconds of crowd noise – just cheering – embedded in the middle of a soundbite (ABC, 13 October 1972). Today the cues are instant, and there is virtually no time when someone is not speaking. Research on audience comprehension suggests that this pace takes its toll on the ability of viewers to understand television news.[21]

It seems likely, moreover, that whoever may have 'started it,' the modern form of TV news encourages exactly the kind of campaigning – based on one-liners and symbolic visuals – that journalists decry. There is clearly irony in a television journalist complaining about the candidates' one-liners in a report in which the soundbites average 8.5 seconds. The truth is that one-liners and symbolic visuals are what get on the air, and it is hardly surprising that the candidates' 'handlers' gravitate toward them. Journalists frequently threaten, as NBC's Andrea Mitchell recently said, to 'walk away,' if a 'photo opportunity of the day is simply a visual with no substantive core.'[22] But this is not in fact what they do. Campaign managers, for their part, seem to be convinced that visuals are effective regardless of what journalists say about them. Whether they are right in this assumption or not, symbolic visuals and their counterpart soundbites clearly have come to dominate political communication. Soundbite news and the packaged campaign now seem locked in a mutually reinforcing cycle, with campaigns packaging their events to fit the demands of television and TV journalists counter-packaging all the more tightly in response.

SOUNDBITE NEWS AND HORSE-RACE JOURNALISM

Finally, the rise of mediated TV news is connected with an increasing preoccupation with campaign technique and a kind of 'inside dopester' perspective that puts the image-making at the center of politics and pushes real political debate to the margins. If we look back to Figure 7.2, we can see that although issue coverage has gone up in the 1980s, the strongest trend as news has become more mediated is toward greater emphasis on 'horse-race' coverage. The numbers here, in fact, probably do not do full justice to the dominance of horse-race or 'technical' themes, since they measure raw amounts of time and do not take into account the organization of the story.

Table 7.5   Correlations between average soundbite length and percentage of story devoted to horse-race and policy issue themes

Horse-race	−0.33**	−0.21	−0.42**	−0.16	−0.22	−0.22*
Issue	0.48***	−0.06†	0.28*	0.14	0.46***	0.21

Notes: *p < 0.05 (one-tailed test) **p < 0.01 ***p < 0.001
† If Watergate stories (which have long soundbites but are classified campaign issue rather than policy issue) are eliminated, r = 0.03.

Even when a modern campaign report devotes significant time to issues, the main story-line typically focuses on strategy and tactics – often on the question of whether the candidate has made a 'good move' in focusing on a particular issue. This is reflected in the fact that in 1988 82 per cent of correspondents' 'wrap-ups' – which in modern TV news strongly reflect the basic organizing theme of the story – focused on 'horse-race' themes. It is important to emphasize that 'horse-race' coverage as defined here is reporting that focuses on the effectiveness of campaign techniques. There were, by contrast, some stories that dealt with campaign techniques as an ethical issue – was campaigning becoming too negative, or too superficial for the good of democracy? This kind of reporting, amounting overall to a very small proportion of the total, was not counted as horse-race coverage.

The connection between horse-race coverage and soundbite journalism is very strong. Not only do the trends coincide historically, horse-race coverage increasing as soundbites shrink, but a substantial correlation between soundbite length and horse-race emphasis shows up in each year of the study (see Table 7.5).

Stories with high percentages of time devoted to horse-race themes tended to have short soundbites, while more issue-oriented stories tended to have longer ones. If we translate this into regression terms, taking 1976 as an example, a story that was 75 per cent issue-focused and 15 per cent concerned with horse-race themes (the rest of the time taken up with unrelated themes) would be expected to have soundbites averaging about 29 seconds. A more typical story, though, in which those percentages were reversed would be expected to have soundbites averaging only 18 seconds.[23]

Why should this connection exist between mediated news with its short soundbites and horse-race coverage? Focusing on the election as a contest, for one thing, gives the news the kind of dramatic narrative structure valued by modern television. Even in 1968, 69 per cent of film reports had horse-race 'wrap-ups' (though recall that wrap-ups in that era did not necessarily reflect a story-line carried through the whole report). It also helps to solve a problem of authority created by the television journalist's increasingly active role. The mediated, journalist-centered form of modern TV news places journalists in a difficult position. They are expected to take center stage as interpreters of the campaign, to serve as surrogates for the largely empty public sphere. Yet 'no one elected the media,' as the phrase goes and their role can easily become a focus of political controversy. Hence, television journalists feel most comfortable making essentially technical judgements about campaign performance, judgements which can be presented as non-partisan and verified by polls and the judgements of other political professionals; election coverage is one of the best examples of the 'technical angle' introduced in Chapter 2. Thus Roger Mudd, then NBC's chief political correspondent, opened and closed his analysis of the first Reagan–Mondale debate (8 October 1984) like this:

> Who won or lost was largely a matter of expectations. By most accounts, including Republican ones, Ronald Reagan did not live up to his own standards. By most accounts, including Republican ones, Walter Mondale exceeded his . . . .
>
> As jubilant as the Mondale campaign might be about the debate and its impact on morale, no one is claiming last night's debate was enough to close the enormous gap with Ronald Reagan.

In between, Mudd showed high points and low points of each man's performance. This he did without the slightest reference to the substance of what they said ('from time to time Mondale's voice grew whiney as he fell back on his old stump speech'), nor was there discussion anywhere in the broadcast of the substance of the debate. But this is to be expected: it is precisely those non-substantive aspects of candidate effectiveness that the community of political professionals can agree upon ('by most accounts . . . no one is claiming').

Similarly in 1988, when Dukakis began criticizing the Bush campaign's furlough ads as racist, Bruce Morton of CBS handled the story like this:

> Morton: The question is, can this kind of attack on the process, on the negative style of the Bush campaign, do Dukakis any good? He badly needs something to shift momentum his way.
>
> Norman Ornstein: If you can somehow exploit and underscore the disillusionment that an awful lot of people feel with the negative tactics of the campaign and the less than adequate choices presented to them, you've got the potential for a turnaround.

Ornstein, based at the American Enterprise Institute in Washington, is independent of both campaigns and yet very much a political insider – a perfect sort of person to offer this kind of technical analysis, with the aura of objectivity it provides. Political experts like Ornstein, including academics (mostly from Washington think-tanks) and campaign consultants not involved in the current campaign, first appeared in large numbers in the sample in 1988. Aides for the major campaigns, the so-called 'spin doctors,' first started appearing in large numbers in 1980. Ordinary voters, meanwhile, have been a diminishing presence in the news, dropping from over 20 per cent of soundbites in 1972 and 1976 to 3 to 4 per cent in 1984 and 1988 (in the sample, incidentally, 95 per cent were white and two-thirds male, with only a faint trend over time toward greater diversity). Remember, too, that soundbites for voters are vanishingly small, averaging 4 seconds in 1988. Voters appear in the news essentially to illustrate poll results, and almost never contribute ideas or argument to campaign coverage. The journalists' increased focus on technique is thus accompanied by increasing dominance of campaign discourse by political insiders.[24]

Here again the position of TV news is ironic. Just as TV decries photo-opportunity and soundbite campaigning, yet builds the news around them, so it decries the culture of the campaign consultant, with its emphasis on technique over substance, yet adopts that culture as its own. There are moments, indeed, when it is hard to distinguish the journalists from the political technicians, as when Dan Rather, in live coverage following the first Bush–Dukakis debate, asked a series of pollsters and campaign aides questions like, 'You're making a George Bush commercial and you're looking for a sound bite with George Bush . . . . What's his best shot?'[25] The dominant tone that results from all this, as Todd Gitlin has pointed out, is a kind of knowing, 'postmodern' cynicism, that debunks the image and the image-maker, yet in the end seems to accept them as the only reality we have left.[26] It is hard to be nostalgic either for the politics of 1968 or for the passive television journalism of that era. But it must be said that in 1968 one did have a feeling that the campaign, as it appeared on television, was at its core important, that it was essentially a debate about the future of the nation. As sophisticated as it is, modern television news no longer conveys that sense of seriousness.

NOTES

*   I would like to thank Judith Gregory, who was the principal coder for the study, as well as Sandra Au-Young and Monica Genewich for research assistance. I would also like to thank Kathy Frankovic, Herbert Gans, Michael Grossman, Shanto Iyengar, Lawrence Lichty, Samuel Popkin, Jay Rosen, William Schneider, and Michael Schudson for comments on earlier drafts.

1   Sample sizes – in terms of number of soundbites rather than number of broadcasts – for the six election years are, beginning with 1968: 113, 123, 119, 201, 179, and 284.

  A number of methodological issues arise in measuring soundbites. Their effects on the overall results are not dramatic, but they are nevertheless important to note. Stories that were strictly interviews, without voice-over narration by the anchor or a correspondent, were excluded from the analysis. These have a distinctive structure of their own, and the notion of a soundbite does not really apply to them. The sample contained ten such stories, one in 1968, four each in 1976 and 1980, and one in 1988. (If one were to include them, and count each segment of speech by the interviewee as a 'soundbite,' it would raise the average soundbite each year by about a second.)

  When film or tape of an interview or press conference was shown in a film report, a continuous exchange between a reporter and source was counted as a single soundbite. Continuous exchanges between two or more people, for example in film of a congressional hearing, were also treated as single soundbites.

Finally, two kinds of jump-cuts were handled differently. The first could be called the ellipsis jump-cut, in which two or more segments of the same person speaking in the same setting are spliced together. These were treated as single soundbites. The second is what could be called the juxtaposition jump-cut – a true jump-cut – in which contrasting segments, usually from different settings, are spliced together in a way that the discontinuity is evident. These were treated as separate soundbites.

The three networks did not differ significantly and are merged in all the figures that follow.

Another study (K. Adatto, 'Sound bite democracy: network evening news presidential campaign coverage 1968 and 1988,' Joan Shorenstein Barone Center, Harvard University, Research paper R-2, 1990), looking at the full universe of coverage for the same period covered by this study in 1968 and 1988, found a very similar figure for 1968 – an average soundbite of 42.3 seconds – but a slightly larger figure, 9.8 seconds, for 1988. The difference is not of great substantive importance, but it is large enough that it is not likely to be due entirely to sampling fluctuation. It may be due to differing choices involving some of these measurement problems.

2 Here interview stories (see note 1 above) are included.

3 In 1976 the difference between campaign and non-campaign stories was barely significant at the 0.05 level. But for other years it was not significant, and if the four years are combined an analysis of variance shows no significant difference.

4 A. Westin, *Newswatch: How TV Decides the News*, New York, Simon & Schuster, 1982, pp. 49–50.

5 D. Hallin, *The 'Uncensored War': The Media and Vietnam*, New York, Oxford University Press, 1986, pp. 115–26.

6 D. Hallin (ed.), *The President, the Press and the People*, La Jolla, Calif., University of California Extension, 1993, p. 158.

7 J. McGinnis, *The Selling of the President, 1968*, New York, Trident, 1969.

8 S. Kernell, *Going Public: New Strategies of Presidential Leadership*, Washington DC, Congressional Quarterly Press, 1986.

9 'Blurred image in the electric mirror,' in M. Barrett (ed.), *The Politics of Broadcasting, 1971–72*, New York, Thomas Y. Crowell, 1973. See also S. Mickelson, *From Whistle Stop to Sound Bite*, New York, Praeger, 1989.

10 New York, Ballantine, 1974.

11 M. J. Robinson and M. A. Sheehan, *Over the Wire and on TV: CBS and UPI in Campaign '80*, Beverly Hills, Calif., Sage, 1983, p. 111.

12 Only film reports and voice-over stories are included here. Commentaries are excluded, as are 'tell' stories read by the anchor without film (which are almost always neutral). Our measure is slightly different from Robinson and Sheehan's. We coded only for the tone of the journalists' commentary, and did not consider other sources of information within the story. We followed Robinson and Sheehan (op. cit.) in excluding 'horse-race' judgements about the candidates' chances of winning.

13 4 September 1968. This report, by the way, was coded as neutral, but its closing line illustrates the more respectful tone of earlier coverage, which was manifested in many subtle ways not always picked up by the content analysis.

14 J. Greenfield, 'Making TV news pay,' *Gannett Center Journal*, 1987, vol. 1.

15 One account refers to film clips in local news being 'shortened to about 20 seconds' (M. Barrett, *Moments of Truth*, New York, Thomas Y. Crowell, 1975, p. 112). This would probably put the local stations ahead of the networks in shortening soundbites, especially if it is meant that soundbites were usually 20 seconds or shorter.

16 P. J. Boyer, *Who Killed CBS?*, New York, St Martin's, 1989; Greenfield, op. cit.; B. Matusow, *The Evening Stars*, New York, Ballantine, 1983.

17 T. E. Patterson, *The Mass Media Election: How Americans Choose Their President*, New York, Praeger, 1980; Robinson and Sheehan, op. cit.; B. Buchanan, *Electing a President: The Markle Commission Report on Campaign '88*, Austin, Tex., University of Texas Press, 1991. See also H. E. Brady and R. Johnston, 'What's the primary message: horse race or issue journalism?', in G. R. Orren and N. W. Polsby (eds.), *Media and Momentum: The New Hampshire Primary and Nomination Politics*, Chatham, NJ, Chatham House, 1987.

18 For the most part, I have followed the categories used in the content analyses of Robinson and Sheehan op. cit. and Patterson op. cit. In defining the horse-race category, however, I did not include coverage of 'campaign hoopla' – the enthusiasm of the crowd, etc. – unless it was tied to analysis of campaign strategy or 'momentum.' Like Patterson and Robinson and Sheehan, we also coded for two categories of content besides horse-race and policy issue. The first was campaign issue coverage, focusing on the conduct of the campaign, including issues of whether a certain candidate would or wouldn't debate, for instance, or something like the Eagleton affair in 1972 (which concerned whether George McGovern should keep his vice-presidential nominee, who had undergone psychiatric treatment). The second was candidate coverage, focusing on candidates' qualifications and personal qualities (was Carter too mean, Reagan too old, Dukakis too cold?). Both these occurred with much less frequency than policy issue and horse-race coverage (except campaign issue coverage in 1972), and there was no significant trend over time. These data do not support the common notion that television coverage of elections focuses heavily on candidate personality; candidate coverage never rose above about 15 per cent.

19 The year 1972, which shows a drop in both horse-race and issue coverage, was unusual in part because of Watergate. Watergate was not defined here as a policy issue, but as a 'campaign issue' since in this early phase it was seen as a question of the conduct of Nixon's campaign rather than the management of government.

20 Adatto, op. cit., p. 8.

21 J. P. Robinson and M. R. Levy, *The Main Source: Learning from TV News*, Beverly Hills, Calif., Sage, 1986.

22 W. Boot, 'Campaign '88: TV overdoses on the inside dope,' *Columbia Journalism Review*, January/February 1989, vol. 27, p. 26.

23 These estimates are based on a regression of average soundbite length (AVBITE), on percentage of time devoted to issues (ISSUPCT), and to horse-race themes (HORSPCT): AVBITE $= 25.80 + 0.0685$ (ISSUPCT) $- 0.1139$ (HORSPCT).

24 The only trend running the other way is the increased use of issue experts. In 1988, 58 per cent of soundbites showed candidates, 9 per cent other public officials, 8 per cent political experts, 4 per cent campaign aides, 6 per cent issue experts, 3 per cent interest group representatives, 4 per cent non-élites, including voters and rank-and-file campaign workers, and 8 per cent others.

25 Boot, op. cit., p. 27.

25 Todd Gitlin, 'Blips, bites and savvy talk,' *dissent*, winter 1990.

Chapter 8

Summits and the constitution of an international public sphere

The Reagan–Gorbachev meetings as televised media events*

During the Cold War, now at an end after nearly half a century, US–Soviet summits have been seen above all as symbolic events. Beyond any concrete agreements reached during their closed-door meetings, they have typically been evaluated by the 'spirit' they created, by the sense of common commitment, transcending political antagonism and presumably leading to further political accomplishment, which a successful summit was expected to produce.

In this sense, US–Soviet summits seem to fit fairly closely the model of 'media events' put forward by Elihu Katz and Daniel Dayan.[1] Dayan and Katz define 'media events' as planned, symbolic performances staged for a media audience. Besides summits, this definition would include such events as inaugurations and coronations, public commemorations of historical events, launchings and landings of space missions. It excludes unplanned events covered by the media: an assassination is not a media event in this sense; the state funeral following it is. Adapting the Durkheimian view of the social function of ritual, Dayan and Katz have argued that media events tend to integrate societies: they dissolve or de-emphasize social divisions, and bring the members of a community together around shared values and a shared sense of identity. At the funeral of a statesman like Kennedy or Berlinguer, for example, references to partisan divisions are considered inappropriate.[2] The experience, shared primarily through television, is for 'everyone.' And the event is as much a celebration of the common identity of the audience – as Americans, or Italians, or simply as human beings – as it is a tribute to the individuals who stand for the community.

All of these, of course, are primarily national media events. They may be covered by the media of the entire world, but the ceremonies involved are addressed primarily toward national audiences. A summit, on the other hand, is truly an international media event, part of a small category of such events addressed directly toward global audiences. It would follow from Dayan and Katz's analysis – and also fit with the common understanding of the symbolic effects of summitry – that summits should push toward international integration, toward a sense of common identity that transcends the nation state. This is the hypothesis we would like to take up here, using the example of the three major summits between Reagan and Gorbachev, at Geneva in 1985, Washington in 1987, and Moscow in 1988.[3]

What makes the US–Soviet summits particularly interesting, as we shall see, is that the definition of community becomes highly problematic at these moments. Several different levels of community, for one thing, come into conflict – the nation, the bloc, and humanity as a whole. This creates familiar difficulties for the consensual Durkheimian framework. Beyond the problem of consensus versus conflict, however, is an issue of how to conceptualize community, which will ultimately become our focus. We shall explore, in particular, the distinction between the Durkheimian conception of civil religion and the very different notion of the public sphere.

THE SUMMIT AS AN 'INTEGRATING' EVENT

There is, in fact, a good case to be made that the summit, as a media event, pushes in certain ways in the direction of some form of global integration. Three specific effects of the summit – all of them closely interrelated – seem to us particularly important: first, expansion of the global communication flow; second, the symbolic constitution of a global community; and third, a tendency to humanize the Other.

Expansion of global communication flow

The most obvious effect of summits as media events is that they change the structure of the world communication flow, increasing the flow of communication through international, as opposed to national channels. This has always been true of east–west summits, but it was particularly so in the Gorbachev era, as the Soviets sought both to communicate more effectively outside their borders and to open up their own communication system.[4] A summit offers an extraordinary opportunity for the states involved to override normal limitations on communication, taking the spotlight worldwide and even opening direct channels of communication with the population of other states, something which was, at the height of the Cold War, normally impossible across its major line of division.

What makes this really significant, however, is that in order to take advantage of this opportunity, a state must allow itself to be drawn into a process which it cannot completely control; it must accept the rules of the international game it seeks to play. At Geneva, for instance, the Soviets held far more press conferences than they had at previous summits. But when they did, they had to be prepared to answer numerous questions about human rights, posed both by journalists and by demonstrators who had themselves come to Geneva to seek a place on the world stage. Gorbachev could seize the headlines in Washington by meeting with political leaders outside the administration and by stopping his limousine to 'press the flesh.' But he in turn had to grant Reagan the right to meet with religious dissidents in Moscow and to proselytize the Soviet public, when the two leaders exchanged televised New Year's greetings at the beginning of 1988, about elections, religion, and the American 'standard of living.' The Reagan–Gorbachev summits opened up an unusual global process of communication, and anyone who wished to participate had to be prepared to hear and to answer voices that were not normally present in national political discourse.

The implications have been particularly great for the Soviets, since the international communication process tends to be dominated by western conventions. In a society in which divisions among the political élite were until recently excluded from public communication, for example, the sight of Mikhail Gorbachev responding in a televised press conference to the comments of demoted party leader Boris Yeltsin, who granted interviews during the Moscow summit to CBS and the BBC, was a truly dramatic break from the past. So was the prominent role of Raisa Gorbachev. Western audiences expect political leaders to appear with their wives. Without this balancing of civil and political roles – leader and husband or wife – they are not seen as properly part of the community; and it is unlikely that Gorbachev could have become such a celebrity had he and his mate not met this expectation so well.

The role of the media in this process is a relatively active one. The media are active, first of all, in building up a global audience for the event. Their promotion and dramatization, though these take different forms in different countries, are in each country essential to the constitution of the event as something that exists for everyone; without it the sense that the 'whole world is watching' that surrounds the event would not exist. The media are active also in shaping the conversation that emerges in the summit, through their role as interrogators and interpreters of the summit participants. If the international communication process has certain rules which participants must follow, the journalists are among the most important arbiters of those rules.

Events like the Reagan–Gorbachev summits thus raise the issue of whether the media might be developing into a genuinely international institution – not merely conduits linking each national audience with the central event of the summit, but an actual transnational institution, with common norms and routines, capable of playing an autonomous role in world politics. Certainly, the extent of transnational institutionalization of the media should not be exaggerated. In fact, as we shall see, the summits show dramatically how nationally-centered journalists still are, both in their political views and in their professional culture. Until there are international institutions around which journalists congregate on a regular and not a sporadic basis, internationalization of the press corps cannot be expected to develop beyond a limited extent (it is most developed today in the case of the world financial press, the *Financial Times* and the *Wall Street Journal*, which of course are tied to increasingly internationalized economic institutions.[5] But the internationalization of journalism is a process that is at least under way, and the increased intensity of interaction among national media that takes place during summits – even to the the point of producing joint news broadcasts, as the US and Soviets did during the Washington summit – seems likely to accelerate it.[6] The consequences for world politics might in the long run be quite significant. Perhaps, indeed, the dramatic changes in Eastern Europe during 1989 are in part – in their form and timing if not in the fact of their occurrence, which is no doubt rooted in deeper structural and cultural factors – the result of the intensified communication between east and west during the 1980s.

Symbolic constitution of a global community

It is a common hypothesis that electronic communication tends to break down the barriers of established social groups. There are both utopian and anti-utopian versions of this argument, ranging from McLuhan's vision of the 'Global Village' on one side to theories of mass society and cultural imperialism on the other. Dayan and Katz's theory of media events of course is utopian; extending it to superpower summitry, it could be argued that the power of television to override social boundaries should combine with the integrative effect of ritual to produce at least temporarily a global sense of community.

And in fact something like this did happen with the Reagan–Gorbachev summits. Because it takes place on a world stage, the summit constitutes international society for a brief period as a tangible, salient community. All the actors involved are acutely aware that they stand before a worldwide audience, and this has substantial impact on political discourse, shifting it away from the standard national frame of reference, toward a global frame. Journalists, for example, will frequently use the term 'we' to refer not to the inhabitants of a particular nation state, but to all humanity (or in some cases to the people of both superpowers). 'We' comes to mean not the particular national audience the journalists normally address, but the international audience that a summit brings temporarily into being.[7] The anchor of the main Italian news broadcast summed up Geneva by saying,

> Thus the first Russian/American summit for over six years has come to a close . . . . Grounds for divergence do persist, and they are deeply rooted, but an important page has been turned. The hope of all mankind is that this day shall remain in history, that it truly marked the beginning of a process for which we all long – that is to say: may the arsenals indeed be emptied, and the granaries be filled. Of this the world undoubtedly has great need.

Once global society has been invoked values considered appropriate to that society tend at least partly to displace more particularistic values of ideology and national sovereignty; as these examples suggest, the value of peace clearly takes center stage during a summit. The celebration of international harmony, in fact, was not confined to news during the Reagan–Gorbachev summits, but spilled into other parts of mass culture as well. Coca-Cola ran a commercial showing children of all races singing together and embracing one another: 'As the leaders of the world come together, we offer this message of hope.' And Parker pen offered the image of Reagan and Gorbachev signing the INF treaty, with the slogan, 'The pen is mightier than the sword.'

The role of the media in the symbolic constitution of global community is complex: they are not only the channels through which a world audience is created, but also themselves represent global community. The global audience itself is invisible during the summit, for the most part, aside from a few occasions when journalists interview citizens or other observers. But the 'muro di giornalisti,' as the Italians put it, the wall of journalists, about 6,000 strong (up from about 1,000 during the superpower summits of the early 1960s), is extremely visible; the journalists are one of the key visual images of the summit as a televised media event. Their role in summit coverage is double in an interesting way: they are both the narrators of the drama, and a character in it. They appear as a stand-in for the world community, witnessing and interrogating the two leaders on its behalf. Another interesting illustration of the symbolic role of the world press can be taken from the Washington summit, during which American and Soviet television produced a live joint broadcast, seen simultaneously on ABC's *Nightline* and the Soviet morning program *90 Minutes*. At one point during that broadcast, the camera lingered over the front pages of *Pravda* and the *Washington Post*, revealing common expectations and a common sense of the historical importance of the occasion, reflected in part in identical photographs of that day's meeting of the two leaders.

Even if the institutionalization of the world press corps remains limited, their symbolic role is certainly powerful during a summit. It is parallel in an interesting way to the chorus in another kind of civic ritual – Greek tragedy. The structure of tragedy, according to Vernant and Vidal-Naquet, involved

> [a] tension between the two elements that occupy the tragic stage. One is the chorus, the collective and anonymous presence embodied by an official college of citizens. Its role is to express through its fears, hopes, questions and judgements, the feelings of the spectators who make up the civic community. The other, played by a professional actor, is the individualized character whose actions form the core of the drama and who appears as a hero from an age gone by, always more or less estranged from the ordinary condition of the citizen.[8]

Like the chorus, the media at the summit represent world community. It is above all in the 'wall of journalists' and the interaction of world leaders with them that the world community seems no longer abstract but physically present and undeniably real – an imagined community, in the words of Benedict Anderson.[9]

Humanization of the Other

This leaves us to consider the role of the other symbolic element of the summit as media event, the 'individualized characters' of Reagan and Gorbachev. Consider the 'tea summit' (or 'style wars') of Nancy and Raisa, or the sight of Gorbachev shaking hands with stunned Americans on a Washington street; these events suggest a third way in which the summit, as a media event, tends toward international integration. As Dayan and Katz have argued, media events are planned and presented as *narratives*, centering around certain characters understood as the heroes of the story. Here, for example, is how NBC opened its broadcast on the eve of the Geneva summit:

> Tom Brokaw [over video]:   Soviet leader Mikhail Gorbachev arriving in Geneva today. [Pause.] President Reagan already in place. Said to be eager for tomorrow's opening session of the summit.
>   Announcer: NBC Nightly News with Tom Brokaw, tonight from the Geneva summit.
>   Brokaw: Good evening from Geneva where the final countdown is under way. This long-awaited summit meeting between President Ronald Reagan of the United States and Mikhail Gorbachev, Secretary General of the Communist Party of the Soviet Union, is now less than twelve hours away. The pre-summit maneuvering, the warnings, the speculation – all that fades now as these two men, representing the most powerful forces in civilization, come together to see if they can begin the process of working out their differences.

Brokaw went on to summarize the careers of the two men.

During a media event, television moves away from the usual modes of political reporting and toward a dramatic mode. The dramatic mode does two things simultaneously. First, it celebrates the event as something standing above the routine of political life. In the Italian coverage, this is manifested in a shift of journalistic roles from neutral announcing to a more active interpretation of the significance of the event, as in the comment about granaries and armories quoted above. In the American coverage, where the normal mode is analysis focused on policy conflicts, the elevation of the event above routine politics is symbolized in part in the fact that the journalists 'stand back' at certain moments to put the event itself rather than their own analysis in the foreground, pausing to let the image and sound of the event fill the screen without words from the journalist to define their meaning, something very unusual in American TV news. The visual is often privileged in this sort of coverage. So, for example, the morning the Geneva summit began the host of NBC's morning program *Today* opened the broadcast by repeating the image of the two leaders shaking hands: 'The moment was so special,' he said, 'it bears repeating. This is the picture you will see again and again.' And one of the things that is presented as special in this dramatic presentation – here we come to the second characteristic of the dramatic mode – is a personal meeting of two human beings. As a dramatic ritual, the event is both elevated above routine politics and 'brought down' to human scale.[10]

The consequences of dramatization are also twofold. First, again following Dayan and Katz, it opens up a sense of possibility: 'Media events testify that *voluntarism* is still alive, that the deeds of human beings – especially great ones – still make a difference and are worth recording.'[11] Both the sense of occasion of a media event and the fact that it centers around particular human individuals rather than anonymous social institutions, contribute to an impression that the laws of politics are suspended and the future is open – a naive view, certainly, but one that may at the same time encourage people to think about what *could be*. Normally political news is rigidly focused on what *is*; media events change the ontology of news, introducing what Dayan and Katz call, following Turner, a 'subjunctive mode.' Summits are traditionally occasions when, for a brief period at least, the Cold War no longer seems natural, and we are allowed to speculate about the possibility of a different international order: 'may the arsenals be emptied and the granaries be filled.'

Second, because of the personal focus of the dramatic mode, the person who represents the Other also comes before each audience not as a political abstraction but as a human being. Personalization obviously can have many uses and consequences. Khrushchev functioned in a highly personalized way as a negative symbol of the Other in an earlier era; Saddam Hussein was a personal *causus bellum* during the Gulf War. During the summits of the 1980s personalization clearly benefited each leader within his own country. In the Soviet Union, television followed every word of Mikhail Sergeyevich Gorbachev as he made his odyssey for peace. In the United States, the audience watched as the journalists awaited the arrival of the president's helicopter, which delivered him, in prime time, to address Congress and the nation as the returning hero:

> Good evening everyone, and in the skies over Capitol Hill you see President Reagan's helicopter. He has just arrived at Andrews Air Force Base moments ago and he is helicoptering now to a dramatic appearance before a joint session of Congress in Washington. He's had about a twenty hour day wrapping up his Geneva meeting with Soviet leader Mikhail Gorbachev .... The President has had by his standards a triumphant day, a joint session with Mr. Gorbachev this morning in which he described a fresh start in US/USSR relations.

The parallel with Greek tragedy is again striking:

> 'Even as the setting and the mask confer upon the tragic protagonist the magnified dimensions of one of the exceptional beings that are the object of a cult in the city, the language used brings him closer to the ordinary man.'[12]

Approval of Reagan's handling of foreign policy jumped dramatically in American opinion polls following both Geneva and Moscow.[13]

But when the political context is right, the dramatic mode of the media event can mean that the person who represents the Other can also benefit from this humanization. Thus in Washington we saw Mikhail and Raisa singing along with great emotion as the pianist Van Cliburn played 'Moscow Nights' at the White House, while the Reagans smiled warmly next to them. We also saw Gorbachev and Reagan, with big smiles, looking at their watches as the two wives came in 10 minutes late to a scheduled photo opportunity. Demon images of the enemy are obviously eroded by this sort of thing, especially when the leaders of the two superpowers are as charismatic and as active in using the media as Reagan and Gorbachev. (Notice that in the image of the two husbands looking at their watches, Cold War stereotypes are displaced by gender stereotypes.) A *Newsweek* poll after the Washington summit showed 32 per cent of Americans saying their opinion of Gorbachev was better than before the summit, 1 per cent that it was worse, and 64 per cent that it was the same; this came on top of an already greatly improved public image of the Soviet leader.[14]

MEDIA AS NATIONAL INSTITUTIONS

In certain ways, then, it makes sense to think of summits, as media events, pushing toward international integration. But this is only part of the story. Here the limitations of the Durkheimian approach to ritual and the media event become clear.[15] The Durkheimian theory abstracts both from structures of power and from processes of change and conflict, assuming that civic rituals produce a sense of community that stands above politics. Thus Shils and Young wrote that the coronation of the British Queen promoted 'the common sentiment of the sacredness of communal life and institutions . . . people became more aware of their dependence on each other [and] more sensitive to the values which bound them all together.'[16] Communal life and mutual dependence are assumed here to be equally shared and essentially unproblematic.

The summit is a good illustration of the limitations of this perspective. The primary political identities of each of the countries in this study are after all national identities strongly connected to the structure of conflict known as the Cold War. The global sense of community invoked by the summits threatened to disrupt integration at the national and bloc level and the media in each country, tied as they are to national political institutions, simultaneously celebrated global community *and* played the role of reinforcing patterns of understanding and commitment rooted in the Cold War. This was particularly true in the United States, where television journalists are more autonomous and more active as ideological interpreters than in Italy or the Soviet Union, and therefore felt a heightened sense of responsibility to uphold the dominant political consensus. We cannot summarize the political content of the American coverage in detail here; it will have to suffice to say that for American television the summits provided an occasion for an exceptional emphasis on the ideological division between east and west. Journalists were fond of quoting a description of Gorbachev as having a 'nice smile, but iron teeth.' This illustrates the political problem they faced. The summit as media event threatened in significant ways, as one journalist put it, to create a situation in which 'feelings ran so warm the entire history of the Cold War was wiped away;' and the journalists were determined that this should not occur.

AN INTERNATIONAL PUBLIC SPHERE?

Clearly considerable difficulties arise in applying the traditional Durkheimian framework to the divided and conflictual global 'community' of the Cold War world.[17] It makes sense, therefore, to relate the media event to another, different conception of common social space: that of the public sphere. The concept of the public sphere refers to the arena of civic discourse, in which citizens enter into an ongoing dialogue about the common concerns of the society.[18] It involves a conception of community centered around *participation in a common conversation* rather than *sharing of common values*. As we focus on this different conception of community, a new set of questions arises.

Does it make sense to say that the Reagan–Gorbachev summits, as media events, opened up an international public sphere? Just as when we asked whether the summit could be seen as leading to international integration, the answer is yes and no. Certainly in some ways the summits opened a semblance of an international public sphere. The two superpowers entered into a conversation with one another before the 'court' of world public opinion; they entered into a conversation with the world press; journalists from the two superpowers entered into conversation with one another. Dialogue on a global scale was the order of the day. At the same time, however, the nature of the civic discourse surrounding the summit was extremely restricted in the television coverage of each of the countries examined here.

In order to make this case in more detail, we need to begin to break down the notion of a 'global dialogue' into more specific components. In particular, we need to distinguish between two different conceptions of international society. International society is most commonly conceived as a kind of second-order society, the 'citizens' of which are states. If we focus on this level, the most important thing to say about the public sphere opened by the summit is that participation in it was extremely uneven, with the voice of the two superpowers overwhelmingly dominant. The notion of a world audience was invoked, of course. But the views of other members of the world community were little represented. On American television, for example, less than 5 per cent of Geneva coverage was devoted to the reactions of the nation's West European allies; virtually none to the views of the rest of the world. Italian television did devote significant attention – a little more than 11 per cent of its coverage – to the reactions of Italian political parties and other West European countries; but these actors appeared in the passive role of hoping for superpower reconciliation, and were rarely shown expressing independent political views. Soviet television gave the most attention to views outside the superpowers. Indeed about a third of Soviet coverage was devoted to reactions of West Europeans and the Third World, as well as non-government voices in the United States (an issue we will take up in a moment). But these voices functioned in the Soviet coverage mainly to praise Soviet policy, or, as in the Italian coverage, to praise summitry itself. In this sense, the summit as a media event would seem to reinforce what Fred Halliday has called hegemonic internationalism: 'the belief that the integration of the world is taking place but on asymmetrical, unequal terms, and that this is the only possible and desirable way for such an integration to take place.'[19]

International society can also be seen, however, as composed of individuals or associations of individuals. Among the provisions of the Helsinki Final Act, for example, is the directive that the Final Act be publicly disseminated in each signatory state. Implicit in this provision is the idea that, though the Final Act resulted from an agreement among states, the matters it deals with, particularly human rights, are the concern not just of states, but of *people*, and it is hoped that public opinion will play some role in achieving the goals of the final act. This is not the dominant conception of international society, certainly. But it seems likely to become increasingly important, at least if the trend toward public transnational institutions like the European Parliament continues.

This issue is significant in the context of the Reagan–Gorbachev summits because this was a period when there was considerable tension between the points of view of government leaders and those of citizens. The years preceding Geneva were after all a period of significant public protest in the west against policies of political leaders in the area of arms control and US–Soviet relations, and also of more widely shared uneasiness with the whole regime of deterrence and Cold War.[20] In Europe, NATO governments deployed the intermediate-range nuclear weapons eventually eliminated by the INF treaty without the support of a majority of their populations, and in the face of massive demonstrations in many countries. In the United States, as well, the peace movement became extremely influential; nuclear freeze resolutions, for example, were passed as referenda or by legislatures in many states. The Catholic bishops produced a pastoral letter condemning the use of nuclear weapons, a document which was powerful enough to produce some resignations from the military.[21] And the issue of nuclear war made important inroads into popular culture, particularly with the television movie, *The Day After*, which was watched by two-thirds of the American public, making it one of the most-watched programs in the history of American television. Polls showed fear of war and concern about the arms race to be among the most important public anxieties.[22] Even the reaction to Reagan's 'Star Wars' speech, with its promise to make nuclear weapons 'impotent and obsolete,' can be seen as a manifestation of deep public anxiety about the possibility of annihilation inherent in a world order based on nuclear deterrence.

These manifestations of unhappiness with deterrence were diverse, of course; but, as a number of studies of the discourse of international peace and security have shown, they have tended (Reagan's Star Wars speech would be no exception here) to speak a language very different from the language in which élites were accustomed to talking about US–Soviet relations: 'civil discourse' about nuclear war has been sharply different, as Robert Karl Manoff has put it, from 'statist discourse.'[23] Peace movements have tended, for example, to use a 'contextualized' language emphasizing the consequences of nuclear war for concrete human beings ('if you were here when the bomb fell in the center of your town, this is what would happen to you') rather than to speak in the abstract about the capabilities of the two sides.[24] They have often invoked moral language; that is, spoken in terms of right or wrong rather than rational or irrational. At times, as for instance in the notion of 'détente from below,' or the focus of certain East European activists on 'civil society,'[25] they have explicitly counterposed the conception of international society as a society of individuals against the state-centered view of international order.

The media, of course, even if they have close formal or informal ties to the state, are oriented toward the ordinary citizens who make up their audience. It might be thought, therefore, that the summit, as media event, would tend at least temporarily to promote the notion of public opinion as an important basis for world order, and to shift attention from the statist to the civil point of view. Certainly to some extent this is true. Because it invokes the standpoint of humanity as a whole, for example, and because it humanizes political leadership, the summit as media event can be seen as pushing toward the civil voice. And yet in each country there are strong journalistic forces pushing the other way.

We can begin here with the US coverage, which on this point is probably the most complex. It might be tempting to conclude simply that the American summit coverage privileged a state-centered point of view. Certainly foreign policy coverage in the US media is largely dominated by the official sources on whom journalists rely,[26] and much of the summit coverage reflected, as one journalist put it during the Moscow summit, an 'inside baseball, professional arms negotiator point of view.' But if American journalists see themselves as 'insiders,' they at the same time see themselves as representative of the point of view of the ordinary citizen; indeed they often stress in coverage of US–Soviet relations that while the east exalts the State, the west exalts the Individual. How are the two points of view reconciled?

Here it will be useful to consider a particular text, a commentary by Bill Moyers of CBS during the Geneva summit. The commentary began with Moyers in the room where Reagan and Gorbachev had met earlier in the day.

> They were alone in those two chairs with only interpreters in the room. But if some magic camera could have flashed here, a multitude of faces would have been revealed looking on . . . . [Here Moyers mentioned domestic factions in the two countries, East and West Europeans, and public opinion.]
>
> Public opinion is fickle. 'My hope is for peace in the world,' a voter said to a pollster. 'But if not that, the complete destruction of Russia and China.' It is a thought to justify a summit.
>
> You may wince, as I do, to realize that in a world of such diversity and talent, the destinies of so many ride into a single room with just two men. But as a friend of mine said this morning, 'People don't want to be blown up, and these are the two guys who can do something about it.' We were all in that room.

Here we see the 'magic' of the media event. Because all the world is looking toward Geneva, Geneva becomes a place from which we can 'see' humanity (Dan Rather, in introducing Moyers, described the room as 'a special room with a view, a *world* view'). It is 'humanity,' above all in the form of the invisible audience of ordinary people, that is the addressee of the commentary. Moyers identifies himself with and purports to present the perspective of the 'little guy' who doesn't 'want to be blown up,' the 'we' who were 'in that room.' At the same time, Moyers was 'in the room' in a different sense than 'we' were: when the commentary begins he is physically present in the room where the two leaders met; later he comes out into the street to speak directly to 'us.' We are 'present' in the room vicariously, both through our leaders and through Moyers, who represents himself as a bridge between the powerful and the powerless. The journalist mediates between state and society, leader and citizen. But he clearly mediates in such a way that the dominant position of the state is affirmed: 'public opinion is fickle. . . these are the two guys who can do something about it.'

Public opinion, although it was in a sense presented by American journalists as extremely potent – there was great preoccupation in American summit coverage with the possibility that Gorbachev would win a propaganda victory – was also seen either as an essentially passive force, subject to manipulation by the two sides, or as a disturbance interfering with the rational conduct of international affairs. The journalists granted it little positive role, actual or potential, in the establishment of international political order. It was normally excluded, for instance, when journalists explained the process by which the US and the Soviets came together to conclude the INF treaty. At the same time, the American coverage was generally very hostile toward more active manifestations of public opinion (at least within the west; human rights activists in the east typically were given more favorable coverage). At Geneva, for instance, Dan Rather invoked a standard stereotype in American coverage of political protest, that of the cacophony of causes, all equally meaningless:

Voltaire called Geneva 'proud, noble, wealthy, deep and sly.' To which might be added this week, *noisy*. With both Mikhail Gorbachev and President Reagan in town, there are more pleaders, petitioners and protesters here, with more axes to grind, than a Swiss army knife. Afghans, Cambodians and Romanians mad at Gorbachev. Peace demonstrators and various people in odd costumes mad at President Reagan. Hare Krishnas mad at absolutely nobody.

Certainly we are a long way here from the original liberal view that the basis of progress and of political order lies in an active civil society, and the subjunctive mode of the media event does not bring us a bit closer.

For the Soviet journalist, at the time of the Reagan–Gorbachev summits, the theory of the vanguard party eliminated any feeling of tension between the statist and civil perspectives. The vanguard party made state and society one, and the Soviet journalist had no problem speaking explicitly for the state. Looking at the side of domestic politics Soviet summit coverage was strictly statist: the problem of peace was presented as one that the Soviet government would resolve; the citizen had no independent role or perspective. This assumption was powerfully present in the Soviet coverage of Geneva in many ways. No ordinary Soviet citizen, for instance, appeared in the news. Beyond Soviet borders the picture was more complicated; in the international arena a lively public sphere of peace movements and active citizens sprang into being, along with a wide community of nations clamoring for peace. Soviet, like American television, payed homage to the value of citizen activism by celebrating its role in the *other* bloc. The West European peace movement, especially, was given far more attention by Soviet than American television, accounting in fact for almost a third of the people appearing in *Vremya*'s coverage. These were not, however, independent voices: their function in the news broadcast was to praise Soviet policy. The handling of Jesse Jackson's meeting with Gorbachev illustrates this well. Extensive Soviet coverage of the meeting eliminated all reference to an appeal on human rights, and presented Jackson simply as endorsing Soviet arms control policies.

In Italy, television journalism normally is centered around what could be called the institutionalized public sphere of organized political forces like parties. The summit introduced a significant change, with the journalist adopting the point of view of the 'man on the street:' 'Let us wish for them [the leaders] and for ourselves that they will make it [that is, agreement].' 'We' here is the ordinary citizen, whatever his or her political affiliation, and the whole story of the summit is told around this ordinary citizen's hope for peace: Will it be realized or not? A few ordinary people even appear in the Italian summit coverage – something very unusual for Italian television – though these are Soviets and not Italians. In a sense, the Italian coverage is the most civil-centered of the three countries. Yet the public sphere of the Italian coverage remains passive and largely devoid of content. The very word 'hope' – which could be considered the key theme of the Italian coverage – sums up the nature of the community that is invoked: it is a community of *spectators*, who have no ability to influence the outcome of the process they are watching.

As the term 'spectators' suggests, the extent and nature of participation by the 'audience' is a key problem in assessing the media event as a force for the construction of community. Dayan and Katz argue, against mass society theory, that the audience for a media event is not a passive one. This is as important for the Durkheimian as for the Habermasian and Millsian conception of community; Durkheim certainly saw civil religion as a generator of active involvement in social life. And indeed media events clearly involve some increase in participatory activities linked to social concerns beyond those of everyday private life (summits, because they are more routine than moon shots and state funerals, do this less than other media events). They even, to a limited extent, involve the kind of participatory activities, centered around voice and dialogue, which are of primary concern to Mills and Habermas: the Reagan–Gorbachev summits were, after all, occasions for many social groups to make themselves part of the spectacle/conversation, even if the mass media were generally uninterested in their presence.

Consider, though, the difference between the kind of popular participation described by Dayan and Katz, as characteristic of the media event, and the sort that characterizes the opening of something resembling a real public sphere.

> The space of leisure – home and privacy – is no longer the antithesis to the public dimension of social life. Public space invades the home. People no longer undress to watch television; they may actually dress up. The event becomes the occasion for a spectatorial contract. Friends are invited in to watch the show. The apathetic television viewer . . . drifting from program to program in an endless 'strip' . . . is replaced by the active viewer, a sociable being full of purpose, ready to assume his role of spectator.[27]

Recent events in Eastern Europe provide an excellent contrast. Here, for example, is an excerpt from a speech by Christa Wolf, an East German intellectual, to a rally in Berlin at the height of the upsurge of popular participation there in November 1989:

> Every revolutionary movement also liberates language. What we used to have a hard time articulating flows easily, all at once, from our lips . . . . Never before have people been talking the way they're talking now, talking to one another. Never before have they expressed so much passion, so much anger and grief, and also so much hope . . . . We make friends with mobs of

people, and we quarrel with each other bitterly. All this is known as 'dialogue.'[28]

CONCLUSION

The Reagan–Gorbachev summits, as televised media events, were a mixture of internationalism and nationalism, of communitas and structure, of openness and exclusion. How can this ambivalence be summed up? One way might be to see the summits, following Murray Edelman, as rituals of pacification.[29] Elaborate 'lip-service' is given to international reconciliation, but in a way that gives it only the most vague and general content. People are reassured that something is being done about the threat of nuclear war by established political authorities and structures, loyalty to which is simultaneously reaffirmed. Popular activism is discouraged, and in its place is found the 'quasi-democracy of intimate access' to political leaders.[30] There does seem to have been a pattern of demobilization of peace movements and consolidation of the Cold War following limited but symbolically celebrated moves toward détente. The disarmament movement of the early 1960s died out after the Test Ban Treaty. And there is some evidence of a similar process following the INF treaty. There was, for instance, much less coverage of western peace activists in the American coverage of the Washington than at the Geneva summit. Events in the Soviet Union and Eastern Europe, of course, subsequently pushed the discussion of east–west relations far beyond what most thought possible as late as the Moscow summit. But even if we put aside this history, and ask what might have happened if the Soviet bloc had not crumbled from within, the pacification view of the summits is probably too simple. It seems to us that the contradictory character of these summits as media events is real and irreducible, expressing a genuine tension in human consciousness in this era between what was and what could be, and probably functioning – though this essay does not pretend to address directly the long-term effects of the summit – both to limit and pacify a discourse looking beyond the Cold War and simultaneously to keep that discourse alive.

NOTES

*   Co-authored with Paolo Mancini. This research was funded by the Institute on Global Conflict and Cooperation of the University of California and by Regione dell'Umbria, Amministrazione della Provincia di Perugia, Lega delle Cooperative dell'Umbria. We would like to thank Joyce Evans for assistance with the content analysis and Jay Rosen, Robert Hackett, Herbert Gans, James Ettema and the UCSD 'discourse group' for useful comments on earlier drafts. Earlier versions of the paper were presented at the meeting of the Union for Democratic Communications, Ottawa, 1988, the Second Annual Conference on Nuclear Discourse, Ballyvaughan, Ireland, 1988, and the Congress of the International Communication Association, San Francisco, 1989. A different version, with additional discussion of problems of comparative method, appears in J. G.

Blumler, Jack M. McLeod, and K. E. Rosengren (eds), *Comparatively Speaking: Communication and Culture Across Space and Time*, Newbury Park, Calif., Sage, 1992.

1 D. Dayan and E. Katz, 'Articulating consensus: the ritual and rhetoric of media events,' in J. C. Alexander (ed.), *Durkheimian Sociology: Cultural Studies*, Cambridge, Cambridge University Press, 1988; E. Katz with D. Dayan and P. Motyl, 'Television diplomacy: Sadat in Jerusalem,' paper presented at the conference on World Communication: Decisions for the Eighties, Annenberg School of Communication, University of Pennsylvania, 1980; E. Katz with D. Dayan and P. Motyl, 'In defense of media events,' in R. W. Haigh, G. Gerbner, and R. Byrne (eds)., *Communications in the Twenty-first Century*, New York, Wiley, 1981; E. Katz and D. Dayan, 'Media events: on the experience of not being there,' *Religion*, 1985, vol. 15, pp. 305–14; D. Dayan and E. Katz, *Media Events: The Live Broadcasting of History*, Cambridge, Mass., Harvard University Press, 1992.

2 P. Mancini, 'Rito, leader e mass media: Enrico Berlinguer,' AAVV, *Leadership e Democrazia*, Padova, Cedam, 1987; S. Verba, 'The Kennedy assassination and the nature of political commitment,' in B. S. Greenberg and E. B. Parker (eds), *The Kennedy Assassination and the American Public: Social Communication in Crisis*, Stanford, Calif., Stanford University Press, 1965.

3 Information on the methodology of the study, as well as a more detailed account of the coverage of the three summits, can be found in D. Hallin and P. Mancini, *Friendly Enemies: The Reagan–Gorbachev Summits on U.S., Italian and Soviet Television*, Perugia, Provincia di Perugia, 1990.

4 R. Lyne, 'Making waves: Mr. Gorbachev's public diplomacy, 1985–6,' *International Affairs*, 1987, vol. 63, pp. 205–24.

5 C. Sparks, 'The popular press and political democracy,' *Media, Culture and Society*, 1988, vol. 10, pp. 209–33.

6 Obviously there is more to the question of the internationalization of the media than we can deal with here. There is, for example, a trend toward internationalization of ownership of the media in the west, as well as continuing development of the international market in news and cultural products, represented, for example, in CNN's international operations and European responses to its success.

7 Cf. G. Urban, 'The pronomial pragmatics of nuclear war discourse,' *Multilingua*, 1988, vol. 7, pp. 67–93; J. V. Wertsch, 'Modes of discourse in the nuclear arms debate,' *Current Research on Peace and Violence*, Tampere Peace Research Institute, Tampere, Finland, 1987.

8 J.-P. Vernant and P. Vidal-Naquet, *Tragedy and Myth in Ancient Greece*, Atlantic Highlands, Humanities Press, 1981. The parallel with the chorus in Greek tragedy was pointed out to us by Eric Vollmer.

9 *Imagined Communities: Reflections on the Origin and Spread of Nationalism*, New York, Verso, 1983.

10 In humanizing political leaders the summit would seem to involve at least to a limited extent the leveling V. Turner discusses in connection with liminality in *The Ritual Process: Structure and Anti-Structure*, Ithaca, NY, Cornell University Press, 1969.

11 'In defense of media events,' op. cit., p. 53.

12 Vernant and Vidal-Naquet, op. cit., p. 10.

13 *Public Opinion*, March/April 1988, pp. 22–3.

14 *Newsweek*, 21 December 1987, p. 22. A *Wall Street Journal*/NBC poll done during and after an NBC interview with Gorbachev before the Washington summit showed 53 per cent of Americans with favorable impressions of Gorbachev and 20 per cent unfavorable (the figures for Reagan, from a poll reported 4 December 1987

in the *Wall Street Journal*: 59 per cent favorable, 35 per cent unfavorable). More general attitudes toward the Soviet Union in the United States also became less hostile in the mid-1980s, though the shift was gradual and did not show dramatic changes directly tied to the summits. In the early 1980s, for instance, 30–39 per cent of Americans believed that 'Russia seeks global domination and will risk a major war to achieve that domination if it can't be achieved by other means.' By January 1988, the percentage holding this view of Soviet intentions had dropped to 11 per cent. *Public Opinion*, March/April 1988, p. 28.

15 D. Chaney, 'A symbolic mirror of ourselves: civic ritual in mass society,' *Media, Culture and Society*, 1983, vol. 5; D. I. Kertzer, *Ritual, Politics and Power*, New Haven, Conn., Yale University Press, 1988; S. Lukes, 'Political ritual and social integration,' *Sociology*, 1975, vol. 9.

16 E. Shils and M. Young, 'The meaning of the coronation,' *Sociology*, 1953, vol. 1, p. 74.

17 In their later work Dayan and Katz give increasing attention to the hegemonic side of media events, though still remaining primarily in a Durkheimian framework.

18 J. Habermas, *The Structural Transformation of the Public Sphere: An Inquiry into a Category of Bourgeois Society*, Cambridge, Mass., MIT Press, 1989; N. Garnham, 'The media and the public sphere,' in P. Golding, G. Murdock, and P. Schlesinger (eds), *Communicating Politics: Mass Communication and the Political Process*, New York, Holmes & Meier, 1986; also C. W. Mills, *The Power Elite*, New York, Oxford, 1956.

19 F. Halliday, 'Three concepts of internationalism,' *International Affairs*, 1988, vol. 64, pp. 187–98.

20 H. Mehan, C. E. Nathanson, and J. M. Skelly, 'Nuclear discourse in the 1980s: the unravelling conventions of the Cold War,' *Discourse and Society*, 1990, vol. 1, no. 2, pp. 133–66.

21 J. Newhouse, 'The abolitionist,' *The New Yorker*, 2 January 1989.

22 Public Opinion, July/August 1988, pp. 34–5.

23 R. K. Manoff, 'Covering the bomb: the nuclear story and the news,' *Working Papers*, summer 1983; see also J. Rosen, 'Democracy overwhelmed: the press and the public in the nuclear age,' occasional paper, Center for War, Peace and the News Media, New York, 1988.

24 Wertsch, op. cit.

25 For example, G. Konrad, *Antipolitics*, New York, Henry Holt, 1984.

26 L. V. Sigal, *Reporters and Officials*, Lexington, Mass., D.C. Heath, 1973; D. C. Hallin, R. K. Manoff, and J. W. Weddle, 'Sourcing patterns of national security reporters,' *Journalism Quarterly*, 1993.

27 Dayan and Katz, 'Articulating consensus,' op. cit., p. 162.

28 *Sonntag*, 1987, no. 47, translated by Maryellen Boyle.

29 M. Edelman, *The Symbolic Uses of Politics*, Urbana, Ill., University of Illinois Press, 1967; M. Edelman, *Constructing the Political Spectacle*, Chicago, Ill., University of Chicago Press, 1988.

30 D. Chaney, 'The symbolic form of ritual in mass communication,' in Golding, Murdock, and Schlesinger (eds), op. cit.

Chapter 9

The passing of the 'high modernism' of American journalism

My first encounter with a professional journalist was an interview with Peter Arnett, then at the Associated Press. It was the late 1970s, and I was a bearded graduate student from Berkeley writing my dissertation on the media and Vietnam, a story which Arnett had covered since the early 1960s. He assumed from my background that I would want to know why journalists hadn't taken a stronger stand against the war; this was the era when advocacy journalism enjoyed a heyday of sorts – quite brief and marginal, really – as a challenger to the journalistic mainstream. So he launched into an articulate defense of what he called 'Establishment journalism.' Just by reporting the facts, he said, journalists had contributed more effectively to ending the war than they could have done in any other way.

What impressed me most strongly in this interview was the sense of wholeness and seamlessness in Arnett's vision of journalism, or to put it the other way around, the absence of a sense of doubt or contradiction. I remember being quite surprised by this, which I suppose reflects my very different generational experience, as someone who came of age politically just as the polarization that ended the 1960s reached its height. Arnett's view reflects very well the consciousness of American journalism at the peak of the country's power and prosperity: this was an era when American journalists felt they had overcome all the basic contradictions which historically have troubled the practice of journalism. And in fact – consciousness never fundamentally standing apart from material reality – they had achieved resolutions of these contradictions which for the moment seemed solid and stable.

Politically, it seemed possible for journalism to be independent of party and state, and yet fully a part of the 'Establishment.' Thus James Reston, the premier journalist of the era, recounts delivering through his column a threat of nuclear war if the Soviets failed to back down in Berlin, the exact wording approved by President Kennedy but presented on Reston's own authority. With John Foster Dulles, Secretary of State under Eisenhower, who 'liked . . . philosophical wanderings with a fellow Presbyterian,'[1] he had a continuing relationship of this sort. These kinds of ties were not entered into without an occasional pause to weigh their implications. But they were not seen by journalists as a conflict of interest or surrender of independence. They were, after all, voluntary agreements in which the journalists gained extraordinary access to the inner workings of politics. The journalists felt they had bargaining power of their own, could criticize without losing access, and indeed could uphold the old ideal of press as a scourge of the powerful. 'When they tried to bully our reporters,' Reston writes, 'I reminded them that we had been around before they arrived, and would probably still be in Washington when they were gone.'[2] But most important, they felt confident that all of it was done in the defense of the Free World, a cause that stood above politics.

In their internal organization, the news media seemed to have resolved the twin problems of private ownership and personal bias. Owners had largely ceded day-to-day control of the news columns to the journalists. With the shift of the *Los Angeles Times* toward neutrality in the 1960 election and the death of Henry Luce in 1967, the last important survivors of the days when the news media were essentially political tools of their owners were gone.

The journalists, for their part, had accepted the bureaucratic hierarchy of the newsroom and the constraints of the professional norms of neutrality and 'objectivity.' Lichter, Rothman, and Lichter note that they found contemporary journalists much less likely to complain about editors interfering with their news judgement than were the journalists of the 1930s, when Leo Rosten found a majority complaining that stories had been altered or killed for 'policy' reasons.[3] They interpreted this as an indication that individual journalists now had more or less complete autonomy. But I think it reflects something else, besides the undeniably greater professional autonomy of the contemporary journalist. Contemporary journalists have internalized the constraints of professionalism far more than the writers of the 1930s had done, and are also far less politicized than their predecessors. They are committed more strongly to the norms of the profession than to political ideas.

We know, of course, that politics never disappeared. It was there all along, in sources, in routines, in consensus assumptions that major political actors didn't disagree about, and which therefore weren't seen as political. Still, we shouldn't allow the critique of objectivity, which has occupied so much of the media scholarship of the last couple of decades, to obscure the real historical change represented by professionalization. Journalism took on a role in this period which felt to most of those involved and which appeared to most of the society to be genuinely 'above politics.'

Finally, in economic terms, prosperity meant that the 'profane,' commercial side of the news organization didn't have to conflict with its 'sacred,' public service side. Not that everything was well with every paper. Newspapers, in fact, were dying right and left. But the ones that remained were for the most part so prosperous in their new, usually monopoly status, that journalists could think of themselves more as public servants or as keepers of the sacred flame of journalism itself than as employees of a profit-making enterprise. It

was the same at the television networks, where the separation of the news
divisions from the commercial side of the enterprise was reinforced by the
regulatory injunction that broadcasters serve the public convenience and
necessity. The prosperity of these organizations was closely connected with
their universality: their audience knew no bounds of class, politics, or other
social distinction. And that prosperity lifted both the status and income of the
individual journalist. Think of the change in the journalist's image in popular
culture, from the rowdy, corrupt, politically-entangled ambulance-chasers of
The Front Page to the altruistic professionals of *All the President's Men*.

This was the high modernism of American journalism,[4] an era when the
historically troubled role of the journalist seemed fully rationalized, when it
seemed possible for the journalist to be powerful and prosperous and at the
same time independent, disinterested, public-spirited, and trusted and beloved
by everyone, from the corridors of power around the world to the ordinary
citizen and consumer. Two major social conditions made this possible. The
first was political consensus, rooted in the New Deal and the Cold War. The
second was economic security, both for the society at large and for media
industries specifically. Both have substantially broken down. How far their
disintegration will go or what new political and economic forces will replace
them we cannot know. But it is clear that the changes underway are already
shaking up the profession of journalism. I will organize the remainder of my
discussion around these two broad themes: the collapse of political consensus
and intensification of economic competition.

THE COLLAPSE OF POLITICAL CONSENSUS

From the beginning of the Second World War to the late 1960s, political
debate in the United States was extremely muted. In domestic politics the
liberal policies of the New Deal commanded a majority solid enough to leave
the far left marginalized and the conservatives with little choice but to join the
fold. In foreign policy wartime consensus was converted into the bipartisan
policy of Cold War containment, whose basic outlines came essentially to
define the bounds of political reason. Consensus was accompanied by a high
level of public confidence in political institutions. In this environment, it was
possible for social scientists to proclaim the 'end of. ideology' and to put
forward a vision of social science as a source of neutral expertise, closely tied to
governing institutions, and at the same time serving society as a whole. And in
a similar way consensus made it possible for journalists to feel that they could
be part of the political 'Establishment,' and yet remain neutral and
independent.

A series of major changes in political life have undermined this consensus.
First, and probably most basic, the New Deal majority has broken apart,
destroyed by racial and other social divisions and by economic conditions.
Second, the Cold War consensus has disappeared, first undermined by

Vietnam and detente, and now made irrelevant by the collapse of the Soviet bloc. Third, public confidence in political authorities has declined. To a large extent, this has probably been a biproduct of the general decline of political consensus. But I think it also has a more specific and simple cause, namely that the instrumental attitude toward communication developed during wartime became institutionalized, and officials were caught again and again in blatant falsehoods, from the U-2 incident to the Dominican invasion to Watergate.

Finally, important institutional changes have taken place in the relations among major political actors. The political system has become increasingly fragmented, individualized and adversarial, with central structures weakened and individual actors looking out for themselves. The parties have weakened substantially: voters identify with them far less strongly, they exercise less discipline in Congress, and their organizations play a diminished role in the electoral process. Relations between the president and Congress are more adversarial: as Samuel Kernell has shown, presidents bargain less with congressional leaders and rely more on the mobilization of public pressure.[5]

As this last point suggests, changes in political communication were central to these developments. It is likely, for instance, that the advent of television was an important factor: television made it much easier for presidents to go 'over the heads' of congressional leaders by appealing directly to the public, and gave candidates a new way of reaching the voters without relying on the old party ward leaders. And certainly public communication – or if one likes, propaganda – became more central to the political process. And the news media were affected by the changes in similar ways to other political actors: their relations with those actors became more adversarial, less bound by a sense of reciprocal obligations. Gone is the clubby atmosphere of the Roosevelt years, when the president met with reporters every week and the reporters agreed not to print photographs showing his leg braces. Press conferences are far rarer today, and are less occasions for give and take between the president and the press corps, than confrontations staged by the president to impress the television audience. And the media are more reluctant to honor politicians' wishes about what will be publicized: consider the networks' decision to broadcast tape of President Bush vomiting in the lap of the Japanese prime minister.

All of this was beginning to change journalism substantially by the late 1960s. Journalists were becoming bolder about challenging political authority, as they did most dramatically by publishing the Pentagon Papers. And more profoundly, the old model of 'objective journalism' was giving way to a more active, mediated, journalist-centered form of reporting, whose rise is detailed in Chapter 7.

Before going on to discuss some of the implications of that change, a qualification is necessary. It is important not to exaggerate the extent to which American journalism has become either more adversarial toward political authority, or more interpretive in mode of presentation. The relation between the news media and political power is still tight and symbiotic; and it seems to me that the news media are still very much the junior partner. The statistics on news sources, for instance, have changed little since the early 1970s, when Leon Sigal found that about half the sources in front-page stories in the *New York Times* and the *Washington Post* were US government officials.[6] The large percentage of these that are unnamed suggests the degree of trust that still prevails between reporters and officials. And one has only to think of the way the media image of Saddam Hussein's regime changed as he shifted from ally to enemy to realize how much official policy still shapes the news. American journalists, moreover, remain far more comfortable with the role of reporter than that of commentator.

Still, the changes that have taken place since the 1960s are substantial. And there are reasons to think they may continue to develop. One such reason is the end of the Cold War. It was the Cold War above all that made a relatively passive, state-centered model of journalism appear reasonable. Truth and power seemed united in the Washington headquarters of the Free World, and the basic job of the reporter, in a phrase I have often heard from reporters covering national security policy, was to 'reflect the thinking' of official Washington. Given the prestige of the national security beat, moreover, this model of journalism tended to influence the rest of the profession, just as the national security paradigm influenced the rest of political thought. (We still talk about a war on drugs and argue for education or economic reform on the grounds that they will promote 'national security.' This is one of the only ways we have of talking about the public good.) As foreign policy consensus has broken down, reporters have had to think for themselves much more, about which voices to listen to, for example, and how to synthesize for their audience a political reality that is not black and white. The end of the Cold War raises the prospect that this will become a normal condition.

Another reason to expect continuing change has to do with the anguished state of electoral politics, which became a major subject of discussion following the 1988 election and subsequent polls showing intense voter dissatisfaction with political leadership. It is naive, of course, to imagine that there was once a golden age when political discussion in America was a model of reason. But I do think it is true that there have been periods when the political identities of the two parties were relatively clear, and when the bulk of the electorate felt represented by one or the other. This was the case during the New Deal era, and it made the journalists' job relatively easy: covering politics meant above all relaying to the voters what the candidates were saying about whatever issues they chose to stress. Since the break up of the New Deal coalition in 1968, however, the identities of the parties have become muddled. This has interacted with – perhaps it opened the way for – the domination of campaigning by professional consultants, to produce the substanceless politics of 1988.

And the latter in turn has provoked considerable discussion among journalists about how to cover elections. Should journalists, as the *Washington Post*'s David Broder has proposed, take a more active role in defining the agenda of the campaign,[7] or is that, as others argue, a presumptuous and unrealistic usurpation of the role of the parties and candidates? Coverage of the 1992 campaign seemed to move modestly in the direction Broder advocated. For example, the *New York Times* ran as its right-hand lead a story under the head:[8]

DEMOCRATS VYING IN '92 RACE OFFER PAINLESS RECOVERY

ECONOMISTS ARE SKEPTICAL

Except for Tsongas, Candidates are Avoiding Remedies that
Might Antagonize Voters

No candidate was quoted until the tenth paragraph.

For the most part, the changes of the past two decades have made American journalism better, and I think we should welcome the prospect of further change, especially in the direction of greater independence from the state, greater sensitivity to diversity of viewpoints, and more sophisticated interpretation. But the changes also confront American journalism with some rather difficult questions about its role. One way to think about what has happened is this: key institutions of political debate and interpretation in America have weakened in recent years. The presidency, in particular, has lost credibility (even as it has become more aggressive and sophisticated in the practice of public relations); and the parties – especially the Democrats – have fragmented, lost a sense of what they stand for, and resorted increasingly to instrumental forms of communication that cannot be taken seriously as political discourse. The interpretive role of the journalist has expanded to fill part of the vacuum.

Up to a point this is fine. Better the journalists than the flacks. But in many ways journalists are neither well positioned nor well qualified to fill the void of political discussion. They remain, for one thing, too much insiders, too close to the powerful institutions whose actions need to be discussed. And they are too constrained by the need to avoid offense to any major political faction or, most powerfully, to the majority sentiment of the moment. In the case of elections, again to recall the argument of 'Soundbite news' and other essays in this volume, journalists tend to steer the discussion in the direction of technical questions that don't seem political: which candidate is running the most effective campaign? A similar thing happened, by somewhat different means, during the Gulf War – the kind of emotional political issue that arouses the most intense fears in the media of being on the wrong side of public opinion. The television networks hired as consultants retired military and Defense Department experts, who could provide seemingly neutral technical analysis, and who also had a base of authority outside journalism, and turned over much of the interpretation directly to them.

This problem – the emptiness of the American public sphere – is not one that can be solved solely or primarily by the news media. It is first of all a political problem. But assuming it is not going to disappear quickly or easily, journalism will have to adapt to it. And it seems to me that this may require journalism to be reattached to the all-but-forgotten republican notion of citizenship. This is too large a problem for me to explore fully here.[9] But I would like to make two points about what it might mean in practical terms. First of all, journalists need to move from conceiving their role in terms of mediating between political authorities and the mass public, to thinking of it also as a task of opening up political discussion in civil society, to use the term popular in the new democracies of Eastern Europe. If the candidates in an election campaign, for instance, don't seem to have much to say, why not look for someone else who does? Because Broders's critics are ultimately right: journalism has a thin political skin, and if it blows itself up too big it will burst.

Second, it might be time for journalists themselves to rejoin civil society, and to start talking to their readers and viewers as one citizen to another, rather than as experts claiming to be above politics. I am not arguing here for a revival of advocacy journalism. That kind of journalism has an important role to play, and it is too bad that forms like the 'authored' documentary have become so marginalized. But the front page of a monopoly newspaper is not the place for it. I am also not arguing for the kind of pseudo-populist identification with popular sentiments that is often seen today on television news (more on this in a moment). All I am arguing is that the voice and judgement of the journalist may have to be more honestly acknowledged. The style of modern American journalism, with its attributions, passive voice constructions, and its substitution of technical for moral or political judgements, is largely designed to conceal the voice of the journalist. But as journalism has become increasingly interpretive, it seems to me this form has become increasingly problematic – both alienating in the wall it throws between the journalist and the reader, and fundamentally dishonest. Journalists used to speak sometimes in the first person – listen to Edward R. Murrow or Bill Shirer. Perhaps it wouldn't be a bad thing if that practice came back.

THE COMMERCIALIZATION OF NEWS

Economics, meanwhile, has eroded the barrier between journalism and the profit-making business of selling audiences to advertisers. And this is likely to bring into question both the notion of journalism as a public trust and the existence of the common public culture that news once provided. To some extent, all news media have been affected by these changes, as declining audiences and the proliferation of new advertising media have squeezed the bottom line, and as the news media have increasingly become part of media conglomerates for which news is only one more form of 'software.'[10] But the changes have been most dramatic by far in television, and I shall focus here on that medium.[11]

News never was 'the core of the asset' in television as it was in the newspaper industry, as Jack Welch, CEO of NBC-owner General Electric put it.[12] But it did have a privileged and insulated place in the networks for a relatively brief period, from about 1963 until the mid-1980s. That special position was based primarily on two things: the secure profitability of the networks, and the fact that broadcasting was a regulated industry. A series of developments beginning in the 1970s have eroded it. In the first place, local TV news emerged as a highly profitable form of programming, far too important to the bottom line of local stations to be left under the control of journalists. It has since evolved into a powerful hybrid of news and show business. It is also the main training ground for network journalists, who in earlier days were trained in radio or print. Then in the 1980s, the advent of cable and the VCR threw the television industry into a period of intense competition which has seen the network share of the television audience decline from near 90 to near 60 per cent. Broadcasting, meanwhile, was being substantially deregulated, and all three networks were taken over in deals that involved the assumption of substantial debt by the new parent companies. All of this combined to force both budget cutbacks and increased pressure to worry about the ratings.

The character of the evening news has already changed substantially. Its pace has come to resemble more closely the pace of the rest of commercial television, with 10-second soundbites and tightly packaged stories. The agenda of news has changed, with fewer traditional political stories and more stories that 'tug at the heart strings.' And the pressure is far greater today for the stories to have high 'production values,' both narrative and visual: drama, emotion, and good video. These changes are not all bad; and the common view that sees television history as a simple decline from the supposed Golden Age of Murrow and Cronkite (extremely different eras, actually!) seems to me seriously misleading. News in the 'classical age' probably was, for example, far too centered on Washington; and I see nothing wrong with a switch toward greater attention to health or family life or other subjects which are both closer to the lives of the viewers and significant political issues in their own right.

Still, many of changes in television news are indeed disturbing. If the news agenda has been democratized in certain ways, it has been trivialized in others, with more attention to stories like celebrity trials and beached whales. The networks have also to some extent adopted the local news practice of dropping neutrality and presenting the journalist as a 'regular person' who shares and champions the emotions of the audience. This is an old practice of the tabloid press, with its language of outrage and pathos. In TV news it is most common in stories of crime, heroism, or tragedy that are at least on the surface nonpolitical. But it often spills over into the political arena when emotions are high and consensus seems present. There was plenty of it at all levels of American television during the Gulf War. Often the temptation in TV news is to push a political story into the sphere of consensus: so war becomes a story not of political decisions but of individual heroism, and the journalist, like the politician, can ride the crest of the emotions that pour into such a story. This is what I referred to earlier as 'pseudo-populism.' It heightens emotion, makes black and white what is in fact far more ambiguous, and tramples dialogue in the rush to an easy, pre-packaged consensus. Here, I think, we can see the urgency of the need for journalists, hungry to build a bridge to the public, to think about what a 'public' really is and what role they might play in constituting it.

The network news divisions, of course, still have one foot firmly planted in the traditional profession of journalism. But they now face competition that is purely commercial, and it is possible that this will have a profound impact eventually on the nature of television news. One of the most significant effects of deregulation and the proliferation of television outlets is the growth of what is often called 'trash television.' The term has been applied to a number of different kinds of programming, and may be unfair to some of it. It includes, for example, popular daytime talk shows, some of which combine sensation with a significant amount of serious social content, and might be seen as a democratization of the talk-show format, which used to be reserved for discussions among Washington's movers-and-shakers, journalists prominently included. These shows played an important and I think in many ways a constructive role in reawakening public interest in the political process during the 1992 election.[13] But the ones that seem to me most likely to affect television journalism are the 'tabloids,' seen in most markets in the evening, at the beginning of prime time: *A Current Affair, Hard Copy,* and *Inside Edition.* These shows are both cheap to produce and successful in the ratings. They borrow the form and aura of journalism – *Hard Copy* uses a typewriter ball in its promotional imagery – but are produced purely as commercial products. And they involve an intertwining of 'real' and 'fictional' material: they report on 'actual events' using a combination of documentary material and re-creations, the lines between the two blurred by a heavy use of music and visual effects.

The tabloids are, it seems to me, a deeply problematic development for the culture. They exist, for one thing, primarily in the emotional realm of fear. Violent crime, often linked to sex, is their most cherished material, and they handle it in a way that maximizes the feeling of omnipresent threat. One typical story, for example, about a transvestite stockbroker who murdered a client, ends with the principal character saying, 'Do I have to live in fear until that man gets caught?' This line comes over video of the killer in a courtroom, turning toward the camera – that is, the viewer – with a smile; his gaze is then frozen for a moment at the end of the segment. They are also pervaded by irrationalism both in their content, which is full of UFOs and ghosts, and, probably most important, in form: the core of what they say is not stated directly, but insinuated in cryptic lines and visuals (they are much like political commercials in this respect).

Perhaps these shows should be dismissed as 'just entertainment,' with no relevance for understanding American journalism. But I doubt that this will prove correct. A number of them are produced, for one thing, by people who have moved over from the network news divisions, and it seems likely that personnel movements will continue to cross-fertilize the different programming forms. Beyond that the tabloids are simply too successful not to be tempting to those in local and network television news who are also, in the new language of television, in the business of 'reality-based programming.'

It is also possible that significant parts of the public will one day be exposed to no other sort of 'news' than the tabloids. And this brings me to my final point. In the period I have called the high modernism of American journalism, the news audience was close to universal. The metropolitan newspaper and the network evening news provided rich and poor, political and apolitical alike with a source of relatively serious reporting on public affairs. These media served some members of the audience better than others, to be sure, but almost everyone did at least belong to the audience. It is not clear that this common audience will survive. Newspapers have lost circulation generally. But it is likely to be in television that a really dramatic change takes place, reproducing something like the split in the newspaper market of many European countries between the quality and mass press.

Serious public affairs programming was never economically rational for the television industry. It developed to begin with because of regulatory pressure, and it is not likely to survive unmodified the combination of increased competition and deregulation. Some form of serious television journalism will certainly survive. CNN is doing well with its low-budget operation, and it seems likely that at least one network will continue to produce a major evening news show. But there is already considerable talk in the television industry about whether three such programs can survive.

If they do not, 'the public' becomes fragmented in a way that is potentially very significant for American politics and culture. Fragmentation of the news audience might not necessarily be a bad thing. One can imagine a system in which, for example, distinctive forms of journalism emerged for middle-class and working-class audiences (and subgroups of these), reflecting the different tastes and concerns of the audiences but providing each with serious discussion of the world of politics in the widest sense. (Public broadcasting has long served to provide the educated middle-class – but not other groups, who were assumed to be served adequately by commercial television – with a specialized kind of news programming the market does not deliver.) Unfortunately, this is not what is likely to happen. What is likely instead is a division of the audience into one part, mostly wealthier and better educated, which 'consumes' news of perhaps a higher quality than we have yet seen, and another far larger part, poorer, less educated, and substantially drawn from minority ethnic groups, which consumes nothing but *A Current Affair* and a sort of soft tabloid style of local news. And this would mean not only a widening of cultural barriers, but also an intensification of the knowledge gap.

NOTES

*   This essay was written while I was a fellow at the Freedom Forum Media Studies Center at Columbia University.

1   *Deadline: A Memoir*, New York, Random House, 1991, p. 232.

2   Ibid., p. 205.

3   S. R. Lichter, S. Rothman, and L. Lichter, *The Media Elite: America's New Powerbrokers*, Bethesda, MD, Adler & Adler, 1986; L. Rosten, *The Washington Correspondents*, New York, Harcourt, Brace, 1937.

4
>   High modernist art, architecture, literature, etc. became establishment arts and practices in a society where a corporate capitalist vision of the Enlightenment project of development for progress and human emancipation held sway . . . . The belief 'in linear progress, absolute truths, and rational planning of ideal social orders' under standardized conditions of knowledge and production was particularly strong. The modernism that resulted was, as a result, 'positivistic, technocratic and rationalistic' at the same time as it was imposed as the work of an elite avant-garde . . . .
>
>   D. Harvey, *The Condition of Postmodernity: An Enquiry into the Origins of Cultural Change*, Cambridge, Mass., Blackwell, 1990, p. 35.

5   S. Kernell, *Going Public: New Strategies of Presidential Leadership*, Washington DC, Congressional Quarterly Press, 1986.

6   L. Sigal, *Reporters and Officials*, Lexington, Mass., D. C. Heath, 1973.

7   D. Broder, 'How to stop a political mudbath in five easy steps,' *Washington Post National Weekly Edition*, 22–8 January 1990, p. 4.

8   D. E. Rosenbaum, 'Democrats vying in '92 race offer painless recovery,' *New York Times*, 18 January 1992, pp. A1, A7.

9   J. Rosen (ed.), *Recovery of the public world* (special issue), *Communication*, 1991, vol. 12, no. 4.

10 L. Bogart, 'The American media system and its commercial culture,' *Media Studies Journal*, 1991, vol. 5, no. 4, pp. 13–33.

11 On similar developments in the the newspaper industry, see J. Squires, *Read All about It: The Corporate Takeover of America's Newspapers*, New York, Random House, 1992.

12 Quoted in K. Auletta, *Three Blind Mice: How the TV Networks Lost Their Way*, New York, Random House, 1991, p. 569.

13 P. Taylor, 'Political coverage in the 1990s: teaching the old news new tricks,' in J. Rosen and P. Taylor, *The New News v. the Old News: Press and Politics in the 1990s*, New York, Twentieth Century Fund, 1992.

Index